Narrating Knowledge in
Flannery O'Connor's Fiction

Narrating Knowledge in
Flannery O'Connor's Fiction

Donald E. Hardy

University of South Carolina Press

Published in Columbia, South Carolina, by the
University of South Carolina Press

Manufactured in the United States of America

07 06 05 04 03   5 4 3 2 1

Library of Congress Cataloging-in-Publication Data

Hardy, Donald E., 1955–
  Narrating knowledge in Flannery O'Connor's fiction / Donald E. Hardy.
    p. cm.
  Includes bibliographical references and index.
  ISBN 1-57003-475-3 (alk. paper)
  1. O'Connor, Flannery—Technique. 2. O'Connor, Flannery—Philosophy.
  3. Knowledge, Theory of, in literature. 4. Narration (Rhetoric)
  I. Title.

PS3565.C57 Z685 2002
813'.54—dc21   2002010881

For Tom and Dolores

Contents

Figures

Tables

Acknowledgments

Narrating Knowledge in Flannery O'Connor's Fiction contains parts of essays that I have published elsewhere, distributed over various chapters. In all cases, the essays have been extensively rewritten, reorganized, and expanded. In some cases, even the statistical significance of quantitative tests has changed because of expanded coverage of the data in the book. Parts of my "Narrating Knowledge: Presupposition and Background in Flannery O'Connor's Fiction," *Language and Literature* (London) 6 (1997): 29–41; "Presupposition and the Coconspirator," *Style* 26 (1992): 1–11; and "Free Indirect Discourse, Irony, and Empathy in Flannery O'Connor's 'Revelation,'" *Language and Literature* (San Antonio) 16 (1991): 37–53, appear in chapter 3. Chapters 4 and 5 are loosely based on Hardy and Newton's "Why Is She So Negative? Negation and Knowledge in Flannery O'Connor's *A Good Man Is Hard to Find*," *Southwest Journal of Linguistics* 17, no. 2 (1998): 61–81. Parts of Hardy and Durian's "The Stylistics of Syntactic Complements: Grammar and Seeing in Flannery O'Connor's Fiction," *Style* 34 (2000): 92–116, appear in chapters 6 and 7. And parts of Hardy's "Linguistic and Literary Theory: The Dancer and the Dance," *Southwest Journal of Linguistics* 10, no. 2 (1991): 1–29, and Hardy's "Introduction: Tracing the Crosscurrents of Influence: Literary vs. Ordinary vs. Scientific Language," in *Crosscurrents of Influence: Linguistics and Literary Theory*, ed. Donald E. Hardy, special issue of *Language and Literature* (San Antonio) 17 (1992): 1–17, appear in chapter 8. I thank these journals for permission to reprint portions of these essays in *Narrating Knowledge*.

The Hardy and Newton paper and the Hardy and Durian paper were both supported by Northern Illinois University's Undergraduate Research Apprenticeship Program. In particular, I thank Dean Fred Kitterle of the College of Liberal Arts and Sciences for support of this innovative and important program designed to involve undergraduates as apprentices in faculty research. I also thank Heather Hardy for reading parts of *Narrating Knowledge* and providing valuable comments. Finally, I thank Northern Illinois University for a sabbatical taken in spring 1998, which allowed for considerable uninterrupted work on *Narrating Knowledge*.

Abbreviations

O'Connor's Works

CFOBC	*The Correspondence of Flannery O'Connor and the Brainard Cheneys*
CS	*The Complete Stories*
CW	*Collected Works*
ERMC	*Everything That Rises Must Converge*
GM	*A Good Man Is Hard to Find and Other Stories*
HB	*The Habit of Being*, ed. Sally Fitzgerald
MM	*Mystery and Manners: Occasional Prose*
VBA	*The Violent Bear It Away*
WB	*Wise Blood*

Grammatical Terms

ADV	Adverb
AUX	Auxiliary
COMP	Complement (narrative element)
comp.	Complement (figures)
CONJ	Conjunction
DD	Direct Discourse
FID	Free Indirect Discourse
I	Instrumental
ID	Indirect Discourse
L	Locative
M	Manner
p	Probability
SUBJ	Subject
T	Time
VB	Verb
~	Not
>	Implicates
>>	Presupposes

Chapter 1

Knowledge and Grammar in O'Connor's Fiction

I think the reason I like chickens is that they don't go to college.

—Flannery O'Connor (*CFOBC,* 123)

Somewhat paradoxically, since this study is a qualitative and quantitative analysis of Flannery O'Connor's fiction, *Narrating Knowledge* will show that an "understanding," or interpretation, of O'Connor's fiction leads us to appreciate the limitations of knowledge. All of the "understanding" that is the nature of a book of this sort is dangerous ground, since O'Connor made it clear in both her letters and her occasional essays that one of her least favorite intellectual products was that of the hyperactive literary-critical mind. She complained in her letters of one set of Vanderbilt students that "they try to make everything a symbol" (*HB,* 465). In particular, in their interpretations of "A Good Man Is Hard to Find," the students seem to have fixated their Freudian critical minds on The Misfit's hat and the name of Red Sammy's combination gas station/barbecue shop/dance hall "The Tower." O'Connor did not save her scorn for outrageous interpretations from students alone. In one letter, she complains of a "teacher" at Wesleyan who wanted to know "the significance of the Misfit's hat." She told him that "it was to cover his head" (*HB,* 334). As her reply indicates, O'Connor could be brusque and even rude, however much that rudeness might sometimes seem justified. In 1961, a professor of English suggested in a letter to O'Connor that he, three of his colleagues, and their students had performed some sort of group interpretation on "A Good Man Is Hard to Find" and concluded that The Misfit and his gang, and all the events that involved them, were simply the products of Bailey's imagination. O'Connor's reply began, "The interpretation of your ninety students and three teachers is fantastic and about as far from my intentions as it could get to be." In a letter written soon after to her friend John Hawkes she expressed some remorse for being so "harsh" in her response to the professor (*HB,* 437, 438–39).

However, O'Connor spared not even her friends from her complaints of overwrought interpretation. She wrote to William Sessions the following about his impressions of *The Violent Bear It Away*: "your critique is too far from the spirit of the book to make me want to go into it with you in detail. I do hope, however, that you will get over the kind of thinking that sees in every door handle a phallic symbol and that ascribes such intentions to those who have other fish to fry. The Freudian technique can be applied to anything at all with equally ridiculous results. . . . My Lord, Billy, recover your simplicity. . . . Don't inflict that stuff on the poor students there; they deserve better" (*HB*, 407).

My analyses in *Narrating Knowledge* will explicitly avoid symbol hunting, although that in itself doesn't mean that O'Connor would, or even should, approve of my approach. I believe that she would probably respond to *Narrating Knowledge* in the same way that she responded to an interpretive inquiry from another English professor just two months before she died: "I think you folks sometimes strain the soup too thin" (*HB*, 582). Indeed, I will be straining the soup in this study, but I hope not too thin. *Narrating Knowledge* will concentrate on three linguistic patterns that are spread throughout O'Connor's stories and novels: presupposition, negation, and verbal complements. Crucially, my investigation of these grammatical signals will serve the investigation of an equally diffuse but well-recognized thematic concern in O'Connor's fiction: the limitations of human knowledge. One of the reasons that this theme is so well recognized is that O'Connor herself frequently commented on it.

O'Connor scholars are blessed with collections of her letters and essays, the contents of which frequently shed significant light on her literary intentions. There are certainly both prescriptive and proscriptive threads in those collections.[1] O'Connor repeatedly provides explicitly Christian readings, as in her suggestions for understanding the grandmother and The Misfit in "A Good Man Is Hard to Find." This "nutshell guide" is embedded in a letter to John Hawkes about, among other things, misinterpretations of her work: "Grace, to the Catholic way of thinking, can and does use as its medium the imperfect, purely human, and even hypocritical. . . . The Misfit is touched by the Grace that comes through the old lady when she recognizes him as her child, as she has been touched by the Grace that comes through him in his particular suffering. . . . In the Protestant view, I think Grace and nature don't have much to do with each other. The old lady, because of her hypocrisy and humanness and banality couldn't be a medium for Grace. In the sense that I see things the other way, I'm a Catholic writer" (*HB, 389–90*). One of the themes that O'Connor returns to again and again in her letters and essays is the limitations of human knowledge, not only as a key to understanding her fiction but also as an occasional warning against too much "theorizing" about literature and how it gets written. She writes in an essay on regional fiction that "to know oneself is, above all, to know what one lacks. It is to measure oneself against Truth, and not the other way around" (*MM, 35*). She writes in a letter about "The Enduring Chill," "It's not so much a story of conversion as of self-knowledge, which I suppose has to be the first step in conversion" (*HB, 299*). Lamenting the failure of modern authors, and hence their characters, to "go out to explore and penetrate a world in which the sacred is reflected," O'Connor argues in an essay on the relationship between the novelist and the Christian that the novelist must necessarily construct a believable world but that fiction should lead the reader beyond the merely believable: "The virtues of art, like the virtues of faith, are such that they reach beyond the limitations of the intellect" (*MM, 158*). However, in a letter to Brainard Cheney in which she comments on brutality as a method to communicate as a Catholic writer, she also writes, "I don't believe in theorizing about it though. In the end you do just what you're able to and don't know what that has been" (*CFOBC, 6*).

Knowledge, in all of its manifestations (spiritual, rational, emotional) and as possessed by all the central participants in the narrative (e.g., narrator, narratee, character), permeates the style of Flannery O'Connor's fiction, "style" here understood as enveloping both content and form. Concerns with what can be known in the material and spiritual worlds are spread throughout the earliest to the latest fiction. In this chapter, I establish O'Connor's concern with the theme of the limitations of human knowledge so that the theme can serve as the background against which the bulk of *Narrating Knowledge* may be read. "The Barber," from O'Connor's 1947 M.A. thesis, has as its main character an academic "liberal," Rayber, who is considerably less liberal than he thinks and much less persuasive in arguing with his racist barber than he hopes. His wife tells him, "Just because you teach doesn't mean you know everything" (*CS, 22*). Enoch Emery of the 1952 *Wise Blood*, O'Connor's first novel, has a divided brain, one calculating side in touch with his wise blood but wordless, the other just "stocked up with all kinds of words and phrases" (*WB*, 87). As Enoch is preparing his shrine for the new Jesus, the narrator comments, "For the time, he knew that what he didn't know was what mattered" (*WB*, 131). In the same novel, the shyster Onnie Jay Holy attempts to sell Hazel Motes's new "Church Without Christ" as the "Holy Church of Christ Without Christ" with a familiar American anti-intellectual theme: "'Now I just want to give you folks a few reasons why you can trust this church,' he said. 'In the first place, friends, you can rely on it that it's nothing foreign connected with it. You don't have to believe nothing you don't understand and approve of. If you don't understand it, it ain't true, and that's all there is to it. No jokers in the deck, friends'" (*WB*, 152). Hazel Motes himself, the central character of *Wise Blood*, is driven by his denial of his knowledge of Christ into the clutches of a thoroughgoing empiricist epistemology. He engages a boy working at a filling station in a one-sided conversation on theology and knowledge: "He said it was not right to believe anything you couldn't see or hold in your hands or test with your teeth" (*WB*, 206). In "A Good Man Is Hard to Find," The Misfit—a literary avatar of our contemporary fascination with the serial killer—is spiritually and emotionally tortured because he wasn't present when Christ raised the dead. If he had been there, he "would of known" and perhaps not have become the killer that he is (*GM*, 29). Old Tarwater, in *The Violent Bear It Away*, O'Connor's second and last novel, lives with his schoolteacher nephew, Rayber, for three months while Rayber secretly makes a sociological study of him. Old Tarwater discovers the betrayal and kidnaps his great nephew (Young Francis Tarwater) to live with him in the woods and "instruct" him "in the hard facts of serving the Lord" (*VBA*, 6). He explains to Young Tarwater the importance of his having kidnaped him: "'I saved you to be free, your own self!' he had shouted, 'and not a piece of information inside his head! If you were living with him, you'd be information right now, you'd be inside his head, and what's furthermore,' he said, 'you'd be going to school'" (*VBA*, 16). Old Tarwater accurately sums up Rayber's character: "He don't know it's anything he can't know. . . . That's his trouble. He thinks if it's something he can't know then somebody smarter than him can tell him about it and he can know it just the same" (*VBA*, 56). And in "Revelation," finished in the last year of O'Connor's life, we meet Ruby Turpin, a self-satisfied farm owner who is sure of her elevated position in the hierarchy of creation until she is hit in the head by a book entitled *Human Development* thrown by a college student from Wellesley. Ruby does not begin to understand her true place until her defiant shout to God ("Who do you think you are?") "returned to her clearly like an answer from beyond the wood" (*ERMC,* 216–17). This small sample of O'Connor's children, intellectuals, prophets, criminals, and farm matrons reveals the wide range of character types in O'Connor's fiction who are obsessed with what they know, or don't know, or can't know, or don't want to know.

O'Connor appears to have narrowed her critical epistemological focus to a particular type of character as her writing career developed, a type we might label as the failed, or ineffectual, intellectual. In her M.A. thesis, there is one ineffectual academic—Rayber in "The Barber"—and one failed writer—Miss Willerton in "The Crop." Later in her career, O'Connor sometimes combined the types in overly intellectualized failed writers. Miss Willerton is full of abstract literary phrases like "literary venture," "tonal quality," and "phonetic art." A large portion of "The Crop" is concerned with the narration of Miss Willerton's hunt for an appropriate topic for her fiction. As the narrator tells us, "She spent more time thinking of something to write about than she did writing" (*CS,* 33–35). *Wise Blood* has no intellectuals, although there is the occasional glancing satiric blow to intellectual trends. The taxi driver who drops Hazel off at Leora Watts's house is properly horrified by Hazel's denial that he is a preacher and his claim that he doesn't "believe in anything": "That's the trouble with you preachers. . . . You've all got too good to believe in anything" (*WB,* 31–32). In the short story collection *A Good Man Is Hard to Find*, we find O'Connor's first fully developed intellectual, Hulga Hopewell of "Good Country People." Hulga's self-deception is exceeded only by her naïveté. In her imagination, she sees "profound implications" in her planned seduction of the "innocent" Bible salesman Manley Pointer. She lay "in bed imagining dialogues for them that were insane on the surface but that reached below to depths that no Bible salesman would be aware of" (*GM,* 184). The eventual humiliation that Hulga faces once she discovers that she was the one seduced and taught a lesson in duplicity becomes typical of the harshness with which O'Connor's intellectuals are treated in her mature short fiction. The plot of *The Violent Bear It Away* is in part an extended battle for the soul of Francis Tarwater between the forces represented by the great-uncle Tarwater, a backwoods prophet, and the younger uncle Rayber, a high-school teacher. All we know of the details of Rayber's academic career is that he is an expert on testing methods and that he publishes a study of the elder Tarwater in "a schoolteacher magazine" (*VBA*, 114, 4). While each of O'Connor's collections and novels up to and including *The Violent Bear It Away* has one or maybe two satiric characterizations of intellectuals, arguably six out of the nine stories in her last short story collection, *Everything That Rises Must Converge*, have a failed, or at least flawed, intellectual figure. In the eponymous story, Julian, the "writer" who sells typewriters "until he gets started," spends "most of his time" withdrawn in a "mental bubble" where he believes himself "safe from any kind of penetration from without" and where he believes he sees "with absolute clarity" (*ERMC*, 10–11). Wesley May, in "Greenleaf," teaches in a university, but "he hate[s] the second-rate university and he hate[s] the morons" who go there. His mother believes that a childhood bout with rheumatic fever "was what had caused him to be an intellectual" (*ERMC*, 28–29, 35). Asbury Fox, the failed writer in "The Enduring Chill," blames his mother in a hazy, puerile way for his own complete lack of talent. In "The Comforts of Home," it is not clear what kind of career the historian Thomas has. His mother says simply that he writes history and is the current president of the "local Historical Society." However, it is clear that he relies on "the fruits of his mother's saner virtues" for his daily comforts, including the home he lives in and the meals he eats (*ERMC*, 123, 119). Thomas's well-ordered life, which is merely threatened by his mother's Christian charity towards Star Drake (Sarah Ham), ends with his accidental shooting of his mother, caused at least in part by his emotionally clueless rationalism. Sheppard, in "The Lame Shall Enter First," loses his own son to suicide, partially as a result of his intellectual hubris and elitism. And in "Revelation," Mary Grace, the "lunatic" college student from Wellesley, may well be the messenger for Ruby's revelations, but she is carted off— sedated—in an ambulance to a hospital.

O'Connor's treatment of the theme of the inadequacy of intellectual knowledge alone in the perception of truth, whether religious or otherwise, is widely recognized. For example, Jane Carter Keller demonstrates the limitations of both empiricism and rationalism in O'Connor's fiction while Jane Marston focuses on the limitations of empiricism. John McCarthy generalizes quite accurately that "O'Connor's intellectuals usually aspire beyond their capacities." John Desmond argues that "a major theme in her work" is "deceptive consciousness[—]the mind's capacity for distortion in apprehending the real and its proneness to closure when impinged upon by the divine." Carol Shloss writes of the story "Good Country People" as "exploding the myth of rational control." Edward Kessler stresses the function of metaphor, whose power "demands the death of the understanding," in bringing readers to "a new consciousness." Stephen Behrendt argues that in "The River" the drowning of the child Bevel is "the culmination of a series of linked experiences that turn upon knowledge and illusion" and that in the same story "Mr. Paradise is trapped in a crisis of knowledge." Bob Dowell says of O'Connor's typical fictional character that in "rebelling against belief, [he] forces a crisis that reveals to him his haughty and willful misconception of reality." Michael Schroeder explores the similarities in pride of knowledge between Ruby Turpin of "Revelation" and the biblical Job.

Many of O'Connor's critics who simply touch on the topic of rational knowledge stress either the horror of rationality or the mystical beauty of revelation.[2] It is certainly the case in O'Connor's fiction that spiritual knowledge is radically opposed to rational knowledge, at least in the minds of her fundamentalist characters, such as Hazel Motes: "He knew by the time he was twelve years old that he was going to be a preacher. Later he saw Jesus move from tree to tree in the back of his mind, a wild ragged figure motioning him to turn around and come off into the dark where he was not sure of his footing, where he might be walking on the water and not know it and then suddenly know it and drown" (*WB*, 22). Hazel, thus, has an instinctive understanding that rational knowledge spells death to spirituality, both of which he seems to fear equally. Others of O'Connor's characters, like Hulga of "Good Country People," Thomas of "The Comforts of Home," Julian of "Everything That Rises Must Converge," Wesley of "Greenleaf," Asbury of "The Enduring Chill," and Sheppard of "The Lame Shall Enter First," are successful rationally (or at least they think they are) but abysmal failures spiritually until the limits of their rationality are exposed. My study, like those of McCarthy, Joyce Carol Oates, Richard Rupp, and Joseph Louis Zornado, recognizes both sides of the knowledge issue in O'Connor—the limitations of human rationality as well as the promise of grace once those limitations are realized or, at least, reached.[3] O'Connor does not propose a "leap into the absurd," as she phrases it in a letter to Alfred Corn, an Emory University student interested in theology. She explains, "I believe what the Church teaches—that God has given us reason to use and that it can lead us toward a knowledge of him, through analogy. . . . I find it reasonable to believe, even though these beliefs are beyond reason" (*HB,* 479). Thus, O'Connor is not so much opposed to the intellect as opposed to the misuse of the intellect. What O'Connor intends her protagonists to understand is the reality of their fundamentally ignorant selves; her narratives strip them of the many self-delusions that allow them to function without Christ. The frequently violent self-revelations of intellectual and spiritual hubris prepare O'Connor's characters for Christian grace (*MM,* 112).

As striking as O'Connor's prose is, one would expect a great deal of stylistic interest in her writing. However, compared to the overwhelming number of studies concentrating on her social, psychological, or religious thematic content, the number of specifically stylistic or linguistic works is quite small. Among the stylistic devices that have been analyzed are metaphor and simile, modes of speech presentation, onomastics, and rhetorical exhortation.[4] In most O'Connor criticism, the best that one can usually hope for in the way of stylistic analysis can be represented, for instance, by Shloss's passing reference to the conjunction *but* in one sentence from *The Violent Bear It Away* and her mysterious reference to the use of the passive in O'Connor's fiction in general (but without unambiguous examples).[5] Thus, I hope that one of the attractions that *Narrating Knowledge* both promises and delivers to the reader is an exemplification of what can be achieved in a stylistic investigation of O'Connor's fiction. Another of the book's attractions is, I believe, the demonstration of some of the methodologies of corpus linguistics in stylistics.

Corpus Linguistics, Corpora, and Text Analysis Tools

Narrating Knowledge is in the tradition of corpus linguistics, which in America was almost totally eclipsed by the ascendancy of nonempirical, rationalistic Chomskian linguistics in the 1960s.[6] Corpus linguistics, however, has flourished in Europe and did not altogether disappear even in America since the 1960s and 1970s saw the construction of several important corpora: the Lancaster/Oslo-Bergen, the London-Lund, and the Brown, the last of which is an American-made corpus. In this study, I compare the

Brown general-fiction corpus to O'Connor's texts in order to demonstrate the statistical significance of the stylistic patterns of both negation and verb complements that I examine in O'Connor. As we will see later in *Narrating Knowledge*, the statistical significance of these patterns supports the argument that O'Connor's concerns with human knowledge permeate her stories at a remarkable level of detail. Computational stylistics, a subfield or development of corpus linguistics, shares many concerns with corpus linguistics but has a few specific concerns of its own, given the place of stylistics within literary studies and its specialized use of corpora. Computational stylistics, like any field, may define its object of inquiry narrowly or broadly. In this book, I assume a moderately narrow object of inquiry, a single author's works, rather than an even narrower object, such as an individual story, or a potentially broader object, such as southern American literature. However, no matter the size of the object of inquiry or even its identity, one of the central concerns of computational stylistics is methodology. Under the broad umbrella of methodology lie issues such as obtaining or even planning and creating the corpora themselves, including any markup language; the computational tools used to access the data within the corpora, whether those tools are prepackaged or written by the investigators themselves; and the basic design and implementation of statistical tests to determine the significance of distributional patterns.

In stylistics, to determine anything of real comparative value about an author's work, one normally needs a comparative corpus, one that is as similar as possible to the author's "linguistic peers" and gathered with as little bias as is possible. Without a comparative corpus, to say, for example, that O'Connor uses a large number of "as if" quasi similes, however exact that number might be, is to say merely that in the analyst's opinion O'Connor's quasi similes outnumber those of most American authors, or perhaps all authors—an unverifiable intuition. To make a valid comparison for an author such as O'Connor, an analyst would ideally seek a corpus of American fiction published in the early 1960s. Fortunately, there is such a subcorpus in the Brown Corpus, which contains one million words of American English in excerpts of around two thousand words. The elements of the corpus were all published in 1960 or 1961. Most were randomly sampled from the Brown University Library and the Providence Athenaeum. The K subcorpus contains American "general fiction" and totals 58,120 words in twenty-nine excerpts.[7] The random nature of the sampling ensures that one type of general literature is not sampled more frequently than another. For instance, a story such as Hemingway's "Hills Like White Elephants," which is heavy in dialogue and thus potentially in negation, would not be statistically over represented as a type in the Brown Corpus. In this study, then, O'Connor's texts are compared to the statistical literary "norm," as represented by the Brown K subcorpus of general fiction (hereafter, "the Brown general-fiction corpus").

Another methodological imperative is that the comparative corpus must be tagged in similar ways to the main corpus under investigation. Thus, for this study, I coded both the Brown general-fiction corpus and the electronically scanned O'Connor texts for dialogue and narration, some of which had to be done manually in the Brown corpus because not all of the selections use quotation marks to indicate dialogue. Central to the methodology of any computational stylistic analysis is a text analysis tool. There are several available on the Internet, some of them free (TACT [Text-Analysis Computing Tools]; http://www.chass.utoronto.ca/cch/tact.html), and some of them for a reasonable cost (e.g., Wordsmith Tools; http://www.liv.ac.uk/~ms2928/homepage.html). Harald Klein has created a useful list of these programs and many other similar programs and a basic description of each (http://www.intext.de/TEXTANAE.HTM), and Eric Rochester has written a review of the strengths and weaknesses of both TACT and Wordsmith Tools.[8] Most of these programs will allow keyword-in-context searches, which are crucial for gathering contextual information about the use of particular linguistic constructions. However, there are inevitable limitations in any prepackaged text analysis tool, either in the size of texts that the program can work with effectively or in the output that is generated by the program. As Douglas Biber, Susan Conrad, and Randi Reppen point out, there are many advantages to writing one's own program for text analysis.[9] Foremost among those reasons, as far as I am concerned, are the allowable size of the corpus and accuracy in the processing of that corpus, both of which are frequently compromised in prepackaged text-analysis tools. TEXTANT (©2001 Donald E. Hardy), a program that I created specifically for the analysis in *Narrating Knowledge*, is written in PERL (Practical Extraction and Report Language), a computer language that is especially useful and well suited for Internet web programming (e.g., password protection and database management) and stylistics (e.g., text manipulation). TEXTANT (TEXT ANalysis Tools) makes use of both of the primary areas of strength in PERL: text manipulation, because TEXTANT is a text-search engine, and the web, because it runs on the Internet so that the interface (i.e., radio buttons, drop-down menus, and text-input boxes) is provided by the use of freely available web-browsers. The primary use of TEXTANT in my study was to search for and count tokens of morphological and syntactic patterns such as *not* negation and *see* + clausal or phrasal complements. TEXTANT was also used to count all words in dialogue and all words in narration. Using TEXTANT, I was able to process all of O'Connor's fiction in one text file, whose size makes economical processing impossible in programs such as TACT, for example. By processing O'Connor's fiction in one file, I was able to perform many tasks at once that otherwise would have necessitated several repetitive, and potentially error-inducing, processing runs. For example, I was able to create one "suspect-words" list in the final check of the accuracy of the electronic scanning of the texts into ASCII files. Greater accuracy in text searches is made possible by the ease with which the results of searches can be double-checked against multiple versions of the corpus, ensuring the identification and correction of any errors introduced by coding the corpora for contextual variables such as dialogue and narration.

The Organization of Narrating Knowledge

The three syntactic and semantic-pragmatic patterns that I explore in this book are (1) dependent clauses and presupposition, (2) *not* negation and supposition, and (3) nonfinite complements and implication. Because each of these complex patterns is what William Labov calls "a departure from basic narrative syntax" and is therefore fully understandable only within the context of narrative structure, chapter 2 introduces and summarizes Labov's influential account of the structure of oral narrative in his 1972 essay "The Transformation of Experience in Narrative Syntax," which is based in part on Labov and Joshua Waletzky's 1967 article "Narrative Analysis: Oral Versions of Personal Experience."[10] Making use of Labov's analysis of oral narrative, I then turn in chapter 2 to a description of the linguistic structure of narrative syntax and my analysis of how O'Connor's narrative makes reference to that structure. Each of the three constructions that I explore in depth in this book, as we will see, has its own complex grammatical and epistemic qualities. And each is intimately and subtly involved in the production and management of knowledge in O'Connor's fiction.

Chapter 3 explores some of the stylistic issues involving presupposition in O'Connor's fiction. To lay some preliminary groundwork for presupposition analysis, consider the following sentences:

1. Bill realizes that you are sick.
2. Bill doesn't realize that you are sick.

In both (1) and (2) the truth of the clausal complement to the main verb of cognition *realize*, "that you are sick," is presupposed, as is proved by the negation of the main verb in (2). What remains true after the negation of the main verb is the propositional material that is presupposed. What is asserted in (1) and (2) is that Bill either realizes or doesn't realize the presupposed fact that "you are sick." One of the many patterns of presupposition in complements to cognition verbs used by O'Connor is the presentation of ironic, questionable propositions that can be attributed to the thought of the character under consideration. For example, consider the following description of what the mother and grandmother are wearing in the car on their way to their Florida vacation in "A Good Man Is Hard to Find":

> The children's mother still had on slacks and still had her head tied up in a green kerchief, but the grandmother had on a navy blue straw sailor hat with a bunch of white violets on the brim and a navy blue dress with a small white dot in the print. Her collars and cuffs were white organdy trimmed with lace and at her neckline she had pinned a purple spray of cloth violets containing a sachet. In case of an accident, anyone seeing her dead on the highway would know at once *that she was a lady*. (*GM*, 11)

Italics will be used in this book to draw the reader's attention to selected constructions in quotations. Italics are mine unless indicated otherwise. The italicized clause "that she was a lady" occurs as a complement to the cognition verb *know*. If the truth of a clause is unquestionably presupposed and if the clause expresses a positive judgment such as this one does of a character established as having questionable judgment, the claim is most likely to originate from the narrator's mimicking the character's thoughts or words.

Chapters 4 and 5 consider the quantitative and qualitative stylistic patterns of negation in O'Connor's fiction. The following examples may be used to explore some initial basic pragmatic issues with respect to negation:

3. I sat down at the restaurant table, ordered the best steak on the menu, but didn't eat it.
4. I sat down at the restaurant table, ordered the best steak on the menu, but didn't wear it as a hat.

Although (3) and (4) are nearly identical in structure, (3) strikes the reader as unremarkable while (4) seems very odd. Example (3) is unremarkable because one expects to eat a steak if one orders it, but (4) is odd because one does not expect to wear a steak as a hat, no matter how good it is. As we will see in detail later, negatives are normally felicitous only if they respond to a background expectation to the contrary. That background expectation can tell one a great deal about what particular speakers have in mind as they speak; in other words, background expectation is a location of knowledge, whether shared or not among speakers and listeners, or characters and readers. In "Greenleaf," Mrs. May despairs of her sons' ability to deal effectively with the hired help on their farm, particularly Mr. Greenleaf. When she finds out that it is Greenleaf's sons who own the bull that is loose on her farm, she asks Wesley—the intellectual—a series of parental questions that seem designed to encourage guilt or at least responsibility in him. The series ends with the following question:

> "Do you see that if I hadn't kept my foot on his neck all these years, you boys might be milking cows every morning at four o'clock?"
> Wesley pulled the paper back toward his plate and staring at her full in the face, he murmured, "I wouldn't milk a cow to save your soul from hell."
> "I know you wouldn't," she said in a brittle voice. (*ERMC*, 36)

The background expectation for Wesley's negation, "I wouldn't milk a cow to save your soul from hell," is double-edged. First, the negation responds to the expectation on the part of his mother that he would actually milk a cow. Second and oddly, it creates the expectation that he might do so to save her soul from hell. There will be much more to say in chapters 4 and 5 about "creating" background expectation through the use of negation. Note also that Wesley's mother somewhat incongruously says in return that she already knows that he wouldn't milk the cow to save her soul.

In part, chapters 6 and 7 continue from chapter 3 the exploration of presupposition in O'Connor's fiction since they treat the differences between implication and presupposition as they are signaled in the various phrasal and clausal complements to the verb *see*. We will be concerned with both

nonfinite (i.e., tenseless) complements and finite (i.e., tensed) complements to the verb *see*, as in the following examples, which may be used to
explore some preliminary points about the differences between those complement types:

5. Liz saw *the dog leave.*
6. Liz saw *the dog leaving.*
7. Liz saw *the dog left on the porch.*
8. Liz saw *that the dog left.*

Examples (5), (6), and (7) contain nonfinite complements to the verb *see*,
the first being an infinitive (or bare stem), the second a present participial,
and the third a past participial. For our purposes, "tense" is not signaled in
the participials. Even though they are traditionally labeled the "present" participial and the "past" participial, they are actually without tense. Example
(8) contains a finite complement, finite by the presence of the past tense.
Nonfinite complements to the verb *see* are implicational. That is, the truth
of the main clause "Liz saw the dog leave" guarantees the truth of the complement "the dog leave." For example, in (5), if Liz saw the dog leave, the
dog must necessarily have left. The same is true of the examples "Liz saw the
dog leaving" and "Liz saw the dog left on the porch." At first glance, example
(8) seems to be implicational as well. However, there is a difference between
nonfinite and finite complements to the verb *see*. Finite complements are
presuppositional in nature, not implicational. The details of this technical
and subtle difference are covered in chapters 6 and 7, so I will leave exposition of that difference until then. However, now we may illustrate a few of
the stylistic problems involved in nonfinite and finite complements in the
following O'Connor passages:

9. "I said long ago, you get you a signature and sign everything you do
   and keep a copy of it. Then you'll know what you done and you can
   hold up the crime to the punishment and see *do they match* and in the
   end you'll have something to prove you ain't been treated right. I
   call myself The Misfit," he said, "because I can't make what all I done
   wrong fit what all I gone through in punishment." (*GM*, 27–28)
10. [The Misfit's] voice seemed about to crack and the grandmother's
    head cleared for an instant. She saw *the man's face twisted close to her
    own as if he were going to cry* and she murmured, "Why you're one of
    my babies. You're one of my own children!" (*GM*, 29)

In (9), two of the important characteristics of finite complements to *see* are illustrated: (1) the relative syntactic independence of the complement such that inversion of subject (*they*) and auxiliary (*do*) is possible and (2) the cognitive content of the complement (i.e., it is a question about a judgment). In (10) at least one of the important literary characteristics of nonfinite complements of *see* is illustrated: literal physical vision. It is from the vision that the grandmother receives the grace to conclude that she and The Misfit are of one humanity and that she is to care for him, as she does in the sense that she touches him both physically and spiritually.

In the concluding chapter 8, I will turn to the subject of the history of the interaction of linguistics and literary study in America, after having demonstrated in the bulk of *Narrating Knowledge* that a productive interaction between the two is attainable without the sacrifice of either the methodological rigor of linguistics or the interpretive subtlety of literary study. Chapter 8 will also place in historical context the type of stylistic analysis that is practiced in this book.

I have written *Narrating Knowledge* with the general educated audience in mind so that readers unfamiliar with linguistics will be able to follow the linguistic arguments. It is the nature of stylistics to be a bit technical in parts; however, I sincerely hope that readers will conclude in their cost-benefit analysis that the details of the linguistically driven analyses and interpretations help them to enjoy and appreciate deeply the total effect of O'Connor's fiction. Interpretation is not necessarily the weakest link in the stylistic chain, but its constitution is probably the most surprising to the outsider because it most frequently relies on the linguistics that guides the analysis in the first place. Thus, just as Lacanian analysts might go looking for mirror stages and such in O'Connor's multiple doppelgängers because a Lacanian framework predetermines a search for mirror stages, a stylistician might go looking for presuppositional clauses in the language of O'Connor's idiot savant prophets and prophet enablers because a linguistic perspective on narrative predetermines, among many other things, a search for significant uses of presuppositional dependent clauses. Furthermore, as will be evident in parts of this book, stylistic analysis can give as much back to linguistics in the form of supports for refinements of linguistic hypotheses as it takes in the form of interpretive and analytic models. For example, chapters 4 and 5 will demonstrate a new type of negative supposition, and chapters 6 and 7 will provide literary data that will reinforce a pragmatic rather than semantic interpretation of implication. Both of these refinements are in part a result of the kind of data that are examined—literary prose.

Readers may finally judge for themselves the strongest claims of this book: that linguistics has a continuing relevance in literary theory and interpretation and that in particular it enriches our appreciation and understanding of O'Connor's struggles with both the promises and the limitations of human knowledge.

Chapter 2

The Linguistic Structure of Narrative

I hope you realize that your asking me to talk about story-writing is just like asking a fish to lecture on swimming.

—Flannery O'Connor (*MM*, 87)

Stylistics, as I practice it in *Narrating Knowledge*, is a merger of concerns with the traditional objects of investigation—oral language and literary language—in linguistics and literary studies. That merger is a result of the interest of stylistics in the analytic tools of linguistics since many of those tools (subdisciplines) have been developed through an analysis of oral language. It is well-established doctrine within most traditional areas of linguistic theory that oral language has diachronic and synchronic primacy over written language.[1] Indeed, the theoretical dominance of the oral over the written in linguistics is frequently given as a legitimation for the existence of linguistics as a field of study separate from other social sciences and humanistic disciplines. However, even in linguistics, there are radically different approaches to orality. In light of frequent complaints that linguistics is more reliant on written language for its data, intuitional or otherwise, than is sometimes supposed or claimed, it is important to realize that orality is a multifaceted issue, as Monika Fludernik points out in some programmatic detail.[2] The influences on the understanding of orality in stylistics, for example, minimally include studies in formulaic orality, corpus linguistics, and oral-narrative study.

Scholars in orality studies such as Milman Parry, Albert Lord, Eric Havelock, and Walter Ong have written extensively of the psychological, cultural, and sociological effects as well as forms of formulaically oral vs. literate communication. Havelock, for example, argues in his *Preface to Plato* that Plato's literate and rationalist attack on poets and poetry in the *Republic* was motivated by a fear of their orality and consequent irrational control over the public. It should be made clear, however, that orality studies of the type conducted by Havelock, Ong, and others are not primarily or sometimes at all concerned with ordinary oral communication. Have-lock, for instance, argues that a theory of orality should not set itself the goal of accounting for ordinary conversation, and presumably ordinary narra-tive, since the ordinary is "impermanent," unlike the relatively permanent formulaic orality of oral performances in primary oral cultures.[3]

Contemporary linguists who are interested in ordinary orality, including among many others Deborah Tannen, Douglas Biber, Wallace Chafe, John Du Bois, Barbara Fox, Barbara Johnstone, and Sandra Thompson, analyze ordinary oral conversation and narrative, tape recorded and transcribed, for the patterns of everyday orality. Although these researchers find some of the same patterns that researchers in formulaic orality have identified in oral poetry, they are in some of their research interested in the ways in which ordinary oral communication is the same as and different from written communication. Much of this work builds on the enormously influential account of the structure of ordinary oral narrative in William Labov and Joshua Waletzky's "Narrative Analysis" and Labov's "The Transformation of Experience in Narrative Syntax," both of which analyze the structure of ordinary oral narrative in a framework that combines the formal with the pragmatic. The continuing relevance of Labov's 1972 work and the general approach of using frameworks from the analysis of oral narrative in the analysis of literary narrative is revealed in the work of Fludernik and Suzanne Fleischman, for example.[4]

General Narrative Structure

Labov's formal and pragmatic analysis of naturally occurring oral narratives divides the narrative into six parts:

1. Abstract: short summary
2. Orientation: time, place, persons, situation
3. Complicating Action: narrative events
4. Evaluation: justification for narrative
5. Resolution: final narrative event
6. Coda: transitional summary of theme

The abstract is a short summary of the story, with which narrators option-ally begin their stories. The orientation will "identify in some way the time, place, persons, and their activity or the situation."[5] The complicating action is the narrative itself, a series of ordered independent clauses. The evaluation provides the point of the story and thus justifies the telling of the story in the first place. Literary narrators, no less than oral narrators, must justify their taking the literary, or conversational, floor by making their verbal products worthy of the reader's, or audience's, attention. A pointless short story or novel, like a pointless oral narrative, is a breach of literary, or ordinarily polite, protocol. Evaluations in both poetic and natural oral narratives ensure the tellability, or point(s), of the tale. The resolution provides the closure or end of the complicating action. I will go into much more depth on complicating action and evaluation in later sections. The coda indicates the end of the narrative and "may also contain general observations or show the effects of the events on the narrator" (LIC, 365). In other words, the coda frequently summarizes the point of the narrative as it was communicated in the evaluation. The narrative proper consists of only the complicating action and the resolution. All other elements are optional, although a narrative without evaluation is frequently judged to be defective. There is nothing very remarkable about Labov's six-part analysis of the general structure of narrative to those who remember being introduced to Gustav Freytag's analysis in grade school. As Mary Louise Pratt puts it, "Every high school student knows that novels and plays have an introduction, a gradual rising action, a climax followed by a swift dénouement and resolution with the option of an epilogue at the end."[6]

In order to explore the fundamentals of Labov's model, we will first consider an oral narrative that was produced during a dinner party at which hunting stories largely figured.[7] There are actually three narratives in the narrative, two imbedded in an outer narrative frame, a complexity that is by no means rare in oral narratives (or, of course, literary narratives). In the transcription of the story, each abstract, orientation, etc. is labeled with a I, II, or III to indicate which story it serves, although we will see that there is much reflexivity among these stories. I have not reproduced the narratives in close transcription with pauses and overlaps marked because it is only the relatively broad structure of the narratives that is of interest here. The numbered elements are referred to for convenience as sentences although many are simply phrases or clauses and some contain more than one "grammatical" (i.e., punctuated) sentence.

Abstract (I):
7. Tom: But, uh, anyway, they got a story goin' over there, afterwards, later, of me gettin' a deer.

Orientation (I):
8. Well, I'd forgot my Bible and left it up in the stand.
9. Well, I'd got me a deer.

Complicating Action (I):
10. But, anyway, this guy that I hunt with down there found it in this stand,
11. and he came back to Dallas up there at Deb's Diner

Abstract (II):
12. and he said, uh, "Well, we know how Tom Hardy gets his deer."

Orientation (II):
13. He said, "I turned to this pass—, passage, he had it marked,"
14. he said, uh, "ask and ye shall receive.

Complicating Action (II):
15. And he got his deer."

Evaluation (III):
16. I said, "Well, if you think that's, that's bad,"

Orientation (III):
17. I said, "I was down there in that same stand where that bird was that time"

Complicating Action (III):
18. and I said, uh, "I prayed to get me a good buck, a nice big one."

Evaluation (III):
19. And I said, uh, "Now, you may not believe this, but I, I kinda felt foolish shootin' the deer.

Complicating Action (III):
20. The thing, I seen him come up to the fence down all a good ways from me there,
21. and he looked up and down the fence

22. and he just trotted right up there where I was
23. and looked up at me
24. and jumped over the fence
25. and walked under my stand."

Evaluation (III):
26. I said, "He was so pretty, I ju—, I really didn't wanna shoot him."
27. I said, "I felt so bad about it,"

Complicating Action (III):
28. I said, "Then he trotted off out there
29. and turned around
30. and looked at me.

Evaluation (III):
31. And I said, 'Well, you foolish thing.
32. You done the wrong thing.'"

Evaluation (III):
33. Heather: You deserve to die.

Resolution (III):
34. Tom: So:: I shot him.

Coda (III):
35. Heather: Don't need any stupid deer.

Coda (III):
36. Tom: He said, "Yeah, ol' Hardy, he, all he has to do is," he says, "is ask and you shall receive
37. and he gets his deer."

Resolution (I) Coda (III):
38. I said, "Well," I said, "I believe in that,"
39. and I said, "whether you do or not."
40. And I said, "I prayed about that before I even got down there."

Coda (I):
41. But, uh, I said, "Not that you always get your uh, your, uh, uh, prayers answered because sometimes you don't really, you . . . "
42. Heather: you don't need what you're askin' for.
43. Tom: "you don't really need what you're askin' for. I got my meat and that's what I went down there to get."

As will become clear in our discussions of the codas of the narratives and as is already clear in the number of main clauses devoted to each, Tom and Heather find the first and third narratives the more important, the first being the story of the conversation between Tom and the man at the diner who brought his Bible back to him and the third being the story of Tom's shooting the friendly, or stupid, deer. The second narrative in (12–15) is reported by Tom as told to him and others at Deb's Diner, a particularly fertile spot in South Dallas for oral narratives and other things. It is questionable, however, whether we should even call the second narrative a fully formed narrative since it has only an abstract, an orientation, and a one-clause complicating action. Sentence (7) forms a partial abstract of the first narrative, that people talk about Tom's getting a deer. Sentences (8–9) form the orientation, the background, for the narrative of the conversation between Tom and the man who returned Tom's Bible. Sentence (10) begins the complicating action of the narrative of the conversation. Most of the independent clauses in the text begin with "I/he said" or "And I/he said," marking them as belonging at least in part to the complicating action, resolution, or coda of the first narrative of the conversation, even though I have not marked this throughout the narrative—simply for the sake of clarity of marking the embedded narratives. Every sentence in the text serves to further the first narrative, except Heather's comments in (33), (35), and (42), which are either evaluations or codas. Although oral narrators can share the narration of the complicating action, here Heather serves only as an evaluator and coda maker. Narrative I reaches a resolution in (38–40), when Tom tells his friend that he believes in answered prayers whether his friend does or not. We will return later to discuss the coda of Narrative I in (41–43).

Narrative III does not have an abstract, probably because the topic of shooting deer with divine intervention has already been established in Narrative II. Narrative III begins with an evaluation in (16), which promises the tellability of the story by implying that the next story will upset Tom's friend even more. The orientation for Narrative III occurs in (17), in which Tom indicates where he was for the shooting of the next deer, making reference to the setting for an earlier story during the dinner party. The complicating action begins in (18) with prayer. We are taken off the event line (complicating action) in (19), which tells us that Tom felt foolish, for some reason, in shooting this deer. The evaluation, again, ensures the tellability of the tale. The core of the complicating action of Narrative III begins with (20) and continues through (25), as Tom tells of the approach of the deer that he will feel foolish in shooting. Again in (26) and (27), Tom takes his listeners off the event line as he tells them why he didn't want to shoot the deer and that he felt bad about doing so. The complicating action of the narrative event line returns in (28–30), indicating that the deer is still alive and has a chance to live. But in (31–32) Tom again takes us off the event line for an evaluation telling us why he had to shoot the deer. The conflicting emotions revealed in the evaluations of (19), (26–27), and (31–32) serve the purpose of making the tellability of the tale clear. Then in (33) Heather provides further evaluation for Narrative III by indicating why the deer had to die—because he deserved it. The resolution of the narrative and of the tension of the evaluations is provided in (34), when Tom tells his audience that he shot the deer. (The double colon after the vowel of *so* signifies extra long vowel length.)

With (34), all three of the tales are told, except for the resolution to Narrative I in (38–40), and the stories could, of course, end there. But it is typical of oral narrators and even their audiences to provide a coda to narratives in order to bridge the gap between the narrative and the time or context of the storytelling. This coda frequently points to a moral or general point that was perceived to have been made in the narratives.

Since Tom's narrative provides us not simply one coda but four, three by three different speakers, we might assume that the indeterminacy and paradox of high literature would be absent in the "ordinary" prose of his narrative. Heather's coda to Narrative III in (35) is a humorous summary of the point of the story for her as she constructs it, that the deer was killed because we don't need any stupid deer in this world. Tom provides his friend's coda for Narrative III in (36–37), where the friend characteristically or persistently mocks Tom's getting his deer, this time the second one, through divine intervention. Minimally, Tom's friend's coda conflicts with Heather's. They each select only part of the evaluation to abstract from for the point of the entire narrative. Heather concludes that the deer was stupid (compare Tom's evaluation in (31–32) that the deer is foolish and did the wrong thing). Tom's friend takes his coda not from the evaluation of Narrative II, of which there is none, but from the complicating action in (18) and abstract and orientation for his own Narrative II in (12–14). Tom's friend's lame coda for Narrative III in (36–37) provides the occasion for Tom's own coda for Narrative III in (38–40), in which he first asserts that he prayed for the second deer with the implication that the point of the story is that he got what he asked for not once but twice.

So far in Tom's narrative and his own, his friend's, and Heather's codas, or interpretations, we see evidence that narrators and their audiences will disagree on the final interpretation of the significance of a narrative. The parallel with judgments as to the significance or interpretation of literature within literary criticism—New Criticism to post-structuralism—is obvious. But note that in (41–43), Tom and Heather jointly construct a coda for the framing Narrative I. It is here that Tom and Heather get closest to speaking of the paradox in all of the narratives since they are all contained by Narrative I of the conversation between Tom and his friend. Tom tells his friend, with Heather's help, that we don't always get our prayers answered because sometimes we don't need what we ask for. This can hardly be a final coda for any of these narratives since Tom, as he says, gets the "meat" that he prayed for. So, what is the sense of a coda that warns an apparent skeptic that he should be careful of what he asks for? One here has to take a step outside the text itself to interpret the final coda for Narrative I. Tom asked for the second deer, but the evaluations that he provides for Narrative III in (19) and (26–27) tell us that he didn't really want to shoot the deer and that he felt bad about doing so. Was Tom happy about getting his deer or not? Finally, this is a literary question which is unanswerable. We can only point to the text itself and ponder the object of Tom's desire embedded in the "residuary tissue" or the "uncertainty" of his story.[8]

There are several differences between the typical oral narrative and the typical modern literary narrative in the degree to which they follow Labov's six-part general narrative structure. For example, there are usually no abstracts or codas in modern literary narratives. I will not belabor this point here, or argue with scholars like Pratt who maintain that there is greater similarity between oral and literary narratives than I am claiming here or with scholars like Fludernik who work within a theoretical framework at variance with that of Labov's analysis, mainly because my central concern in this book is not the general Labovian narrative structure but instead the particulars of narrative syntax and departures from narrative syntax in Flannery O'Connor's fiction.[9] Thus, instead of attempting to find all six elements of the Labovian narrative structure in an O'Connor narrative, I quote below and analyze in the following section the narrative syntax in a short passage from "A Good Man Is Hard to Find," in which we find the escaped convict The Misfit agonizing over his doubt whether Jesus really raised the dead and the grandmother responding to that agony:

"I wasn't there so I can't say He didn't," The Misfit said. "I wisht I had of been there," he said, hitting the ground with his fist. "It ain't right I wasn't there because if I had of been there I would of known. Listen lady," he said in a high voice, "if I had of been there I would of known and I wouldn't be like I am now." His voice seemed about to crack and the grandmother's head cleared for an instant. She saw the man's face twisted close to her own as if he were going to cry and she murmured, "Why you're one of my babies. You're one of my own children!" She reached out and touched him on the shoulder. The Misfit sprang back as if a snake had bitten him and shot her three times through the chest. Then he put his gun down on the ground and took off his glasses and began to clean them.

Hiram and Bobby Lee returned from the woods and stood over the ditch. (*GM,* 29)

Narrative Syntax

Narrative syntax, according to Labov, is found in the complicating action and resolution of the narrative. Narrative syntax is important because it is by means of that syntax (i.e., the particular order and form of words in clauses) that the ordered events of the narrative proper are expressed. Thus, (44) and (45) are narratives while (46) and (47) are not narratives in Labov's sense:

44. I walked the dog, and then I bathed the dog.
45. I bathed the dog, and then I walked the dog.
46. I bathed the dog after I walked the dog.
47. After I walked the dog, I bathed the dog.

The reason that (44) and (45) are narratives while (46) and (47) are not is explained by Labov's definition of a minimal narrative: "we can define a *minimal narrative* as a sequence of two clauses which are *temporally ordered*: that is, a change in their order will result in a change in the temporal sequence of the original semantic interpretation. In alternative terminology, there is temporal juncture between the two clauses, and a minimal narrative is defined as one containing a single temporal juncture" (*LIC,* 360–61). The reversal of the clausal ordering in (44) and (45), minus the coordinating conjunction and conjunctive adverb, creates different narratives. That is, the order of the walking and bathing are different. But in (46) and (47), although the order of the clauses is reversed in each, the perceived narrative ordering of the events is the same: first I walked the dog; then I bathed him. It is central to the analyses in *Narrating Knowledge* that both of the clauses in (44) and (45) are independent (i.e., foregrounded), while one each of the clauses in (46) and (47) are dependent (i.e., backgrounded). It is the dependent clauses that allow us to reorder the clauses in (46) and (47) with no change in the interpretation of the order of events. The independent narrative clauses may not be reordered without a change in the interpretation of the order of events.

As Labov argues, an independent narrative clause is "one of the simplest grammatical patterns in connected speech" (*LIC*, 375). The following is his outline for the structure of the narrative clause:

a. Conjunctions, including temporals: *so, and, but, then.*
b. Simple subjects: pronouns, proper names, *this girl, my father.*
c. The underlying auxiliary is a simple past tense marker which is incorporated in the verb; no member of the auxiliary appears in the surface structure except some past progressive *was . . . ing* in the orientation section, and occasional quasimodals *start, begin, keep, used to, want.*
d. Preterite verbs, with adverbial particles *up, over, down.* (These particles will occasionally be placed under [f] or [g] by transformations. . . .)
e. Complements of varying complexity: direct and indirect objects.
f. Manner or instrumental adverbials.
g. Locative adverbials. Narrative syntax is particularly rich in this area.
h. Temporal adverbials and comitative clauses.
    (*LIC*, 376)

The only obligatory elements here are the subject, the auxiliary (usually incorporated in the verb), and the verb, as in the sentence "I walked." However, (48) represents all of the narrative elements, obligatory and optional:

CONJ	SUBJ	AUX/VB	COMP	M/IADV	LADV	TADV
a	b	c/d	e	f	g	h
48. And	she	told	the story	loudly	in the store	yesterday

In the following, I have lined up the narrative syntactic elements from a complicating action subset of Tom's narrative, with each of the narrative clauses numbered from (49) to (58):

	CONJ	SUBJ	AUX/VB	COMP	M/IADV	LADV	TADV
	a	b	c/d	e	f	g	h
49.		I	seen	him . . .			
50.	and	he	looked			up and down the fence	
51.	and	he	just trotted			right up there where I was	
52.	and		looked			up at me	
53.	and		jumped			over the fence	
54.	and		walked			under my stand.	
55.	Then	he	trotted			off out there	
56.	and		turned			around	
57.	and		looked			at me.	
58.	So::	I	shot	him.			

The ellipsis in (49) indicates the elision of a bare-stem complement ("come up to the fence down all a good ways from me there"), whose type we will discuss in detail in chapters 6 and 7. The bare-stem complement belongs to a class of structures that Labov terms "departures from the basic narrative syntax," all of which he says "have a marked evaluative force" (*LIC*, 378). The complement is a departure from narrative syntax in that (1) it does not have its own simple subject and (2) the verb is without tense. And by "evaluative force," Labov means the indication of "the point of the narrative, its raison d'être: why it was told, and what the narrator is getting at" (*LIC*, 366). Obviously the entire point of Tom's narrative is not that the deer came "up to the fence down all a good ways from [him] there." Evaluation is diffuse throughout the narrative and is cumulative, as we will see. Thus, the vision (the seeing being foregrounded in (49) in the main verb *see*) of the gift of the deer approaching Tom from a distance is simply one piece of the evaluatory puzzle that creates interest in the narrative.

In the following, I have lined up the narrative syntactic elements from a complicating action subset of the portion of O'Connor's "A Good Man Is Hard to Find" that is quoted above at the end of the previous section, with each of the narrative clauses numbered from (59) to (67):

CONJ	SUBJ	AUX/VB	COMP	M/IADV	LADV	TADV
a	b	c/d	e	f	g	h
59.	She	reached			out	
60. and		touched	him		on the shoulder	
61.	The Misfit	sprang			back . . .	
62. and		shot	her	three times	through the chest	
63. Then	he	put	his gun		down on the ground	
64. and		took off	his glasses			
65. and		began to clean	them			
66.	Hiram and Bobby Lee	returned			from the woods	
67. and		stood			over the ditch	

Note the remarkable similarities in syntactic structure between the oral excerpt in (49–58) and the O'Connor excerpt in (59–67). Both passages, for example, make prodigious use of simple preterite verbs and locative adverbials. The elided departure from narrative syntax in (61) ("as if a snake had bitten him")—a departure because it is a dependent clause and because it contains perfect aspect—is obviously not the point of the entire narrative, but this quasi simile provides background spiritual meaning as The Misfit struggles with the devil that so obviously possesses his soul.[10]

Evaluation and Departures from Narrative Syntax

In Labov's model, there are three basic ways of providing evaluation to the narrative, that is, three basic ways of justifying the telling of the narrative through heightened interest: (1) external evaluation, (2) internal evaluation, and (3) departures from narrative syntax, the last of which is the topic of the next five chapters of *Narrating Knowledge*.

External evaluation occurs when the narrator explicitly tells the listener "what the point is" (*LIC,* 371). External evaluation is normally easily recognized in oral narrative, as we see in the following excerpts from oral narratives, the first of which is from Tom's narrative:

> I said, "He was so pretty, I ju—, I really didn't wanna shoot him." I said, "I felt so bad about it,"

Here, Tom evaluates the shooting of the deer by explicitly telling his listeners that he didn't want to shoot the deer. Note that this external evaluation occurs in the middle of Narrative III, highlighting its importance. Tom's external evaluation is subtle because, as I argue below, it can also be analyzed as internal evaluation. Most external evaluations are intrusive since external evaluation is more usually a relatively crude evaluatory device (compare, "Listen to this. It's a great story.") The following (with the external evaluation italicized)—from another oral narrative—is more typical of external evaluation:

> Cause, so, Jeff was about to fight, to start a fight with this guy. And Frank, my friend Frank, who also was with us, who dressed as a tiger. He's a very small guy, right? And he and Jeff are best friends. And HE the little tiger was holding back the big secret service guy from beating up this big doctor with blood all over him who was dancing in front of the dart board (laughing) that I was standing in the line waiting to throw the darts cause this big guy was in the line. *It's a very funny scene, right?!* . . . And me, the little cowboy, SAT there with my guns doing ABSOLUTELY nothing watching my friends start this big fight.

All except the italicized portion of this excerpt is orientation, but the narrator responds to laughter from his audience by providing the external evaluation "It's a very funny scene, right?!" External evaluation does occasionally occur in literature, although never in O'Connor's fiction.

There are several subtypes of internal evaluation, but they all have in common that the evaluatory comments or material occur within the narrative itself; perhaps a character comments on the significance of the action, as Tom does in quoting himself as a character: "I said, 'He was so pretty, I ju—, I really didn't wanna shoot him.' I said, 'I felt so bad about it.'" As I indicated above, Tom's evaluation in (26) and (27) can be considered internal within Narrative I since he is reporting in Narrative I his own conversation with his skeptical friend. In the following passage of internal evaluation from "A Good Man Is Hard to Find," Bailey first realizes suddenly that he and his family are in the presence of the murdering Misfit and second realizes that he and his son are about to be murdered by The Misfit's gang:

> "Look here now," Bailey began suddenly, "we're in a predicament! We're in . . ."
>
> "Listen," Bailey began, "we're in a terrible predicament! Nobody realizes what this is," and his voice cracked. (*GM*, 21–23)

In the following example from an oral narrative about the speaker's car fire, the first-person narrator and third-person characters provide internal evaluation. The passage ends with one sentence of external evaluation, in which the narrator speaks directly to her audience:

> I said, "Chuck, you have to come over here. *My car is burning down*," and, um, he said, "It is not." You know. "Quit kidding around." And I said, "*It is really burning down*." And Nancy and I were like, "*It's burning down*. You have to get over here now". . . . And we walked back across the street, and he pulled up on the little moped, and he said, "*I swea:r I thought you were kidding*." And he sat there with u:s, and all these people were just sitting there, looking around going, "*This is unbelievable*." Um, the firemen finally got there, and by the time the firemen got there, Nancy and I were pretty well just laughing because we were, we were just in shock. *We, I mean, our ca:rs were burning down*.

We know that the final sentence is external evaluation because the tense shifts from present in the internal evaluation to past.

The third basic type of evaluation, departures from narrative syntax, has four subtypes, and these subtypes have themselves several subtypes each. I will discuss each of the four major subtypes, taking care to place into their narrative context the three formal patterns that are the topics of the remainder of this book: negation, dependent clauses, and participials.

Intensifiers, such as gestures, expressive phonology, quantifiers, and repetition, strengthen an event, and thereby evaluate it. Labov illustrates intensifier strengthening with figure 1.

The bolded arrow represents the intensifying effect of expressive phonology and the other intensifier subtypes. For example, in the burning-car

Figure 1. Intensifiers

From *Language in the Inner City* by William Labov.
Copyright ©1972 University of Pennsylvania Press. Reprinted with permission.

narrative above the narrator uses lengthened vowels to intensify the effect in the words *swea:r, u:s,* and *ca:rs,* and Tom uses extra vowel lengthening in the coordinating conjunction that begins his resolution: "So:: I shot him." Repetition is also frequently used as an intensifier, as in the following passage from "A Good Man Is Hard to Find," in which The Misfit laments his absence at Christ's raising the dead because if he had been there he would have known that Christ did the things that are claimed of him and thus he, The Misfit, would have been a different person.[11] The repetitions are italicized and aligned:

> "*I wasn't there* . . . ," The Misfit said.
> "I wisht I had of *been there,*" he said. . . .
> "It ain't right *I wasn't there*
> because *if I had of been there I would of known.*"
> "*if I had of been there I would of known.* . . ." (*GM,* 29)

None of the intensifiers is of lasting interest to us in *Narrating Knowledge* except in how they differ from the remaining three major subtypes of departures from narrative syntax. The intensifiers all serve to foreground utterances, making them more noticeable, for example through repetition. That The Misfit was not present at the raising of the dead is repeated four times in the passage above; that he would have known whether Christ did what is said of him is repeated once. These repetitions thus highlight, or foreground, The Misfit's doubt and essentially empirical, although vastly flawed, approach to matters of faith and knowledge.[12]

The remaining three subtypes of departures from narrative syntax are all backgrounding devices: comparators, explicatives, and correlatives. Comparators, such as negatives, futures, modals, questions, imperatives, and syntactic comparatives themselves, all "compare the events which did occur to those which did not occur." Labov illustrates comparators with figure 2.

The offset, dashed arrow represents an event or state that either did not occur (e.g., negatives) or that has not yet occurred (e.g., futures). Consider

Figure 2. Comparators

From *Language in the Inner City* by William Labov.
Copyright ©1972 University of Pennsylvania Press. Reprinted with permission.

the following three examples of the quasi simile (*as if*) construction, which Edward Kessler argues "remains, both early and late, O'Connor's poetic signature":[13]

68. "Two fellers come in here last week," Red Sammy said, "driving a Chrysler. It was a old beat-up car but it was a good one and these boys looked all right to me. Said they worked at the mill and you know I let them fellers charge the gas they bought? Now why did I do that?"

   "Because you're a good man!" the grandmother said at once.

   "Yes'm, I suppose so," Red Sam said as *if he were struck with this answer*. (*GM,* 15)

69. She saw the man's face twisted close to her own as *if he were going to cry* and she murmured, "Why you're one of my babies. You're one of my own children!" She reached out and touched him on the shoulder. The Misfit sprang back as *if a snake had bitten him* and shot her three times through the chest. (*GM,* 29)

These examples illustrate just three of the many different specific uses to which O'Connor put the "as if" construction, a construction that most frequently indicates an event that does not occur or a state that does not hold.[14] In (68), the quasi simile is ironic in that Red Sam is not struck with the answer that he is a good man for allowing the men with the "old beat-up car" to charge their gasoline. It is the very response that he was expecting and hoping to get from the grandmother. In (69), the first quasi simile signifies the grandmother's empathetic response to The Misfit. The second quasi simile, although it is literally false, functions anagogically to signal the knowledge that The Misfit gains from his encounter with grace in the form of the grandmother's realization of the spiritual bonds between all humans.

   Not negation is a comparator, like the quasi simile. In *The Violent Bear It Away,* Francis Tarwater's great-uncle gives him the mission of baptizing his retarded cousin Bishop. Tarwater resents and resists this mission. After his great-uncle's death, Tarwater goes to the home of his uncle Rayber and his cousin. When Tarwater comes face-to-face with Bishop and Bishop attempts to make contact by reaching out his hand to touch him, Tarwater rejects him by knocking his hand away. Rayber, who knows nothing of Tarwater's mission, essentially tells Tarwater that Bishop is almost beneath deserving either of their notice. He said earlier, "That's only Bishop. . . . Don't mind him." Now, he tries to reassure Tarwater:

> "You'll get used him," he said.
> "No!" the boy shouted.
> It was like a shout that had been waiting, straining to burst out. "I won't get used to him! I won't have anything to do with him!" He clenched his fist and lifted it. "I won't have anything to do with him!" (*VBA*, 92–93)

This passages illustrates two important patterns in the use of negation. First, ideally, the addressee for a negative will have assumed the positive. That is, for Tarwater to say to his uncle that he won't have anything to do with Bishop, Tarwater should assume that his uncle assumes that he will have something to do with his cousin. But Rayber has been attempting to convince Tarwater that he really need not bother much with the retarded Bishop. Obviously, Tarwater is here in part denying his great-uncle's command that he baptize his cousin. Thus, Tarwater shows himself to be self-absorbed; characters frequently reveal much about themselves in their contextually inappropriate comments. We will see that the negative is a primary device for such self-revelation in O'Connor's fiction. Rayber himself is too self-absorbed to understand either the intensity or the suppositions of Tarwater's negatives. It takes him four days to realize that the elder Tarwater has given his great-nephew the mission of baptizing Bishop.

Consistent with the expectations lying behind the negatives in the passage above is Labov's description of the negative comparator as a construction that "expresses the defeat of an expectation that something would happen." He writes that negatives "provide a way of evaluating events by placing them against the background of other events which might have happened, but which did not" (*LIC,* 380–81). That is, negatives respond to the failure of a backgrounded expected event or state to occur. The sources of the expectedness of an event are numerous. Frequently, the expectedness is simply part of the world view of the speakers, as in the following excerpt, repeated again from Tom's narrative:

I said, "He was so pretty, I ju—, I really *didn't* wanna shoot him." I said, "I felt so bad about it."

In most people's world view, if one goes deer hunting, one wants to shoot a deer; thus Tom's negative indicates the depth at which he appreciates the deer's beauty. We will explore in chapters 4 and 5 the many sources for expectedness in negatives.

Explicatives are dependent clauses, such as qualifications (*while, although*), causals (*since, because*), and relatives (*that, who, whom*) that evaluate the narrative or elaborate the narrative background. Labov illustrates explicatives with figure 3.

The vertical arrow off the fourth arrow to the right represents the off-narrative explications and evaluations of embedded clauses. The following example illustrates a typical use in oral narrative of a particular type of relative clause:

> They had sheep and then they had somethin' *that looked like a little baby llama*, but I don't think it was. It was some kind of goat. It was, YEAH! That's what it was. It was these goats *that were about the size of, uh, a cocker spaniel maybe?*

In the two relative clauses italicized above, we have two intransitive clauses (i.e., the verbs in the relative clauses are intransitive), which as relative clauses characterize new participants to the discourse in ways that make them relevant to the ongoing discourse.[15] The point of these characterizations of goats as harmless, cute animals is that later in the narrative one of the goats attacks a human. Characterization in relative clauses is also common in literary discourse, as in the following description of the unnamed mother in "A Good Man Is Hard to Find":

> Bailey didn't look up from his reading so she wheeled around then and faced the children's mother, a young woman in slacks, *whose face was as broad*

Figure 3. Explicatives

From *Language in the Inner City* by William Labov.
Copyright ©1972 University of Pennsylvania Press. Reprinted with permission.

and innocent as a cabbage and was tied around with a green head-kerchief that had
two points on the top like rabbit's ears. (GM, 9)

The linking of the unnamed mother with an "innocent" vegetable and a defenseless rabbit foreshadows the mother's polite acceptance of her murder much later in the story:

> The children's mother had begun to make heaving noises as if she couldn't get her breath. "Lady," he asked, "would you and that little girl like to step off yonder with Bobby Lee and Hiram and join your husband?"
>
> "Yes, thank you," the mother said faintly. Her left arm dangled helplessly and she was holding the baby, who had gone to sleep, in the other. *(GM, 27)*

Another frequent type of dependent clause in narrative is the complement clause to verbs of speech and cognition such as *say, argue, know, realize,* and *understand.* Labov does not include embedded clauses to verbs of speech and cognition as evaluatory devices because "the use of absolute right-hand embedding with verbs of this type is universal and automatic among all speakers" (*LIC*, 390–91). Labov presumably has in mind the contrast between clausal complements to verbs of speech and cognition and the adverbial and relative clauses mentioned above. A narrator has a choice of whether to use an adverbial or relative clause while the complements to verbs of speech and cognition are usually dependent clauses. However, verbs of speech and cognition are in fact part of the lexicon of foreground narrative events. Just as one need not necessarily subordinate a clause by means of making it a relative clause or adverbial clause, one need not necessarily subordinate a clause as a complement to a verb of speech or cognition. One could, for example, use directly quoted speech with no subordination. Thus, these verbs and the complements to these verbs are choices in narrative. Verbs of cognition are intimately involved in problems of presupposition specifically.

We can get at least a preliminary feel for the effects of literary presupposition in O'Connor's fiction through a brief analysis of the scene in *The Violent Bear It Away* in which Tarwater first sees the poster for the evangelist family the Carmodys. Rayber laughs and says to Tarwater, "All such people have in life is the conviction they'll rise again." Tarwater appears shaken:

> "They won't rise again?" he said. The statement had the lilt of a question and Rayber realized with an intense thrill of pleasure *that his opinion, for the first time, was being called for.*

"No," he said simply, "they won't rise again". . . . He put his hand experi-
mentally on the boy's shoulder. It was suffered to remain there.

In a voice unsteady with the sudden return of enthusiasm he said, "That's
why I want you to learn all you can. . . . This fall *when you start school* . . ."

The shoulder was roughly withdrawn. (*VBA*, 109–10)

This passage is typical of O'Connor in its multiple ambiguity and in its use
of presupposition to encode mistaken assumptions. It is not entirely clear
that the nephew Tarwater is really asking his uncle Rayber whether the
dead will rise again since Tarwater is intensely self-involved and distrusts
his uncle. He could simply be talking to himself. Regardless of Tarwater's
intention, Rayber characteristically selfishly interprets the question as a call
for help. That interpretation—"that his opinion, for the first time, was
being called for"—is narrated as a presupposition; the presuppositional
status of the interpretation is signaled by its form as a clausal complement
to the verb *realize*. Such presuppositional clausal complements are assumed
to be true. The only thing at question in the sentence above is whether or
not Rayber realized the presupposition. Thus, the act of realizing is foregrounded in the long quotation above while the realization itself is backgrounded. Now, what makes that background presupposition interesting is
O'Connor's tendency to make the truth of such backgrounded presuppositions problematic. Rayber's presupposition—that he is being appealed to
for his opinion—leads to his first faux pas with Tarwater: expression of his
assumption that Tarwater would want or at least consent to going to school
to learn more from the likes of Rayber. He presupposes in the adverbial
clause "when you start school" that Tarwater will begin school in the fall.
Adverbial clauses of time are presuppositional, as we will see in chapter 3.
The presupposition that Tarwater will begin school juxtaposes many levels
of knowledge. Rayber doesn't know that one of Tarwater's primary fears is
school, but the reader knows it. Over ninety pages earlier, the narrator
tells us that Tarwater's great uncle "had always impressed on him his good
fortune in not being sent to school. . . . The boy knew that escaping school
was the surest sign of his election" (*VBA*, 17).

Correlatives are phrases, such as participials and appositives, which
"bring together two events that actually occurred so that they are conjoined
in a single independent clause." Labov illustrates correlatives with figure 4.

The horizontal arrow off the fourth arrow to the right represents the
confluence of two events in one clause. The following example illustrates a

typical use in oral narrative of a type of correlative phrase. In this oral narrative, the narrator tells the story of how her young husband behaved in a trip to a health clinic as if he were dying when he had only a mild case of influenza:

> He like . . . he I had to help him stagger out to the car. He *was* like *walking* like this eighty-year-old man all hunched over like this, you know, out to the car. I got into the car and I said, "Look, I'll go pay the bill," and I went back in to pay the bill. And the nurses, and the nurses, (laughter) *going* on about Sam *carrying* on in there about like he *was dying*. (laughter)

The three foregrounded narrative events in this excerpt all occur in the sentence "I got into the car and I said, 'Look, I'll go pay the bill,' and I went back in to pay the bill." However, the italicized participials indicate simultaneous action, some of which occurs simultaneously with Sam's wife helping him to the car, some of which occurs simultaneously with Sam's wife going back to pay the bill, and some which occurs simultaneously with Sam's medical treatment, which was narrated earlier. The following are the first few lines of "A Good Man Is Hard to Find," illustrating the same correlative pattern in literary discourse:

> The grandmother didn't want to go to Florida. She wanted to visit some of her connections in east Tennessee and she *was seizing* at every chance to change Bailey's mind. Bailey was the son she lived with, her only boy. He *was sitting* on the edge of his chair at the table, bent over the orange sports section of the *Journal*. "Now look here, Bailey," she said, "see here, read this," and she stood with one hand on her thin hip and the other *rattling* the newspaper at his bald head. (*GM*, 9)

The event and state of the two past progressives italicized occur simultaneously, while the third participial indicates the grandmother's body action while talking to Bailey.

Figure 4. Correlatives

From *Language in the Inner City* by William Labov.
Copyright ©1972 University of Pennsylvania Press. Reprinted with permission.

As I pointed out in chapter 1, the many differences between participial and finite complements to the verb *see* will occupy our attention in chapters 6 and 7. A short passage from *The Violent Bear It Away* will illustrate for us again one of those regular differences—physical perceptual detail vs. cognitive conclusions—a difference that has obvious ramifications for an exploration of knowledge in O'Connor's fiction. When Francis Tarwater first shows up on Rayber's doorstep, Rayber is momentarily skeptical about whether the elder Tarwater is really dead. He suspects the old man of coming with his great-nephew so that he can sneak in and baptize Bishop. The younger Tarwater has a vision and then a revelation:

> The boy blanched. In his mind's eye he saw *the old man, a dark shape standing behind the corner of the house, restraining his wheezing breath while he waited impatiently for him to baptize the dim-witted child.* . . . With a terrible clarity he saw *that the schoolteacher was no more than a decoy the old man had set up to lure him to the city to do his unfinished business.* (*VBA*, 89)

The complements to the *see* verbs in this passage are typical in many ways of those in O'Connor's fiction. The first—in part, a participial phrase ("standing," "restraining")—contains a mental vision but one that is extraordinarily rich in physical detail. The second contains a cognitive conclusion ("that the schoolteacher was no more than a decoy"), in this case no doubt true, that Rayber is himself almost irrelevant except as a minor diversion on young Tarwater's road to becoming a prophet.

Foreground and Background

My analysis of O'Connor's fiction is heavily influenced by the foreground/background distinction in linguistic studies along with the figure/ground distinction in Gestalt psychology.[16] In the linguistic literature, the Gestalt distinction figure/ground is frequently used to explain a wide variety of linguistic patterns, e.g., subordination, transitivity, topic-marking, given-new distinctions. All of these linguistic patterns seem to mirror the primarily visual patterns of perception that reveal the underlying innate human disposition to separate the visual field into a figure, which is nearer, smaller, and more focused, and a ground, which lies behind the figure and is larger and more diffuse.[17]

There are two relatively minor obstacles to linguistic/literary interdisciplinary applications of the foreground/background distinction. First, Tanya

Reinhart argues that "virtually all" literary theorists understand narrative as primarily representing the *fabula* (the abstract story) rather than the instantiated *sjuzhet* (the form of the story). Although Reinhart's contention is a bit of an overstatement, literary theorists in general do see much more value than linguists do in analyzing the fabula, the story abstracted from its particular form (sjuzhet).[18] A deemphasis of abstract content, or "meaning," in linguistics has always been a site of contention between linguistics and literary study, but this first obstacle to understanding is easily overcome, or at least understood, for the purposes of this book, if we realize that discourse linguistics (of which stylistics is a related field) is primarily interested in *sjuzhet* (Seymour Chatman's "*discourse*") and that it is in the relationship of form to meaning that stylisticians find the foreground/background distinction interesting. The second obstacle to interdisciplinary application of the foreground/background distinction is also easily overcome because it involves primarily a confusion over terminology, mixing a primary interest of literary scholars (the differences between ordinary language and literary language) with an interest of linguists (for the purposes of this study, the difference between narrative syntax and non-narrative syntax). In literary theory, the foreground/background distinction, as Reinhart points out, refers primarily to the difference between poetically foregrounded violations of the standard backgrounded norms of any particular language and those backgrounded norms themselves. But as Jean Jacques Weber points out, the linguistic sense of foregrounding and backgrounding in the work of Labov, Thompson, Paul Hopper, Robert E. Longacre, and others refers mainly to narrative main clauses (foreground) and supporting subordinate clauses and phrases (background).[19] In *Narrating Knowledge*, we will be concerned mainly with the linguistic sense of foregrounding and backgrounding.

Although the figure/ground distinction is primarily a visual one in Gestalt psychology, it is an appropriate framework within which to discuss linguistic form in O'Connor's fiction at least in part because O'Connor not only frequently manipulates main and subordinate clauses to reflect foregrounding and backgrounding issues in knowledge but also frequently draws attention to the visual foreground and background in her fiction, thus indicating a consistent stylistic trait at an abstract level. On the day that Enoch knows in his blood that something important is going happen—he is to steal the museum mummy as Hazel Motes's new Jesus—his conscious mind is in typical conflict with his wise blood:

Town was the last place he wanted to be because anything could happen there. All the time his mind had been chasing around it had been thinking how as soon as he got off duty he was going to sneak off home and go to bed.

By the time he got into the center of the business district he was exhausted and he had to lean against Walgreen's window and cool off. Sweat crept down his back and provoked him to itch so that in just a few minutes he appeared to be working his way across the glass by his muscles, against a background of alarm clocks, toilet waters, candies, sanitary pads, fountain pens, and pocket flashlights, displayed in all colors to twice his height. He appeared to be working his way to a rumbling noise which came from the center of a small alcove that formed the entrance to the drug store. Here was a yellow and blue, glass and steel machine, belching popcorn into a cauldron of butter and salt. Enoch approached, already with his purse out, sorting his money. (*WB,* 135–36)

This passage illustrates at least three important patterns in O'Connor's aesthetics of knowledge: nonnarration, presupposition, and the play of foreground/background in the setting.[20] The break between the paragraphs represents the alienation of what little intellect Enoch possesses and his much wiser blood. Characteristically, his movement to downtown is non-narrated; that is, his movement to downtown is elided between the paragraphs as if we knew he was going to go downtown anyway, in spite of his intentions. Furthermore, the first clause of the second paragraph ("By the time he got into the center of the business district") is presuppositional and backgrounded by means of its subordination, another indication of shared knowledge between narrator and narratee. In the remainder of the paragraph, there are literally two background settings against which the foregrounded Enoch appears: (1) the display of commercial items behind him in the window of the drugstore and (2) the "rumbling noise" that draws him into the exchange with the popcorn vendor. The background against which Enoch moves is twice his height although it is composed of many small commercial items. Jon Lance Bacon argues that this scene illustrates the close identification of Enoch with consumerism in *Wise Blood.* As Bacon points out, Enoch is later driven to buy drapes and gilt to decorate his room for the new Jesus. He argues that in the end Enoch finally submerges his entire identity in the commercial figure of the gorilla Gonga:

"In the uncertain light, one of his lean white legs could be seen to disappear and then the other, one arm and then the other: a black heavier shaggier figure replaced his" (*WB*, 197).[21] Thus, Enoch literally disappears into the background of American consumerism.

O'Connor occasionally goes so far as to reverse what we might take to be normal distributions of foreground and background in visual descriptions. These reversals seem designed to reveal a character's habitual, thoughtless modes of perception and/or to shock the reader into a new consciousness. In "The Displaced Person," Mrs. Shortley, a self-possessed farm worker, herself soon to become displaced, is described early in the story as she faces a peacock's tail that is "full of fierce planets with eyes that were each ringed in green and set against a sun that was gold in one second's light and salmon-colored in the next." This passage, with its own ambiguous foreground/background distinctions, is followed by another that explicitly reverses visual foreground and background: Mrs. Shortley "might have been looking at a map of the universe but she didn't notice it any more than she did the spots of sky that cracked the dull green of the tree" (*GM*, 204–5). In what might be taken to be a normal distribution of foreground and background, the sky would be the continuous and larger background against which the tree would be the smaller foreground. However, here, O'Connor reverses the expected and presents us with a scene in which the smaller foreground consists of the "spots of sky" which interrupt (*crack*) the larger backgrounded "dull green of the tree." The passage could also be used to illustrate one of the most common patterns of presupposition in O'Connor because Mrs. Shortley is characteristically unaware of ("didn't notice") the presupposed, although unexpected, reversal of foreground/background. In a discussion of the prophetic writer as a "realist of distances," O'Connor argues, "In the novelist's case, prophecy is a matter of seeing near things with their extensions of meaning and thus of seeing far things close up" (*MM*, 44). O'Connor used this argument in an attempt to explain the presence of the grotesque in her fiction, but her explanation of the prophetic as the exploration of meaningful connections between the near and far can be understood both metaphorically and literally. The vision of the sky interrupting the dull green of the tree is grotesque and forces us to see the distant as close and the close as distant. But Mrs. Shortley's failure to notice the reversal metaphorically reveals her limited spiritual and psychological vision as well.

There are two obvious stylistically marked pairings of foreground/background with main clauses/subordinate clauses (to take just one pair of grammatical signals of foregrounding/backgrounding for example): (1) the placement of material which is not properly background material in subordinate clauses; and (2) the placement of material which is not properly foreground material in main clauses. Given that dependent clauses (for example, clausal complements to verbs such as *know* and *realize*) frequently signal known, or presupposed, information, and that main clauses do not in themselves signal known, or presupposed, information, we may safely predict that known information will normally be backgrounded while unknown information will normally be foregrounded. Steven Wallace, for example, argues that a main clause is usually more "salient" than a subordinate clause.[22] Compare Labov's analysis of the foregrounded complicating action in a narrative as composed of main clauses, not of dependent clauses. O'Connor's fiction is populated more with characters who "know," "realize," and "understand" incompletely, or wrongly, (i.e., resulting in backgrounded material which is not truly known) than with characters who do not organize their thoughts into a foreground and background (i.e., resulting in foregrounded material which should be uncontestably backgrounded because it is known or of little importance). For this reason the marked pairing of what should be backgrounded material with main clauses is much rarer in O'Connor than the pairing of what should be foregrounded material with subordinate clauses or phrases. A well-known example in American literature of a series of main clauses with at least some material that might more normally be backgrounded occurs in the opening paragraph of Faulkner's *The Sound and the Fury*, in which Benjy as narrator observes the end of one hole of golf and the beginning of another:

> Luster was hunting in the grass by the flower tree. They took the flag out, and they were hitting. Then they put the flag back and they went to the table, and he hit and the other hit. Then they went on, and I went along the fence. Luster came away from the flower tree and we went along the fence and they stopped and we stopped and I looked through the fence while Luster was hunting in the grass.[23]

Here we have a series of fourteen main clauses followed by one subordinate clause that repeats the propositional content of the first main clause. The underlexicalization of the passage (i.e., the absence of lexemes like *golf, green, tee*) as well as the sustained length of main clause parataxis both help represent Benjy's lack of understanding and failure to distinguish background from foreground.

There is only one pattern in O'Connor's fiction of the use of main clauses to present what would seem more normally to belong in subordinate clauses: the character, because of emotional excitement, is unable to process a scene that is currently occurring. In some parts of the O'Connor M.A. thesis story "The Geranium," the resemblance to Faulkner's style is extraordinary. In the following passage, Old Dudley, an elderly southerner, has his first experience with a northern city's subway system after having made what he now realizes is the mistake of leaving his southern home to live with his daughter and son-in-law in the north:

> They went in a "subway"—a railroad underneath the ground like a big cave.
> . . . The people coming out pushed through the people coming in and a noise rang and the train swooped off again. (*CS*, 7)

Here we see a similar underlexicalization as well as a lack of familiarity with the word *subway*. We also see three main clauses in coordination in the last sentence helping to represent Old Dudley's confusion.

In "Wildcat," another of the thesis stories, the main character Gabriel, an elderly blind man, is convinced that a wildcat is coming to kill him and will be breaking into his cabin at any moment:

> He had to get on something high! There was a shelf nailed over the chimney and he turned wildly and fell against a chair and shoved it up to the fireplace. He caught hold of the shelf and pulled himself onto the chair and sprang up and backwards and felt the narrow shelf board under him for an instant and then felt it sag and jerked his feet up and felt it crack somewhere from the wall. His stomach flew inside him and stopped hard and the shelf board fell across his feet and the rung of the chair hit against his head and then, after a second of stillness, he heard a low, gasping animal cry wail over two hills and fade past him. (*CS*, 31)

There are fifteen uses of the coordinating conjunction *and* in this passage. The series of mostly main clauses here helps to signal that Gabriel experiences his panic as one foregrounded event followed by another with almost no backgrounding structure to the events. Compare O'Connor's text to my rewrite:

> There was a shelf nailed over the chimney. He turned wildly, falling against a chair, which he shoved up to the fireplace. Catching hold of the shelf, he pulled himself onto the chair, springing up and backwards. He felt the narrow shelf board under him for an instant. And then because he felt it sag, he jerked his feet up. He felt it crack somewhere from the wall.

Because of its heavy use of subordination and participial phrases rather than coordination, this version lacks the narrated consciousness of O'Connor's text. The rewritten version is more monologically the narrator's language.

Passages such as that about the panicked Gabriel, which occur infrequently even in O'Connor's early thesis work, become exceedingly rare in the more mature work. However, O'Connor returns to the pattern occasionally, as in "Good Country People," in which Manley Pointer, the itinerant Bible salesman, seduces Hulga, who thinks much too highly of her own sophistication, intellect, and Ph.D. (she had planned to seduce the "innocent" Manley). In the following, Manley manages to steal Hulga's wooden leg, which he has just learned how to detach from her body:

> She saw him grab the leg and then she saw it for an instant slanted forlornly across the inside of the suitcase with a Bible at either side of its opposite ends. He slammed the lid shut and snatched up the valise and swung it down the hole and then stepped through himself. (*GM*, 195)

In the first sentence, there are two nontensed phrases embedded under verbs of perception (*see*), a pattern that we will return to in chapters 6 and 7. But in the second sentence, as if to signal an increase in the speed of action and a corresponding failure on the part of Hulga to keep up with the actions of Manley, we have four tensed verb phrases joined by three *and*'s. These tensed verb phrases are formally very close to being independent clauses, the only absent elements being independent grammatical subjects for the last three. The subjects are all identical, so they are gapped for the final three phrases.

Narrating Knowledge furthers the stylistic investigation of O'Connor's literary concerns with knowledge by exploring her literary manipulations of the natural connection of Gestalt ground with negation, dependent clauses, and participials. Each of these three morphosyntactic signals of background respond to or create a different type of background knowledge. Negation pairs with supposition, dependent clauses with presupposition, and participials with implication. Through a manipulation of the quality of knowledge in each background construction, O'Connor is able both to critique the fallibility of human reason and partially to control the reader's response to her characters.

In chapter 3, we explore the form and pragmatics of presupposition in O'Connor's fiction. One of the major themes of *Narrating Knowledge* will be introduced and explored in that chapter—the use of background constructions to create as well as reflect knowledge.

Chapter 3

Presupposition and the
Construction of the Background

*[Haze's] face seemed to reflect the entire distance across the
clearing and on beyond, the entire distance that extended from
his eyes to the blank gray sky that went on, depth after depth,
into space.*

—Flannery O'Connor *(WB, 209)*

As I mention in chapter 2, my analysis of presupposition, implication, and
supposition in O'Connor's fiction is based on a combination of the fore-
ground/background distinction in linguistic studies with the figure/ground
distinction in Gestalt psychology. The fundamental insight of foreground
(figure)/background (ground) studies, whether in psychology or linguistics, is that the perception, or interpretation, of the foreground is heavily
influenced by the background. Tanya Reinhart, for example, uses figure 5 to

Figure 5. Foreground and Background

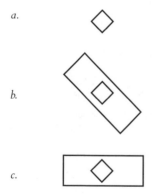

a.

b.

c.

From "Principles of Gestalt Perception in the Temporal Organization of Narrative Texts,"
Linguistics 22 (1984) 779–809, by Tanya Reinhart

Copyright ©1984 Mouton de Gruyter. Reprinted with permission.

demonstrate the influence of background on the perception of foreground.[1] Thus, in (a), we see a diamond because the background is the rectangle of the page on which the figure is printed. Reinhart argues that in (b) we see a square because of the "'direction' of the background." And in (c) we again see a diamond against the background rectangle. Reinhart's analysis of the foreground/background relations in figure 5 is straightforward enough, yet, there is a small problem.

That problem is that (a) and (c) are more "diamond-like" than (b) is "square-like." In fact, (b) is ambiguous between a square and a diamond, depending on whether the rectangle of the page of this book is taken to be the dominant background, in which case it is a diamond, or the smaller drawn rectangle is the dominant background, in which case it is a square. The reason that (a) is a non-ambiguous diamond is that there is only one background, the rectangle of the page itself. And the reason that (c) is a non-ambiguous diamond is that the smaller drawn background is oriented as a rectangle just as is the page, although they differ in orientation of short and long sides, which is irrelevant to determining the foregrounded figure. And, of course, (a) and (c) are only non-ambiguous as long as the reader maintains the alignment of the page on a perpendicular.

A hint to understanding the complex effects of foreground and background on presupposition, implication, and supposition in Flannery O'Connor's fiction is contained in the behavior of foreground and background in (b) and (c) in figure 5. Again, the reason that (b) is problematic is that there is more than one background determining the foreground. One, the drawn and slanted rectangle, determines the foregrounded square; the other, the printed page, determines the foregrounded diamond. Thus, there are three levels of perception in (b): first, the printed page itself; second, the drawn rectangular background; and third, the foregrounded "diamond" or "square." In fact, the intermediate rectangle is at once both background to the foregrounded smaller square and foreground to the rectangular page itself. Its role as foreground to the rectangular page explains why it appears to be slanted. The important issue here for this chapter is that the rectangular backgrounds for the square and the diamond in both (b) and (c), respectively, are constructed. They are not "given" as is the rectangle of the printed page. That is, the rectangular backgrounds in (b) and (c) are deliberately manipulated in order to influence the perception of the smaller, foregrounded figures, which are in fact identical. As we will see in this chapter, presuppositional backgrounds may also be constructed, a lesson that will be of value when we examine supposition and implication in the remainder of the book.

Presuppositions

Presuppositions, primarily investigated in philosophy and linguistics, are background assumptions which are tied to linguistic expressions (presupposition triggers) such as factive verbs, like *know, realize,* and *regret*, and adverbial clauses of time, two of O'Connor's most common classes of presupposition triggers.[2] These background assumptions remain constant under negation, as I indicated in chapter 1. Thus, again, in (1a), the complement to the factive main verb *realize*, "that you are sick," is presupposed, as is proven by the negation of the main verb in (1b).

1. a. Bill realizes *that you are sick.*
   b. Bill doesn't realize *that you are sick.*

It is commonly argued, either directly or indirectly, that what is presupposed is pragmatically backgrounded, in the sense of Gestalt ground.[3] I am here interested more in the pragmatics of presupposition (i.e., the contextual uses of presupposition) than in a precise logico-semantic definition of presupposition. However, I use a conservative standard semantic definition of presupposition in which assumptions are tied to specific linguistic signals because all of the presuppositions that I investigate in O'Connor are tied to such signals. Imagine an absurd scenario—sometimes useful because the absurd helps us to think beyond the ordinary and allows us to concentrate more fully on the linguistic behavior that is so backgrounded in itself that is difficult to realize its constant presence in our lives, language, and literature.[4] The scenario is that you have awakened one morning after your spouse, who is now in the kitchen eating breakfast. You straggle out of bed, sleepy eyed, to the bathroom, hazard a glance at your face in the mirror, and discover that your ears have grown as large as dinner plates overnight. One of the following would be more likely than the other to be your next utterance:

2. a. Oh, fudge! *My ears* are enormous.
   b. ?Oh, fudge! I have ears. They are enormous.

The ludicrous difference in backgrounding between (2a) and (2b) is precisely presupposition. Any referent encoded by a definite pronoun, definite possessor + noun, definite article + noun, or proper noun is presupposed to exist. In (2a), the combination of definite possessor and noun in "my ears" presupposes that the speaker has ears. The reason that (2b) is exceedingly odd is that it foregrounds what is normally taken to be background and can thus be normally presupposed, i.e., "I have ears." Context can make such foregrounding natural; thus, one might say "I have ears" in order to indicate that one has heard, for example, what one might not have been intended to hear. However, it is by means of presupposition that speakers avoid foregrounding that which they have no reason to foreground. Indeed, presupposition is a necessary condition for language itself to function in the everyday world. Imagine a world in which one could presuppose nothing. Even the constructions in (2b) would be impossible as first utterances upon discovering that one's ears have grown as large as dinner plates overnight. First, one would have to assert the existence of the ego, the existence of ears, finally the existence of dinner plates, not to mention the relational concept of possession (*have*) and the existential concept of being (*are*). In chapter 6, where such definitions and distinctions are important to us, I will stop to define and illustrate the precise distinction between presupposition and the closely related phenomenon implication.

Stephen Levinson catalogs ten presupposition triggers—those linguistic devices that signal presupposition. In this chapter, I will refer to the use of four of these triggers in O'Connor's fiction: definite descriptions, factive predicates, temporal clauses, and relative clauses. Wh-question presuppositions will figure briefly in chapter 5. (Wh-questions are formed with a wh-word (e.g., *where, why, who*), as in "who ate the cereal?") The following summary of those triggers uses examples from O'Connor's fiction for illustration. I restrict my investigation to these four because they are the most reflective of knowledge in O'Connor and because I am interested only in those presupposition triggers whose sentences include the presupposition either in phrasal or clausal form. So, for example, comparisons and contrasts, which are presuppositional, are sometimes marked by stress or other prosodic indicators. Consider one of Levinson's examples, in which words in upper case throughout are meant to represent contrastive stress. The symbol ">>" signals "presupposes," as throughout this book:

3. Marianne called Adolph a male chauvinist, and then HE insulted [/didn't insult] HER.
   >> For Marianne to call Adolph a male chauvinist would be to insult him.

O'Connor, like most authors, does not regularly use upper case, or any other signal, to represent contrastive stress. Others of Levinson's presupposition triggers are, as he suggests himself of verbs of judging, "not really presuppositional at all; for, unlike other presuppositions, the implications are not attributed to the speaker, so much as to the subject of the verb of judging." Consider Levinson's example:

4. Agatha *accused*/didn't *accuse* Ian of plagiarism.
    >> (Agatha thinks) plagiarism is bad.

In (4), the speaker and hearer need not think that plagiarism is bad. The only requirement is that the speaker think that Agatha thinks that plagiarism is bad.[5]

As Levinson does, I will italicize the presupposition triggers in the positive and negative versions of the sentences that illustrate the four presupposition triggers referred to above so that readers can check their own intuitions for the presuppositions. I will italicize the presuppositional phrasal and clausal material as well. The original sentence from O'Connor (whether positive or negative) will have the citation information after it. The sentence with the reversed negative/positive polarity will have no such citation.

Definite descriptions:
5. a. *Thomas* withdrew to *the side of the window*. (*ERMC*, 115)
    b. *Thomas* didn't withdraw to *the side of the window*.

In (5a), which is the first clause from "The Comforts of Home," definite description in the forms of a proper noun and two noun phrases modified by the definite article *the* signal the presupposition of the existence of Thomas, the side of the window, and the window. In (5b), the main verb of (5a)—*withdrew*—is negated, leaving the presuppositions of the existence of Thomas, the side of the window, and the window.

Factive predicates:
6. a. As little as he wanted anything to do with the sheriff, he *realized that the man was at least intelligent and not simply a mound of sweating flesh*. (*ERMC*, 136)
    b. As little as he wanted anything to do with the sheriff, he didn't *realize that the man was at least intelligent and not simply a mound of sweating flesh*.

Examples (6a) and (6b) show that factive verbs, so called because they pre-suppose the factivity of their complements, are presuppositional, preserving complement presuppositions in both the positive and the negative. In both (6a) and (6b) "that the man was at least intelligent and not simply a mound of sweating flesh" is presupposed. Other factive verbs include *forget, regret, know,* and *remember.* Predicate adjectives modified by *that* clauses may also be factive, as in *be sorry that, be glad that,* and *be surprised that.*

Temporal clauses:
7. a. The turkey's head flew in his face *as the spitter slung it up in the air and over his own shoulder and turned.* (*CS,* 53)
    b. The turkey's head didn't fly in his face *as the spitter slung it up in the air and over his own shoulder and turned.*

Propositional material in temporal clauses is assumed to be true even on negation of the verb of the main clause. Thus, those propositions, like "the spitter slung it up in the air and over his own shoulder and turned," are pre-supposed. The clausal presupposition in (7a), from O'Connor's M.A. thesis story "The Turkey," mimics the surprise that Ruller must feel on having his turkey stolen by the boys who have been following him. It mimics surprise because it occurs where it does not belong since it is absolutely new, unexpected (at least for Ruller), and important information. This clausal pre-supposition is also much like many others that we will examine in this chapter—problematic for the question of who knows what and how much.

Relative clauses:
8. a. Thomas, *who had not got out of the car at all, or looked at her after the first revolted glance,* said, "I'm telling you, once and for all, the place to take her is jail." (*ERMC,* 129–30)
    b. Thomas, *who had not got out of the car at all, or looked at her after the first revolted glance*, didn't say, "I'm telling you, once and for all, the place to take her is jail."

Levinson argues that non-restrictive relative clauses are presuppositional while restrictive relative clauses are non-presuppositional.[6] In modern formal written English, one fairly reliable signal of a non-restrictive relative clause is the presence of commas surrounding the relative clause, as in (8). Non-restrictive relative clauses do not "restrict" the reference of the noun phrase modified—in the case of (8), "Thomas"—because the referent for

that noun phrase is already uniquely known. Like much presupposed information, the material presupposed in the non-restrictive relative clause in (8) is nonproblematic because it is straightforwardly descriptive although it is literally new information.

Constructing the Presuppositional Background

We can approach some of the basic qualitative issues involved in backgrounding and presupposition by considering three passages from O'Connor's "The Barber," the first of which illustrates a classic case of nonproblematic, or unmarked, clausal presupposition. In the following, Rayber's barber speaks first:

> "Why, lemme tell you this—ain't nothin' gonna be good again until we get rid of them Mother Hubbards and get us a man can put these niggers in their places. Shuh."
>
> "You hear that, George?" he shouted to the colored boy wiping up the floor around the basins.
>
> "Sho do," George said.
>
> It was time for Rayber to say something but nothing appropriate would come. He wanted to say something that George would understand. He was startled *that George had been brought into the conversation. (CS,* 16)

The factive construction "was startled" in the last sentence signals the presupposition of the proposition of the complement clause "that George had been brought into the conversation." The presupposition is nonproblematic because it is mutual knowledge among all participants (narrator, narratee, and characters) that George has been brought into the conversation, this mutual knowledge having been established by the immediately preceding conversation. The proposition of an unmarked prototypical presupposition truly is shared knowledge (i.e., background knowledge) among all participants. But as Robert Stalnaker, T. Givón, and Umberto Eco and Patrizia Violi point out, shared knowledge cannot be an absolute requirement for presupposition because speakers and writers regularly produce presuppositions that are not fully shared, or even sometimes shared at all.[7]

Shared knowledge is a graded phenomenon, just as backgrounding/foregrounding is graded.[8] Presuppositional constructions perform extra pragmatic work to the degree that they encode nonshared knowledge, or to the degree that they construct their own background. In the following passage,

Rayber has been working on a written version of a liberal speech he intends to deliver the next time he visits the barbershop for a haircut:

> He worked on it until suppertime and had four sentences—all crossed out. He got up once in the middle of the meal to go to his desk and change one. After supper he crossed the correction out.
>
> "What is the matter with you?" his wife wanted to know.
>
> "Not a thing," Rayber said, "not a thing. I just have to work."
>
> "I'm not stopping you," she said.
>
> *When she went out*, he kicked the board loose on the bottom of the desk. (*CS*, 21)

The main clause in the last sentence ("he kicked the board loose on the bottom of the desk") is asserted complicating-action material. The introductory time adverbial clause ("When she went out") is presupposed although it is not, strictly speaking, shared knowledge that Rayber's wife "went out" of someplace, presumably Rayber's study, because we did not know that she was there in the first place. Instead, the presupposition helps to construct shared background knowledge: because of it, we assume that the short conversation between Rayber and his wife occurs in his study rather than the dining room. Once we assume that, we know that if someone enters a study at some point that person must leave the study. Sandra Thompson has shown that many adverbial clauses, such as "When she went out" above, which not only are syntactically backgrounded with what is literally new information but also further the narrative in that they are ordered in the text to reflect the presumed order of events in the story, perform additional work besides backgrounding, in many cases creating cohesion with previous discourse.[9] The O'Connor example ("When she went out") is remarkable because it shows that even some of the less striking examples of presupposition in a written text help to construct the very background knowledge that they assume.

The general class of backgrounded, presupposed propositions that are of primary interest in this chapter is represented by our final example from "The Barber." Rayber has delivered his prepared speech, which is ridiculed by the several like-minded overtly racist men in the barber shop:

> He jerked the barber around by the shoulder. "Do you think I'd tamper with your damn fool ignorance?"
>
> The barber shook Rayber's grip off his shoulder. "Don't get excited," he said, "we all thought it was a fine speech. That's what I been saying all

along—you got to think, you got to. . . ." He lurched backward *when Rayber hit him,* and landed sitting on the footrest of the next chair. (*CS*, 25; ellipsis in original)

The time adverbial clause in the last sentence is presupposed although (1) it is not literally shared knowledge that Rayber would hit the barber, and (2) unlike leaving a room once one has entered it, hitting a person is not a natural necessity of any action that could conceivably have occurred before in the text.

Stalnaker says that a speaker "may want to communicate a proposition indirectly" and thus use presuppositional constructions even though the presupposition is not part of the "common background." Givón points out that speakers sometimes "deliberately put [new information] in a *background position*—thus in a sense it is *shielded from challenge*." And Eco and Violi argue that with presupposition "we are not so much interested in what-is-the-case, but rather in what someone tries to make someone else believe to be the case." Thus, through presupposition, the speaker or writer frequently rhetorically constructs a background rather than simply responds to one that is already there. Although Stalnaker, Givón, and Eco and Violi all speak of the effect of backgrounding problematic material as rhetorical in some way, they also all speak as if marked presupposition were mainly a problem to be solved for dyadic conversation.[10]

In narrative, unlike in what is frequently and simplistically taken to be normal dyadic conversation with a single speaker and a single listener, one must question who knows and how well any one participant knows because the narrative act involves at least three core participants—the narrator, the narratee, and the character(s). Because the narrative is told by a narrator to a narratee and because presupposition normally suggests a shared background contained in the presupposition, there is a strong potential for "marked" presuppositions in O'Connor—those involving new information that cannot be deduced from previous information—to be read as an implied conspiracy of knowledge between the narrator and narratee. In the last example from "The Barber," the narratee does not literally know on first telling that Rayber is going to hit the barber. But when the narrator presupposes that the narratee knows, the narratee is invited to construct the background knowledge that would justify the presupposition. If one looks back in the story "The Barber" for justification, one finds that Rayber is in many ways the opposite of what he takes himself to be, prejudiced when he thinks himself not, inarticulate when he thinks himself not (e.g., he kicks the desk board loose when frustrated and angry). It is then not unreasonable to assume that Rayber's attempt at rational argumentation would end in violence on his part.

A marked presupposition does not literally have to be knowledge that does not appear earlier in the text. The knowledge may appear, but the character who is the reflector for the presupposition may be cognitively deficient somehow, as is the case with Mrs. Flood, Haze's landlady in *Wise Blood*. When Mrs. Flood asks Haze what he intends to do with a bucket of lime and water, he tells her he is going to blind himself. Instead of attempting to stop him, she sits and muses on his reasons:

> Perhaps Mr. Motes was only being ugly, for what possible reason could a person have for wanting to destroy their sight? A woman like her, *who was so clear-sighted*, could never stand to be blind. If she had to be blind she would rather be dead. It occurred to her suddenly that when she was dead she would be blind too. She stared in front of her intensely, facing this for the first time. She recalled the phrase, "eternal death," that preachers used, but she cleared it out of her mind immediately, with no more change of expression than the cat. . . . What possible reason could a sane person have for wanting to not enjoy himself any more?
>
> She certainly couldn't say.
>
> [Chapter break in the novel]
>
> But she kept it in mind because *after he had done it*, he continued to live in her house and every day the sight of him presented her with the question. (*WB*, 211–13)

The first presupposition trigger italicized in the passage above, the non-restrictive relative clause, reflects O'Connor's characteristic irony. O'Connor backgrounds in a presupposition an obvious falsehood that represents a character's grossly inaccurate perception of herself. The second presupposition trigger that is italicized, the time adverbial clause, occurs as the very first indication in the text that Haze did indeed blind himself. One would expect that such important information, even if it is hinted at in the previous text, would not be presupposed. Recall that Asa Hawks hesitated at the last minute and did not blind himself although it had been advertised in a newspaper and thus very strongly indicated that he would. Whether readers expect Haze to go through with the blinding or not, the first appearance of knowledge of the event in a presupposed adverbial clause casts a shadow of spiritual and mental vacancy over Mrs. Flood in that it suggests that she did expect it but did nothing to stop it. It also foreshadows her sinister concern for her boarder, whom she later tries to coerce into marriage.

There are four basic types of marked clausal presuppositions in O'Connor's narrative. A useful categorization is the varying quality of the focal character's knowledge of the presupposition: the character (1) "knows" incorrectly, (2) does not know, (3) knows in a way in which the narrator and/or the narratee cannot share, or (4) knows correctly. The result of the first is dramatic irony since there is an obvious collusion of knowledge in which the narrator and narratee share but from which the character is excluded by virtue of being enveloped in false knowledge. When a character is not aware of a presupposition, as in the second category, the narrator and narratee share background knowledge which is, for a variety of reasons, simply not available to the character. So, for example, one might argue that Rayber will eventually come to the realization that he is capable of the violence presupposed in the clause "when Rayber hit him," but there is no indication that he knows it as background when he hits the barber. When a character knows in a way in which the narrator and/or narratee cannot share, as in the third category, the presupposition is distasteful to the narrator/narratee, perhaps for a variety of reasons. Finally, when characters in O'Connor know correctly, they sense the mystery or destiny of their lives. This is a type of knowledge that the narrator and narratee cannot be superior in or even fully share since it comes by grace rather than by human reason.

By far, the most common marked presuppositions in O'Connor are those in which a character has background "knowledge" which is in fact incorrect. When a character "knows" incorrectly and the narrator reports the knowledge with the character as the referent for the grammatical subject, the result is always dramatic irony, whether comic or tragic. The irony results from the contrast between what the narrator and narratee know or suspect to be the case and what the character presupposes. Most of such presuppositions are triggered in a complement clause by a factive verb such as *realize, know,* and *understand*, all of which refer to human cognitive events, the accuracy of which is almost always in question in O'Connor's fiction. In *Wise Blood* Hazel Motes leaves his forty-dollar car unattended as he and Sabbath Lily Hawks are off in a field with Sabbath Lily trying unsuccessfully to seduce Haze and with Haze attempting to explain some of the finer theological doctrines of his Church Without Christ:

> He realized suddenly *that it was parked on a country road, unlocked, and that the first person passing would drive off in it*. (*WB*, 123)

This example is complicated only by the fact that one of the complement clauses to the verb *realize* is correct—Haze's car "was parked on a country road, unlocked." However it is ludicrous to presuppose "that the first person passing would drive off in it." When Haze tries to leave, the car won't even start.

The comedy of presupposed incorrect knowledge is most frequent with childlike innocent characters, as Haze is throughout much of *Wise Blood*. Also like Haze, many of these childlike characters are adults. In "A Circle in the Fire," Mrs. Cope naïvely underestimates her three juvenile visitors—Powell, Garfield, and W.T. Not realizing that the three boys came well-supplied, with food as well as the matches they use to burn her woods, she has an early characteristically condescending realization: "a peculiar look of pain came over her face as she realized *that these children were hungry*" (*GM*, 137). The three boys "only play" with the food that Mrs. Cope prepares for them because they are not hungry for food. These city children, who live in housing "developments," are hungry for Mrs. Cope's land and horses and woods. She has mistaken their predatory stares for physical hunger (*GM*, 141).

O'Connor's childlike characters afflicted with comic presupposed knowledge can occasionally be actual children. In "The River," the child Bevel, who drowns himself to get to the kingdom of Heaven and away from an abusive urban home life, is first subjected to some rural abuse at the hands of his sitter's sons, who manage to get him trampled by a hog after they invite him to pull up a loose board so that he can get a look at the pigs. Bevel's presupposed misunderstanding of the appearance of pigs is encoded in a complement clause to the factive verb *know*: "Bevel had never seen a real pig but he had seen a pig in a book and knew *they were small fat pink animals with curly tails and round grinning faces and bow ties*" (*GM*, 36).

As characters become more and more distasteful, because of overt racism, classism, or hubris, the comic function of the presuppositions in which characters are revealed to know incorrectly is partially or wholly overshadowed by their more sinister implications. In "The Displaced Person," Mrs. McIntyre learns of Mr. Guizac's intent of marrying off his Polish relatives to the black workers on her farm but repeatedly delays firing him because he is a very good worker. She does not begin to question the "morality" of anything until the weight of social opinion begins to bear on her:

> Mrs. McIntyre found *that everybody in town knew Mr. Shortley's version of her business and that everyone was critical of her conduct.* She began to understand *that she had a moral obligation to fire the Pole and that she was shirking it because she found it hard to do.* (*GM,* 248)

Mrs. McIntyre might well have discovered the background to the factive verb *found.* Everyone might, indeed, know Mr. Shortley's version of recent events on her farm and disapprove of her behavior. However, the confusion of moral and social obligations evident in the presupposed complements to the factive verb *understand* is a strong theme in "The Displaced Person" and is a recurrent theme in O'Connor's last short story collection, *Everything That Rises Must Converge.* That confusion eventually leads to the collusional murder of Mr. Guizac. In "Revelation," largely narrated with Mrs. Ruby Turpin as the reflector, Ruby sits in moral and social judgment on everyone in the doctor's waiting room with her. She approves of only three people—herself (most importantly), her husband Claud, and her social twin, the well-dressed "pleasant lady." When the "white-trash woman" lets her views be known on race relations and hog farming, "The look that Mrs. Turpin and the pleasant lady exchanged indicated they both understood that you had to *have* certain things before you could *know* certain things" (*ERMC,* 199, italics in original). The materialist epistemology here is mocked as circular; it is the middle-class pleasant lady and Ruby who can presuppose in the complement of *understood* knowledge of knowledge and how it is obtained. In "The Lame Shall Enter First," the intellectual Sheppard ignores his own child's grief over the death of his mother and concentrates all his messianic energies on saving the juvenile delinquent Rufus Johnson, partially by buying Rufus an orthopedic shoe for his clubfoot. Rufus understands the depth of Sheppard's intellectual and spiritual hubris and rejects both Sheppard and the shoe. However, Sheppard persists in his simplistic social and psychological theories: "He realized *that the boy had refused the shoe because he was insecure*" (*ERMC,* 177). What follows the outrageously inaccurate presupposed complement to *realized* is a series of four sentences in free indirect discourse, each as damning of Sheppard's misunderstanding as the presupposed complement: "Johnson had been frightened by his own gratitude. He didn't know what to make of the new self he was becoming conscious of. He understood that something he had been was threatened and he was facing himself and his possibilities for the first time. He was questioning his identity" (*ERMC,* 177).

Free indirect discourse (FID) is most clearly defined within the context of examples that contrast it with direct discourse (DD) and simple indirect discourse (ID). Consider the following examples, only the last of which actually occurs in "The Lame Shall Enter First":

DD   9.   Sheppard thought to himself, "Johnson has been frightened by his own gratitude."
ID   10.   Sheppard thought to himself that Johnson had been frightened by his own gratitude.
FID 11.   Johnson had been frightened by his own gratitude.

I use *discourse* as a cover term for both thought and speech, even though some analysts write of free indirect thought and free indirect speech. There are some subtle differences between the two, besides the obvious, but they are irrelevant to us here. Two characteristics of DD are illustrated by example (9). The thought of Sheppard is introduced by a cognition verb and is enclosed by quotation marks. A comparison of example (9)—DD—with example (10)—ID—reveals some formal differences. In ID, the thought is introduced with a grammatical subordinator so that the thought does not appear in quotation marks. And the tense in the thought has been shifted to the past to accord with the perspective of the narrator. In example (11)—FID—the verb of cognition has been suppressed, and the only indications that we have that it is Sheppard's thought that is represented are (1) the content itself, which is not likely to be a phrase attributable to either the narrator or the narratee since they both know that Johnson is too cynical and knowing to think such maudlin thoughts and (2) the context, i.e., following the damning statement "[Sheppard] realized that the boy had refused the shoe because he was insecure." Notice that the FID version in (11) and the ID version in (10) differ only by the absence in (11) of the framing "Sheppard thought that." Hence, FID is referred to as free indirect discourse because it is indirect discourse free of the framing attributive clause of thought or speech. None of the four FID sentences in the long quotation above is formally subordinated to the factive *realize*, but again, partly because they follow a complement of *realize* we read them as Sheppard's progressive realizations of preexisting "truths." The layering of misunderstanding by including in these thoughts presupposed complements of the verbs *know* and *understand* deepens the narrator's irony (e.g., "He understood that something he had been was threatened"). Sheppard misunderstands not only Johnson's motivations for refusing the shoe, but also whatever it is that Johnson understands.

When O'Connor's narrator presupposes background knowledge of which the reflector character is clearly not aware, the result is a displacement of knowledge rather than an ironic comment on false knowledge. I use the word *displacement* because it is clear in many cases that the character later realizes the displaced knowledge and in other cases that the narrative may be read as a quest for that knowledge. Some of these displacements are significant thematically, as is Rayber's ignorance of his own violent tendencies in "The Barber." Others are relatively trivial, although they do create narrative suspense, as in the following passage from "The Artificial Nigger," in which Mr. Head and his grandson Nelson arrive on Nelson's first visit to the big city:

> The train was in the station. Both he and Mr. Head jumped up and ran to the door. Neither noticed *that they had left the paper sack with the lunch in it on the seat*. (*GM*, 113)

With the use of the negative pronoun *neither*, the narrator makes it explicit that Nelson and Mr. Head are ignorant of the content of the complement clause of the factive verb *noticed*, although later when they are hungry and lost in the city they do realize it.

Displacement of background knowledge from a character's awareness may be of short duration, as in the example from "The Artificial Nigger," or it may be of much longer duration, as in the very first sentence of O'Connor's *The Violent Bear It Away*, which serves as a partial narrative abstract:

> Francis Marion Tarwater's uncle had been dead for only half a day *when the boy got too drunk to finish digging his grave and a Negro named Buford Munson, who had come to get a jug filled, had to finish it and drag the body from the breakfast table where it was still sitting and bury it in a decent and Christian way, with the sign of its Saviour at the head of the grave and enough dirt on top to keep the dogs from digging it up.* (*VBA*, 3)

The coordinated presupposed adverbial *when* clauses tell us many things that we might assume even at this point in the story that both Tarwater and Buford know. However, the remainder of the novel makes it clear that Tarwater does not know that Buford finishes the grave and buries his uncle. Tarwater returns drunk from the woods and burns his uncle's house, he thinks containing his uncle's body, to the ground. In the final chapter, Tarwater finds his way home again after having completed his prophetic mission, still haunted by the belief that he will find his uncle's charred bones among the ruins of the house. In the final pages, Buford informs him of the knowledge presupposed in an adverbial clause within the first sentence of the novel. In this way, as I argue elsewhere, presuppositions may function to signal Roland Barthes' hermeneutic code, i.e., the enigmas (unanswered questions or unresolved problems) of a narrative that are established and pursued by the narrator and/or the characters themselves.[11]

The realization of displaced knowledge may never be narrated, as in the case of Mrs. Shortley's daughters' understanding of their mother's death in "The Displaced Person." When their mother dies of a stroke, first they don't realize that she has just died, but they also don't know that the whole family has been displaced in turn by Mr. Guizac and his displaced Polish family: "they didn't know *that she had had a great experience or ever been displaced in the world from all that belonged to her*" (*GM*, 223). Of course, the daughters must eventually realize their mother's death although that realization is not narrated. A more significant question is whether they will ever realize the full significance their mother's displacement from the McIntyre farm.

There are several variations on the use of presupposition to encode background knowledge displaced from the character's awareness, including variations on not only the span of displacement but also the cause of the displacement. Tarwater simply cannot know that Buford buried his uncle since he did not notice the grave when he returned to burn the house. There are characters, like Nelson, Mr. Head, and Rayber, who for various major or minor psychological reasons cannot realize certain background knowledge at particular points in the narrative. There are other characters, like Mrs. Hopewell in "Good Country People," who only partially realize certain background knowledge. Mrs. Hopewell—as her name suggests—keeps herself too desperately busy looking on the bright side of life to realize completely the physical condition of Hulga, her maimed child:

> It was hard for Mrs. Hopewell to realize *that her child was thirty-two now and that for more than twenty years she had had only one leg*. She thought of her still as a child because it tore her heart to think instead of the poor stout girl in her thirties who had never danced a step or had any *normal* good times. (*GM*, 173; italicization of *normal* in original)

In the first sentence it is not said that Mrs. Hopewell didn't realize the following presuppositions, only that it was "hard" for her to do so. It is rather unclear whether she has full knowledge of the presuppositions since "hard" is here ambiguous between a reading that says she finds it painful and a reading that says she finds it difficult (intellectually, spiritually, or otherwise) to do so. The following sentence does not resolve the ambiguity since Mrs. Hopewell thinks of Hulga as a "child" or a "girl" regardless of whether she realizes that she is thirty-two years old and that she has spent more than twenty of those years with only one leg. Again, it is likely that Mrs. Hopewell will fully realize Hulga's condition, presumably when after the end of the narrative she will find Hulga abandoned in a hayloft by the Bible salesman who has stolen both her glasses and her wooden leg.

In all examples considered thus far of presupposition used to encode displaced knowledge, the missing knowledge will be, or at least has the potential to be, filled in as the character completes a quest—often an unconscious one—for spiritual enlightenment, including the realization of the background knowledge of their lives that they so stubbornly ignore. Although not as commonly, O'Connor does also use presupposition to present realized knowledge that was previously displaced, as in the following from "The Displaced Person":

> Mrs. McIntyre was looking fixedly at Mr. Guizac's legs lying flat on the ground now. She heard the brake on the large tractor slip and, looking up, she saw it move forward, calculating its own path. Later she remembered *that she had seen the Negro jump silently out of the way as if a spring in the earth had released him and that she had seen Mr. Shortley turn his head with incredible slowness and stare silently over his shoulder and that she had started to shout to the Displaced Person but that she had not.* (*GM*, 249–50)

The long narrative (noncanonical since it is grammatically subordinated) contained in the complement clauses subordinated to the factive *remembered* contains information implicating Mrs. McIntyre, the unnamed black man, and Mr. Shortley in a conspiracy to rid themselves of the very troublesome Mr. Guizac. The displacement of the presentation of this knowledge serves to reinforce not only the unstated (and therefore displaced) background collusion but also the unreality of the sequence of events as Mrs. McIntyre experiences them. Soon afterwards, the narrator says, "Her mind was not taking hold of all that was happening" (*GM,* 250).

A character may also know in a way in which the narrator and/or narratee cannot share or participate comfortably. In *Wise Blood,* Enoch is bothered by the picture in his room of the superior-looking moose and is driven to finding a solution to the problem of bringing the moose down to his own level:

> he realized with a sudden intuition *that taking the frame off him would be equal to taking the clothes off him* (although he didn't have on any) and he was right because when he had done it, the animal looked so reduced that Enoch could only snicker and look at him out the corner of his eye. (*WB,* 133)

The narrator's comment that Enoch was "right" draws attention to the "truthfulness" of his idiotic "sudden intuition." To Enoch, the moose has been made a bit smaller, small enough that he can now snicker at it and hazard glances at it. As with false knowledge, "uncomfortable" knowledge may be comic or sinister. Consider the first paragraph of the story "The Comforts of Home":

> Thomas withdrew to the side of the window and with his head between the wall and the curtain he looked down on the driveway where the car had stopped. His mother and *the little slut* were getting out of it. His mother emerged slowly, stolid and awkward, and then *the little slut*'s long slightly bowed legs slid out, the dress pulled above the knees. With a shriek of laughter *she* ran to meet the dog, who bounded, overjoyed, shaking with pleasure, to welcome *her.* Rage gathered throughout Thomas's large frame with a silent ominous intensity, like a mob assembling. (*ERMC,* 115)

Through definite description, as I pointed out earlier, "Thomas" and "the side of the window" and "the window," among other things, are all presupposed in the first sentence to exist. There is no question of who presupposes the existence of Thomas, the side of the window, and the window itself. Both the narrator and the narratee do. However, if we negate the second sentence of this passage to "His mother and the little slut were not getting out of it," we see that the existence of his mother, the little slut, and it (the car) are presupposed. Furthermore, the little slut is presupposed in the possessive construction "the little slut's long slightly bowed legs." The question is, of course, who presupposes the existence of, and therefore claims the language of, "the little slut"—probably neither the narrator nor the narratee but instead only Thomas, who has so many unpleasant qualities—including hypocrisy and an overwhelming selfishness—that the reader is highly unlikely to sympathize with him. As the reference to "the little slut" shifts to "she" in the third sentence, we have a different point of view on her as "she ran to meet the dog who bounded, overjoyed, shaking with pleasure, to welcome her." In this passage, we again see the intersection of the two literary devices of presupposition and free indirect discourse in the job of creating an unfavorable view of Thomas's mind.

In FID, the narratee is implicitly asked whether he or she along with the narrator can claim the language of the focalized character. When the FID involves existential presupposition signaled by the language of racism or misogyny, for example, the narratee is implicitly asked whether s/he can join with the narrator and/or character in that racism or misogyny, as in the passage above from "The Comforts of Home." If the FID involves simply indefinite noun phrases, presupposition of particular individuals does not result but instead that of generic types (or domains); however, the narratee is still invited to claim that language, as occurs in "Revelation" when Ruby Turpin counts her blessings:

> To help anybody out that needed it was her philosophy of life. She never spared herself when she found somebody in need, whether they were white or black, trash or decent. And of all she had to be thankful for, she was most thankful that this was so. . . . Her heart rose. He had not made her a nigger or white-trash or ugly! He had made her herself and given her a little of everything. Jesus, thank you! she said. Thank you thank you thank you! (*ERMC,* 202–3)

Note the FID use of the word *nigger* here where the reader's relationship to Ruby is defined by pure irony.[12] There is no chance that the reader will be empathetic with her, so there is no reason to separate the reader and Ruby with either DD or ID.

In each of the cases of presupposition that we have examined thus far, the presupposed knowledge has been defective in some way. It has been either just plain wrong, or reprehensible, or correct but displaced from the awareness of the character. Furthermore, if the presupposition is radically at odds with what the narrator and the narratee know, the presupposition is ironic and is used comically or in an effort to reveal serious defects in a character's moral, spiritual, or social judgment. It is not the case, however, that all presuppositions that are in fact new (marked) to the narratee are defective in O'Connor in the sense that the narrator and narratee know more or better than the character due to a conspiratorial use of presupposition by the narrator. Non-defective but still marked presuppositions convey a knowledge of mystery on the part of a character. The sense of mystery in O'Connor's characters is normally more an awareness than a knowledge in the ordinary sense of the word *knowledge*. As we will see, only once does O'Connor give sure and unwavering knowledge of mystery to one of her characters. O'Connor had very definite ideas about the constitution of the writer interested in mystery, as she indicated in "Some Aspects of the Grotesque in Southern Fiction": "Such a writer will be interested in what we don't understand rather than in what we do. He will be interested in possibility rather than in probability. He will be interested in characters who are forced out to meet evil and grace and who act on a trust beyond themselves—whether they know very clearly what it is they act upon or not" (*MM*, 42).

The most common use of presupposition to encode a sense of mystery in O'Connor centers on knowledge of destiny. In *Wise Blood*, after he shows the shrunken man in the glass case to Haze, Enoch senses his destiny although he doesn't know that his specific destiny is to steal the shrunken man and present it to Haze as an icon for his Church Without Christ:

> Enoch Emery knew now *that his life would never be the same again*, because the thing that was going to happen to him had started to happen. He had always known *that something was going to happen* but he hadn't known what. . . . That was a mystery beyond his understanding, but he knew *that what was going to be expected of him was something awful*. (*WB*, 129)

The complements to these uses of the factive *know* contain presupposed knowledge of mystery in the sense that Enoch knows that his life will not be the same although he doesn't know exactly how it will be, that he knows that something will happen but not exactly what, and that he knows that it will be awful but again doesn't know exactly how. Thus, the knowledge of mystery in O'Connor is not viewed ironically, but instead empathetically, and although it is deferred knowledge in that characters typically spend the remainder of the narrative fulfilling their mysterious destinies, a character's knowledge is equal to or even, although rarely, better than that of the narrator and narratee.

Presupposed knowledge of their destiny is usually given to those characters who act positively in the operation of the mystery of grace. In *The Violent Bear It Away*, after his great-uncle dies and before Tarwater goes to the city to baptize, and drown, his own cousin, "The boy knew *he would have to bury the old man before anything would begin*" (*VBA*, 12). In "The River" when Bevel comes back to his parents' apartment after being baptized in the river, "he began to think about the river": "Very slowly, his expression changed as if he were gradually seeing appear what he didn't know he'd been looking for. Then all of a sudden he knew *what he wanted to do*." Bevel proceeds to return to the river and drown himself in an attempt to find "the Kingdom of Christ in the river." Even as he is about to drown, the narrator uses presupposition to narrate his acceptance of his fate: "For an instant he was overcome with surprise; then since he was moving quickly and knew *that he was getting somewhere*, all his fury and his fear left him" (*GM*, 50–52). In "Parker's Back," the central quest of Obadiah Elihue Parker's life—to obtain the image of the Byzantine Christ on his back so that it will lead him in suffering to Christ himself—is set in motion, without his even knowing it, by the vision of a tattooed man at a fair: "It was as if a blind boy had been turned so gently in a different direction that he did not know *his destination had been changed*" (*ERMC*, 223). As an adult, after he wrecks the old woman's tractor, Parker receives the final mysterious push in his quest:

> Parker did not allow himself to think on the way to the city. He only knew *that there had been a great change in his life, a leap forward into a worse unknown, and that there was nothing he could do about it*. It was for all intents accomplished. (*ERMC*, 233)

What Parker "knows" in this three-clause presupposition is quite a bit, but is still a mystery both to himself and to the reader until it is revealed that he is to receive the tattoo of the Byzantine Christ. But even still at the end of the story as we are left with the image of Parker "crying like a baby" after having been beaten and rejected yet again by his wife Sarah Ruth for the "idolatry" of his new tattoo, we and mostly he too are not certain exactly where his "worse unknown" will eventually lead him (*ERMC*, 244).

"The Artificial Nigger" is a prototypical O'Connor story in its central theme and plot: grace and gain of self-knowledge; however, in no other story does O'Connor give her character such a clear and steady understanding and awareness after the destruction of false knowledge. Frederick Asals comments that "revelations in O'Connor's works . . . come only when the consciousness of the protagonist, with all its presuppositions and defenses, is finally overthrown and a deeper awareness forces its way through."[13] Mr. Head, who thinks of himself as having "that calm understanding of life that makes him a suitable guide for the young" means to show his grandson Nelson on their trip to the city that Nelson is "not as smart as he thought he was" (*GM*, 102–4). Nelson is shown that he didn't even know what color blacks are; he is shown cruelly that he is dependent on his grandfather; and he is shown, cruelly also, that the city can be a very hostile environment for children. Thus, consider the following scene in which Mr. Head denies Nelson the protection and comfort that is due to and desperately needed by him:

> "Your boy has broken my ankle!" the old woman shouted. "Police!"
>
> Mr. Head sensed the approach of the policeman from behind. He stared straight ahead at the women who were massed in their fury like a solid wall to block his escape. "This is not my boy," he said. "*I never seen him before.*"
>
> He felt Nelson's fingers fall out of his flesh. . . .
>
> Mr. Head began to feel the depth of his denial. His face as they walked on became all hollows and bare ridges. *He saw nothing they were passing.* (*GM*, 123–24)

In his fear, Mr. Head denies knowledge of Nelson (i.e., his blood relation to Nelson) by claiming that he has never seen him. Then, in his guilt, he becomes symbolically blind, unable to see.

As Nelson punishes Head for his denial by ignoring him, the thoroughness with which Head has been stripped of his false pride and knowledge is
presented in a presupposed clause: "[Head] knew *that now he was wandering
into a black strange place where nothing was like it had ever been before, a long old
age without respect and an end that would be welcome because it would be the end*"
(*GM*, 125). Despite Nelson's own gain in knowledge, it is Head that learns
the most about himself, as is revealed in the following passage, which occurs
after they return from the city and have reconciled:

> Mr. Head stood very still and felt the action of mercy touch him again but
> this time he knew *that there were no words in the world that could name it*. He
> understood *that it grew out of agony, which is not denied to any man and which is
> given in strange ways to children*. He understood *it was all a man could carry into
> death to give his Maker* and he suddenly burned with shame that he had so lit-
> tle of it to take with him. He stood appalled, judging himself with the thor-
> oughness of God, while the action of mercy covered his pride like a flame
> and consumed it. He had never thought himself a great sinner before but he
> saw now *that his true depravity had been hidden from him lest it cause him despair*.
> He realized *that he was forgiven for sins from the beginning of time, when he had
> conceived in his own heart the sin of Adam, until the present, when he had denied
> poor Nelson*. He saw *that no sin was too monstrous for him to claim as his own*, and
> since God loved in proportion as He forgave, he felt ready at that instant to
> enter Paradise. (*GM*, 128–29)

The clauses that are italicized in this passage are presuppositional, all for
the same reasons: they are finite (i.e., tensed clauses), they occur as complements to factive verbs (*know, understand, see, realize*), and the subjects of
the factive verbs are third-person. Robert Brinkmeyer, Jr., argues that in
"The Artificial Nigger" O'Connor comes closer than in any other of her
stories to wedding her own authorial Catholic view with that of her narrator, who is usually a fundamentalist, but who in "The Artificial Nigger" is
very close to Catholic in belief, particularly in the narrator's emphasis on
charity at the end of the story.[14] The device that creates all this good will
between the narrator and the author is nonproblematic presupposition,
that background that is implicit when complements to factive verbs are in
fact shared. Furthermore, O'Connor is kinder to her reader in "The Artificial Nigger" than she normally is. It is widely recognized that O'Connor's
position as a Catholic writer in the Deep South and in an age of unbelief

created difficulties for her in knowing what to assume that her audience either knew or believed. As Carol Shloss argues, O'Connor opts at the end of "The Artificial Nigger" for "a statement of faith" rather than her more usual "oblique insult, which ensues from the intimation that her fictional world is fraught with portentous meanings that we could see if only we were not such monstrous readers, and too limited to understand."[15] Again, the reason O'Connor seems to be kinder toward her reader is that those clauses italicized above are nonproblematically presuppositional for everyone involved in the narrative act, including the reader.

Presupposition has been a topic of only occasional discussion in stylistic and narratological work. In that work, there is a recognition of the literary power of marked presupposition, that in which the narratee or listener does not, in fact, share background knowledge signaled by the narrator or speaker.[16] However, what prior works on narrative presupposition lack is an attempt to explain consistent patterns of theme and marked presupposition across the entire body of an author's works. O'Connor's relatively small corpus of three short story collections and two novels lends itself to this task, a task which should be the first step towards a typology of marked literary presupposition. Such a typology should be based not only on distribution of knowledge among the narrator, narratee, and character(s), but also on the full range of specific literary effects of marked presupposition, e.g., irony, narrative suspense, empathy.

In chapter 4, we move on to another source of background—negated suppositions—and consider the importance of both negation and the unexpected to successful narrative. We also examine in some detail the quantitative basis for determining that heavy analytic negation is a stylistic trait of O'Connor's fiction.

Chapter 4

Negating the Background

*The gist of the story is that H. Motes couldn't really believe that
he hadn't been redeemed.*

—Flannery O'Connor (*CW*, 897)

We continue our exploration of the narration of knowledge in O'Connor's
fiction through the back door—through the negative, that is, through what
is generally understood as a lack rather than a presence. Negation is a promising area of stylistic investigation of knowledge since, as I indicated in chapter 1, negation is used in English typically only when an interlocutor is
assumed to believe in incorrect propositions. The negative corrects the
hearer's incorrect knowledge. This chapter begins with an introduction to
the relationship between negation and the backgrounded incorrect propositions that lie behind the use of negation and then explores the importance
of negation in creating a narratable story. I then examine analytic negation
(*not*, *n't*) in O'Connor's three story collections and two novels and the
Brown general-fiction corpus and find that the frequency of analytic negation in O'Connor's fiction is statistically significantly higher than the frequency of analytic negation in the Brown corpus. Analytic negation (the use
of morphologically separable *not* and *n't*) is opposed to synthetic negation,
in which the negative is bound to a portmanteau morpheme (e.g., *none,
never, nothing*). I show that the higher degree of analytic negation in O'Connor's fiction can be fully accounted for (i.e., statistically predicted) neither
by concentration of dialogue nor by dialogism (operationalized as numbers
of speaker changes), the latter being a modification of Gunnel Tottie's predictive account of higher degrees of negation in oral vs. written language.[1]
That is, I demonstrate that O'Connor's high degree of analytic negation is a
stylistic marker of her writing.

There has been some interest in negation in linguistically influenced literary criticism, primarily focusing on narratological issues, such as William
Labov's tellability.[2] In a much different and more traditionally "literary"

direction, Maire Jaanus Kurrik examines the philosophical and theological foundations of negativity in literature. In spite of Kurrik's claim in her preface to have been allowed to pursue her interest in linguistics, among other disciplines, in the writing of her book, there is very little linguistics in the book and what there is is filtered through postmodern metaphorization: "Negation superimposes itself on an assertion. 'It is not my mother,' is, in Chomsky's view, a negative added to a positive. In this sense, negation is always tantalizing, provocative, and ambiguous, a positive descriptive force which implies and promotes the very idea or thing that it seeks to deny. It is an absence yoked to a presence, or a presence-evoking absence."[3] What Kurrik means by "a negative added to a positive" is the application of the negative transformation to a positive sentence since there are no negative sentences at the deep-structure level. I doubt very seriously that many linguists in the Chomskian tradition—"[i]n this sense"—would ever think of the negative transformation as "always tantalizing, provocative, and ambiguous." In the same school of theologically and philosophically influenced negativity studies but with fewer linguistic pretentions, Joseph Louis Zornado's 1992 dissertation is a sensitive reading of *via negativa* theology as well as deconstructive traits in O'Connor's fiction. That is, Zornado shows that O'Connor's fiction can be profitably read through the theological literature of Pseudo-Dionysius, St. John of the Cross, the author of *The Cloud of Unknowing*, Meister Eckhart, and others as well as deconstructive writers such as Roland Barthes and Jacques Derrida, all of whom have in common the thesis that positive knowledge is an impossibility and that it is only through the failure of both knowing and unknowing that we reach anything like a true appreciation of our abiding ignorance either before the unknowable God or the unknowable text. Kimberly Greene Angle pursues essentially the same "negative" methodology of reading O'Connor with the less ambitious support of "negative-space theory," a collection of insights gathered from studies of right-brain abilities in artistic activities.[4] Unlike *Narrating Knowledge*, none of the literary studies mentioned here has quantitatively examined negation; none has compared negation in an author's work and in a standard corpus such as the Brown general-fiction corpus; and none has examined the location of the linguistic suppositions of negatives in both the (literary) speaker's and hearer's minds.

There are some excellent linguistic analyses of negation in other literary writers' work. J. F. Burrows' *Computation into Criticism* is a detailed

computational and statistical examination of grammatical (function) morphemes such as prepositions, pronouns, articles, and others, including *not*
and *n't*, in Jane Austen's novels. Burrows is primarily interested in using distribution figures to support his contention that one can use the function
morphemes in Austen's novels to distinguish the idiolect of each character
as well as the dialects of subgroupings of characters. What Burrows does not
do, simply because it is not the intended focus of any part of his study,
is examine the particular pragmatic function of any of these grammatical
morphemes. Greg Watson's *Doin' Mudrooroo*, a study of the novels of the
Australian aboriginal writer Mudrooroo, also contains an empirical account
of literary negation, showing, for example, that there is progressively less
negation in the writer's later novels. Watson, who argues that negation is
an involvement device in Mudrooroo's fiction, writes, "The reader becomes
involved on two levels: firstly at a linguistic level, a negative message needs
extra time to decode, and secondly, at an emotional level, we must come
to terms with the emotional response the negative message has incurred."
Watson's first point about involvement depends on Peter Wason's 1959
psycholinguistic study showing that Wason's subjects took more time processing negative statements than positive statements. The extra time involved
in processing negatives is presumably, Wason reasons, due to the extra processing time needed to access the positive version (supposition), which
serves as the background to the negative. In this study, I do not examine the
emotional level that Watson refers to. Rather, I argue that the greater
involvement of negatives, even on an interpersonal level, is due to the
shared background which a negative either responds to or creates itself.
Laura Hidalgo Downing's studies of Joseph Heller's *Catch-22* rely not only
on functional linguistics but also on text world theory, from among others,
Paul Werth. She demonstrates that Heller's novel depends heavily on analytic and synthetic negation to defamiliarize the frustrations and sometimes
irresolvable contradictions in military and modern life. Downing's *Negation,
Text Worlds, and Discourse* is remarkably qualitatively detailed in its comprehensive review of functional and textual theories of negation. The study
also demonstrates that Heller's novel is statistically significantly more
negative than either the American Brown general-fiction corpus or the
Lancaster/Oslo-Bergen general-fiction corpus. While text world theory
is beyond the scope of my own study of negation in O'Connor's fiction,

Werth's negative accommodation, which Downing relies on in part to analyze Heller's novel, is similar to my category of suggested supposition,
which we will take up in detail in chapter 5.[5]

Joanne Halleran McMullen's *Writing against God: Language as Message in
the Literature of Flannery O'Connor* deserves special mention here since she
includes in her stylistic study of O'Connor's fiction an entire chapter on
"The Grammar of Negation." However, besides quoting George Dillon on
the role of negatives in negating an expectation, she makes nothing of
the specific pragmatics of negative suppositions. McMullen's argument is
closer in spirit and substance to the critical literature on the *via negativa* in
O'Connor's fiction than to stylistic analysis. Her chapter on negation, for
instance, shifts in the middle to a long discussion of onomastics in O'Connor, the connection between negation and onomastic anagrams being more
postmodern than linguistic. McMullen's chapter, insofar as it is a stylistic
analysis, is open to some of the criticisms that Stanley Fish raises in his
famous attack on stylistics—"What Is Stylistics and Why Are They Saying
Such Terrible Things about It?" It uses linguistics more as a literary trope
than as a methodology for analysis of the specific linguistic structure of
O'Connor's negatives. However revealing of O'Connor's development of
the *via negativa* McMullen's argument might be, her "grammar of negation"
is insufficiently operationalized for extended comparison with my own
analysis.[6]

Negation and the Suppositional Background

In the extensive philosophical, psychological, and linguistic literature on the
subject, a negative utterance is widely viewed to be a response to a backgrounded affirmative. For example, T. Givón argues, rather broadly, "A
negative assertion is . . . made on the tacit assumption that the hearer either
has heard about, believes in, is likely to take for granted, or is at least familiar with the corresponding affirmative proposition."[7] Thus, consider the two
negatives in the invented dialogue of (1):

1. a. My linguistics professor didn't give us a review guide for the exam.
   b. College professors don't normally give exam review guides.

In (1a), the speaker uses a negative in response to the supposition (the
backgrounded affirmative) that he/she would receive a study guide, and in

(1b) another speaker uses a negative to respond to the more general false supposition on the part of the first speaker that professors normally give such guides. The supposition, or suppositions, of a negative utterance must be "present" in the background; otherwise, the negative calls for correction, as in (1) and (2) in most contexts:

2. I wasn't invited to groom the President's dog yesterday.

If one can imagine (2) as a conversational opening gambit anywhere (absent a cadre of regular dog groomers to the President), one of the few imaginable polite responses might be, "Did you have some reason to expect to be invited?"

There are several problems, some real and some only imagined, with the characterization of negatives as being appropriate only if in the background there is an assumed positive. First, the characterization is an overgeneralization, given the existence of what I call "suggested suppositions." Additionally, it is not just negatives that require a background supposition to be pragmatically felicitous. Thus, consider the following positive propositions from Laurence Horn:[8]

3. a. I went to the meeting of my own free will.
   b. I remember my own name.
   c. Your wife is faithful.
   d. The [2004] presidential election will be held.
   e. The dean is breathing.

All of the examples in (3) are remarkable because they are in most contexts uninformative. Imagine a context in which (3b), for example, would be informative; one would have to assume (i.e., suppose) that the hearer would not expect the speaker to be able to remember his/her own name. Imagine a context in which (3e) would be informative; one would have to suppose that the hearer expected the dean to be dead and/or not breathing.

Contrast the examples in (3) to those in (4):

4. a. I went the meeting, but I didn't want to.
   b. I remembered his name although he was a quiet student of mine fourteen years ago.
   c. The dictator is committed to the citizens' happiness and well-being.
   d. The 2004 presidential election will be free of special-interest funding.

    e. The dean communicates on a weekly basis with the rank-and-file faculty.

In each of these nonproblematic examples, one either communicates a positive against the background of an explicitly present contradictory background (e.g., 4a and 4b), or communicates a positive against a culturally implicit contradictory background (e.g., 4c, 4d, and 4e).

So, if both positive and negative sentences can require background suppositions, what is the suppositional difference between them? The key to this distinction is what Geoffrey Leech calls the *principle of negative uninformativeness* (also referred to by Horn in *A Natural History of Negation*). The principle of negative uninformativeness is that "negatives, all things being equal, are less informative than their positive counterparts." Thus, consider Leech's illustrative examples:

5. a. Abraham Lincoln was not shot by Ivan Mazeppa.
     b. Abraham Lincoln was shot by John Wilkes Booth.

Leech comments that although (5a) and (5b) are both true, (5b) is much more informative than (5a). To follow Leech's argument, one must assume a context in which (5) does not have the supposition that Ivan Mazeppa did shoot Abraham Lincoln but instead simply the felicity conditions of a straightforward wh-question: "Who shot Abraham Lincoln?" In that case, (5a) is less informative than (5b) because it does not help us to exclude any but one of the millions of people who might have shot the president. In most contexts, (5b) excludes all but one person—John Wilkes Booth. As Leech puts it, "The world's population of negative facts is far greater than its population of positive facts." For example, Ivan Mazeppa didn't shoot Lincoln, I didn't shoot Lincoln, you didn't shoot Lincoln, your mother didn't shoot Lincoln, and so on.[9]

Thus, what necessitates a background supposition, either before the utterance of the negative or easily created by the negative, is the relative uninformativeness, outside of context, of negatives when compared to positives. Consider the following variants:

6. The new employee's name is Susan.
7. The new employee's name isn't Susan.
8. The new employee's name isn't Susan. It's Mary.

If (6) and (7) are intended to provide the new employee's name, the positive (6) is more informative than the negative (7). If the addressee of (6) already knows that the new employee's name is Susan, then (6) is informationally redundant. If the addressee of (7) already knows that the new employee's name is not Susan, then (7) is also informationally redundant. But in that context, (7) is noninformative in a way that (6) is not. Example (7) is not only redundant but also noninformative in the sense that it does not provide the name of the new employee. Only (6) and (8) provide that information. Thus, if one is to use a negative, which is inherently less informative than a positive, there must be a reason for that less informative choice. There need not be the supposition in (6) that the new employee's name is not Susan. But the supposition that the employee's name is Susan must be present in (7) and (8). Positives may or may not require suppositions; however, the inherently less informative status of negatives—outside of context—demands background suppositions to make them informative.

All of this talk of background assumptions might tempt some to conclude that the background of negatives is another case of "presupposition" as it was discussed in chapter 3. However, as I indicated in chapter 3, presuppositions remain constant under the negation of the main verb. To review, consider the positive and negative sentences in (9):

9. a. Bill realizes that you are sick.
    b. Bill doesn't realize that you are sick.

In both (9a) and (9b), the complement to the factive main verb *realize*, "that you are sick," is presupposed. What is asserted in these example sentences is that Bill either realizes or doesn't realize the presupposed fact that "you are sick." However similar in background the negative sentences that we have considered thus far in this chapter are to the sentences with factives in (9), the background of negatives is not the same as that for presuppositional constructions. Herbert H. Clark recognizes this fact and labels the background of negatives "supposition," the term that I use as well.[10]

Consider again the negative in (1a), repeated in (10a), and its positive in (10b):

10. a. My linguistics professor didn't give us a review guide for the exam.
    b. My linguistics professor gave us a review guide for the exam.

Although (10a) backgrounds the belief that the speaker would naturally receive a study guide from the professor, that belief, or "supposition," is not presupposed since (10b) does not have the same backgrounded belief. Presuppositions are assumed to hold whether or not the main clause is negated. A reconsideration of (9b), "Bill doesn't realize that you are sick," shows that it has both the presupposition "that you are sick" and the supposition that "you" think that Bill realizes that you are sick. As Givón argues, in a negative, "the hearer **knows wrong**," or **supposes incorrectly**, and "the speaker **knows better**"; in an affirmative, "the hearer **does not know**" and "the speaker **knows**" better (bolding in original). Extending Givón's categorization of the affirmative, I argue that in a presuppositional clause "the hearer **knows**" and "the speaker **knows**." Thus, a very rough epistemological difference between presupposition and supposition is that the hearer knows correctly in presupposition but incorrectly in supposition. Umberto Eco and Patrizia Violi, and I, elsewhere, have shown that presupposition can reflect not so much what both speaker and hearer know but more what the speaker wants to assume or presume that the hearer knows.[11] I will similarly show that supposition sometimes reflects not so much what the speaker knows the hearer to misunderstand but more what the speaker wants to assume or presume that the hearer misunderstands.

In the next section, I consider the influence of negation on the particular shape of some of O'Connor's narratives as well as on the overall shape of O'Connor narratives in general.

Negation and Narrative

This section is concerned with negation as theme and narrative plot, yet it still relies on the linguistic analysis of a negative's response to a supposition. It seems incontrovertible that the high frequency of analytic negation in O'Connor prose (which I quantitatively analyze in a later section) is a result of her thematic fascination with *via negativa*, the approach to God through negativity, or the absence of knowledge. As I have already mentioned, Zornado has shown that O'Connor had a highly sophisticated understanding of the *via negativa*.[12] That sophistication surfaces not only in the general thematic pursuit and flight from knowledge in her stories but also in the very particulars of the narrative within some stories. Consider Hulga's Heideggerian reading material, discovered by her mother, Mrs. Hopewell, in "Good

Country People": "One day Mrs. Hopewell had picked up one of the books the girl had just put down and opening it at random, she read, 'Science, on the other hand, has to assert its soberness and seriousness afresh and declare that it is concerned solely with what-is. Nothing—how can it be for science anything but a horror and a phantasm? If science is right, then one thing stands firm: science wishes to know nothing of nothing. Such is after all the strictly scientific approach to Nothing. We know it by wishing to know noth-ing of Nothing.' These words had been underlined with a blue pencil and they worked on Mrs. Hopewell like some evil incantation in gibberish. She shut the book quickly and went out of the room as if she were having a chill" (*GM*, 176–77). The book that Hulga has been reading is Martin Heidegger's *Existence and Being*. The passage that Mrs. Hopewell reads is an exact quota-tion (in translation) from the essay "What Is Metaphysics?" *Nothing*, a form of synthetic negation, is here presented as the very antithesis of knowledge: "science wishes to know nothing of nothing." Science—rationality—"is con-cerned solely with what-is," the positive what-is, not the negative what-is-not. One could hardly imagine a more positivistic proclamation of the fundamental belief of and hope in modern science. However, if Mrs. Hopewell had continued and read the next paragraph in *Existence and Being*, she would have seen that Heidegger has in the passage above deliberately been painting science into a metaphysical corner: "Science wishes to know nothing of Nothing. Even so the fact remains that at the very point where science tries to put its own essence in words it invokes the aid of Nothing. It has recourse to the very thing it rejects. What sort of schizophrenia is this?" As Heidegger shows, positivistic scientific discourse, which in his car-icature in the first quotation above wants to know nothing of nothing, is sim-ply a specialized and constrained discourse lopped off from philosophy, which does want to know something of nothing. Indeed, one can't know anything of existence without considering nothing. Heidegger, whom both O'Connor and Hulga Hopewell read, begins the first chapter of *An Introduc-tion to Metaphysics* with what he takes as the fundamental question of meta-physics: "Why are there essents rather than nothing?" Heidegger argues that it is impossible to understand, or even seriously ask, this question without a conception of nothing alongside something.[13] Otherwise, how could one rec-ognize something? In other words, the positive relies on the negative. In the spirit of *Narrating Knowledge*, imagine trying to ask "What is white?" if all one saw were white foregrounds on white backgrounds. The "something" in the question "Why is there something rather than nothing?" is similarly inconceivable without an understanding of nothing.

O'Connor's recognition of the thematically negative is responsible at least in part for the prevalence of the grotesque in her fiction. The fundamental reliance of human perception on the contrast between the something and the nothing, or the positive and the negative, is echoed in O'Connor's occasional prose essays several times, but compare in particular Heidegger's argument that the perception of something relies on the consideration of nothing with O'Connor's recognition of the freak on the basis of knowing what the "whole" human looks like: "Whenever I'm asked why Southern writers particularly have a penchant for writing about freaks, I say it is because we are still able to recognize one. To be able to recognize a freak, you have to have some conception of the whole man, and in the South the general conception of man is still, in the main, theological" (*MM,* 44). Whether the freak is the "negative" or the "positive" is irrelevant. The important point is that the freakishness of Enoch Emery, Onnie Jay Holy, Tom Shiftlet, Obadiah Elihue Parker, The Misfit, or any number of other characters is unrecognizable without a consideration of what they lack, individually and as a group. Frequently, what they lack is a balance of the positive (affirmation, acceptance) and the negative (denial, rejection). Nothing—the negative—for O'Connor's characters, prior to their pride-searing revelations, seems to signal metaphorically an emptiness, a prelapsarian, or Christ-denying, or soulless state. Hazel Motes in *Wise Blood* saw in his rejection of his fellow soldiers' invitation to join them at a brothel "the opportunity here to get rid of it [his soul] without corruption, to be converted to nothing instead of to evil" (*WB,* 24). Later, Haze tells the taxi driver who mistakes him for a preacher and who takes him to see the prostitute Leora Watts, "Listen . . . get this: I don't believe in anything" (*WB,* 32). Hulga tells Manley—the ultimate instrument of her awakening—when he pressures her to say that she loves him, "I don't have illusions. I'm one of those people who see *through* to nothing" (*GM,* 191; italics in original). Manley tells her at the last, "I been believing in nothing ever since I was born!" (*GM,* 195).

O'Connor seems to have felt that a recognition and acceptance of what one lacks is important to the process of a deepening spiritual conversion, as is reflected in a 1961 letter to "A": "I think once the process is begun and continues that you are continually turning inward toward God and away from your own egocentricity and that you have to see this selfish side of yourself in order to turn away from it. I measure God by everything that I am not" (*HB*, 430). O'Connor's commitment to the not-self is important not only for her own spirituality but for her characters as well. The arc of many of her stories leads her characters to a revelation of the importance of the not-self, largely through a loss of what is most dear to the self. In "A Good Man Is Hard to Find," the moment of grace comes to the grandmother when she suddenly ceases to think about begging and bargaining for her own life and sees The Misfit as one of her "own children" (*GM*, 29). In "Good Country People," Hulga appears at the end of the story—stripped of her artificial leg (soul) and the spectacles that allow her to sit around "on her neck" all day long reading philosophical treatises about the abhorrence science feels towards "nothing"—ready to look beyond herself (*GM*, 176, 195). At the end of "Everything That Rises Must Converge," the entirely self-absorbed Julian faces an eventual radical redefinition of his self after what appears to be his mother's fatal stroke: "'Help, help!' he shouted, but his voice was thin, scarcely a thread of sound. The lights drifted farther away the faster he ran and his feet moved numbly as if they carried him nowhere. The tide of darkness seemed to sweep him back to her, postponing from moment to moment his entry into the world of guilt and sorrow" (*ERMC*, 23). That guilt and sorrow will come about as the result of the loss of his mother, who protected him and made his smug, self-satisfied life possible. And in "The Lame Shall Enter First," Sheppard realizes too late to save his own son that his self-righteousness and self-absorption are delusional responses to the grief that he refused to face after his wife's death: "His heart constricted with a repulsion for himself so clear and intense that he gasped for breath. He had stuffed his own emptiness with good works like a glutton. He had ignored his own child to feed his vision of himself" (*ERMC*, 190).

The negative is important to the development of not only O'Connor's characters but also her narrative plots in general. Literary theory has shown that there is a very close connection between the negative and the heart of narrative interest. Most narrative and reading theorists—Roland Barthes and Wolfgang Iser, for example—identify obstacles as a crucial narrative element: the defeat of a reader's or protagonist's expectation, or an impediment to either understanding or the protagonist's goals, or an unexpected detour on the way to meaning or denouement.[14] That is, narrative becomes perceptible as literary narrative only through the negative obstacle. Consider the epigraph to this chapter, which is O'Connor's summation to Helen Greene of the point of *Wise Blood* (this, in spite of O'Connor's frequent appeal to New Critical dogma that a story cannot be summarized):

11. The gist of the story is that H. Motes couldn't really believe that he hadn't been redeemed. (*CW*, 897)

This sentence is extraordinarily difficult to process. It contains one positive clause and two negative clauses, the second of which ("that he hadn't been redeemed") serves as the complement to the first ("that H. Motes couldn't really believe"). Thus, an abstraction of the suppositions in (11) requires two steps, the first of which is revealed in (12):

12. a. H. Motes couldn't really believe that he hadn't been redeemed.
    b. H. Motes could really believe that he hadn't been redeemed.

Example (12b) is the underlying supposition for (12a); it is, in fact, the proposition that Haze spends most of the novel attempting to prove, that he could live his life as if Christ never existed, as if he had not been redeemed by Christ. Note that the supposition of (12a) is not "H. Motes couldn't really believe that he had been redeemed." Haze does not struggle throughout the novel attempting to believe that he had been redeemed. The supposition (12b)—for (12a)—is implictly present throughout the text. Consider part of Haze's first sermon on the Church Without Christ:

> "You then," he said impatiently, pointing at the next one. "What church you belong to?"
>
> "Church of Christ," the boy said in a falsetto to hide the truth.
>
> "Church of Christ!" Haze repeated. "Well, I preach the Church Without Christ. I'm member and preacher to that church where the blind don't see and the lame don't walk and what's dead stays that way. Ask me about that church and I'll tell you it's the church that the blood of Jesus don't foul with redemption."
>
> "He's a preacher," one of the women said. "Let's go."
>
> "Listen, you people, I'm going to take the truth with me wherever I go," Haze called. "I'm going to preach it to whoever'll listen at whatever place. I'm going to preach there was no Fall because there was nothing to fall from

and no Redemption because there was no Fall and no Judgment because there wasn't the first two. Nothing matters but that Jesus was a liar." (*WB*, 105)

Haze here denies the miracle work of Christ, the Fall, original innocence, redemption, and judgment. In other words, he claims to believe, by being "a member and preacher to that church where the blind don't see and the lame don't walk and what's dead stays that way," that he has not been redeemed. Of course, given the pragmatics of negation, Haze shows that he "knows" quite a bit about the suppositions of redemption through what he denies.

The most embedded clause in (11), too, has its supposition, as is revealed in (13):

13. a. He hadn't been redeemed.

b. He had been redeemed.

Sentence (13b) is the supposition for (13a). The proposition in (13b) is what Haze spends most of his time in the novel trying to deny. That supposition—that there was a universal redemption—is what moves like Jesus "from tree to tree in the back of [Haze's] mind" (*WB*, 22) and what he can deny no more after the loss of his car, his escape vehicle. The preacher Asa Hawks had "more than ten years before" tried and failed "to blind himself to justify his belief that Christ Jesus had redeemed him." When Hawks and his daughter, Sabbath Lily, fool Haze into thinking that Hawks had blinded himself, Haze replies, "Nobody with a good car needs to be justified" (*WB*, 112–13). After the patrolman pushes Haze's car over an embankment, Haze walks back to town, buys a sack of lime, and blinds himself, finally accepting the supposition that he could not successfully deny—that he had been redeemed—and justifying that belief by the only means he knows.

So in sentence (11) we have both the private, what Haze himself attempts to deny but cannot—that he has been redeemed—and the social, what Haze attempts to prove to the world but cannot—that he can believe that he hasn't been redeemed. O'Connor writes in the author's note to the second edition of *Wise Blood*, "It is a comic novel about a Christian *malgré lui*." Thus, the essence of the novel is the failure of a man both to do and to believe what he fully expected himself to be able to do and believe, as O'Connor indicates in a 1954 letter: "The book is about somebody whose insistence on what he would like to think is the truth leads him to what he most does not want. As I see Haze, he most does not want to have been redeemed. . . . When I say he negates his way back to the cross I only mean that complete nihilism has led him the long way (or maybe it's really the short way) around to the Redemption again" (*CW*, 920). And, of course, this short way back to redemption is just about the last thing that Haze expects.

In an introduction to one of her college readings of the story "A Good Man Is Hard to Find," O'Connor touches on the crucial element of the unexpected in good fiction: "I often ask myself what makes a story work, and what makes it hold up as a story, and I have decided that it is probably some action, some gesture of a character that is unlike any other in the story, one which indicates where the real heart of the story lies. This would have to be an action or a gesture which was both totally right and totally unexpected; it would have to be one that was both in character and beyond character; it would have to suggest both the world and eternity. The action or gesture I'm talking about would have to be on the anagogical level, that is, the level which has to do with the Divine life and our participation in it. It would be a gesture that transcended any neat allegory that might have been intended or any pat moral categories a reader could make. It would be a gesture which somehow made contact with mystery" (*MM*, 111). As I indicated in chapter 3, Mrs. Flood is unable to make any sense at all of Haze's self-blinding. But that is only the first—if the most important—of the many mysteries that pass right over her head in the novel. At the end of each month, Haze throws away any money he has not spent of his government disability pay; he walks with gravel, stones, and broken glass in his shoes; he wraps his torso in barbed wire. When she discovers the wire, she tells him that "it's not normal. . . . There's no reason for it" (*WB*, 224). However abnormal or unreasonable it might be, Haze's self-blinding is the central gesture in *Wise Blood* that makes contact with mystery, and that gesture is the direct result of the gist of the story, which is that Haze was unable to make good on the major supposition of (11): that he could really believe that he hadn't been redeemed.

One could expect that the gist of an equally interesting story, and even equally O'Connoresque story, might be given as follows:

14. The gist of the story is that he couldn't really believe that he had been redeemed.

The "gist" in (14) differs from the "gist" in (11) simply by the positive in the complement "that he had been redeemed." The summary in (14) might be The Misfit's story in "A Good Man Is Hard to Find," he who would have believed had he been there and seen so that he could know whether Jesus did indeed raise the dead. Unlike Haze, The Misfit does struggle as he attempts to believe that he had been redeemed: "'[Jesus] thown everything off balance. If He did what He said, then it's nothing for you to do but thow away everything and follow Him, and if He didn't, then it's nothing for you to do but enjoy the few minutes you got left the best way you can—by killing somebody or burning down his house or doing some other meanness to him. No pleasure but meanness,' he said and his voice had become almost a snarl" (*GM,* 28). The Misfit then laments that he was not there personally to see that Jesus did raise the dead. He says to the grandmother, "Listen Lady, . . . if I had of been there I would of known and I wouldn't be like I am now" (*GM,* 29). In other words, if he had the empirical evidence he could really believe that he had been redeemed.

Thus, sentences (11)—the story of a believer in spite of himself—and (14)—the story of an unbeliever who can never be convinced without empirical evidence in spite of his serious and troubled thought about sin and redemption—are both plausible O'Connor stories. On the other hand, one would not expect either of the following to define the gist of a successful O'Connor story:

15. The gist of the story is that he could really believe that he hadn't been redeemed.
16. The gist of the story is that he could really believe that he had been redeemed.

The reason that sentences (15) and (16) fail as interesting summaries of at least O'Connor stories is that they are completely normal and predictable propositions. Sentence (15) summarizes the story of an untroubled atheist or agnostic; sentence (16) summarizes the story of a untroubled believer. Although there are plenty of atheists and agnostics in O'Connor's fiction, such as Hulga in "Good Country People" and Asbury in "The Enduring Chill," they are never untroubled. Note that the English language has lexical items to name the atheist, the agnostic, the believer. But if we want to refer to the prototype of (11), the believer who fails to not believe, it is surely no narrative accident that we must refer to Paul, the persecutor of Christians. Brian Abel Ragen—who makes much of the connection between Paul on the road to Damascus and Hazel in his rat-colored Essex on the road to a new city to preach his Church Without Christ, both stopped in their tracks, both blinded—argues that Haze also represents the innocence of another biblical prototype—Adam.[15] In the case of the prototype that is represented in sentence (14)—the person who wants to believe but cannot because of a lack of empirical evidence—we also have no common noun specific to that meaning but again we have a biblical precursor: Saint Thomas.

The grace that Haze struggles to reject as he gradually accepts it is in itself a very mysterious process. O'Connor writes to Eileen Hall, "It's almost impossible to write about supernatural Grace in fiction. We almost have to approach it negatively" (*HB,* 144). This, too, is an almost uninterpretable statement until we consider the author's note to the second edition of *Wise Blood.* O'Connor argues that for readers who have a hard time considering that "belief in Christ is to some a matter of life and death," "Hazel Motes' integrity lies in his trying with such vigor to get rid of the ragged figure who moves from tree to tree in the back of his mind. For the author Hazel's integrity lies in his not being able to. Does one's integrity ever lie in what he is *not* able to do? I think that usually it does, for free will does not mean one will, but many wills conflicting in one man." Those many conflicting wills, not only in Haze but also in most of O'Connor's characters, lead to a great deal of analytic negation in dialogue.

In the next section, I quantitatively examine analytic negation (*not, n't*) in Flannery O'Connor's fiction and find that the frequency of analytic negation in the dialogue of her corpus is statistically significantly higher than the frequency of analytic negation in the dialogue of the American general-fiction texts of the Brown Corpus. I examine two possible statistical factors which could account for the higher proportion of analytic negation in O'Connor's dialogue—proportion of dialogue and degree of dialogism (operationalized as number of speaker shifts).

Location and Frequency of Negation

As I pointed out in chapter 1, the K subcorpus of the Brown Corpus contains American "general fiction" and totals 58,120 words in twenty-nine excerpts, each of around two thousand words. I compare the Brown general-fiction corpus with O'Connor's novels, *Wise Blood* and *The Violent Bear It Away*, and her three short story collections, *The Geranium, A Good Man Is Hard to Find,* and *Everything That Rises Must Converge*, the last published in the year following her death in 1964. O'Connor's fiction corpus, which I scanned into electronic text files for this study, totals 293,359 words. The Brown Corpus is one of the standard corpora for performing quantitative work in linguistics and stylistics. The Brown general-fiction corpus is the only publicly available electronic corpus that comes close to representing the fiction of O'Connor's time (the mid-twentieth century) and place (America).

In table 1, I compare the frequencies of analytic *not*'s and *n't*'s to those of other words in the Brown and O'Connor texts. One way to tally words would be to count each contraction with *-n't* as one word, as a negative. Another way would be to count *-n't* as one word and the modal or auxiliary to which it is attached as another. In none of the tests that I run in *Narrating Knowledge* do these two ways of counting words make a statistically significant difference. For the sake of consistency with chapters in which *-n't* is irrelevant as a word in itself, I count the auxiliary or modal and the *-n't* that is attached to it as only one word throughout the book.

The difference in frequencies is significant to the .001 level. The ratio of analytic negatives in the Brown general-fiction corpus is only 9.25 negatives per thousand words while the ratio in the O'Connor texts is 13.58 negatives per thousand words. Because there are five different O'Connor

Table 1. Frequencies of Non-Negative and Negative Words

	Brown	O'Connor	Totals
Non-Negative	57,582	289,373	346,955
Negative	538 *(9.25 per thousand)*	3,986 *(13.58 per thousand)*	4,524
Totals	58,120	293,359	351,479

χ^2=71.266, p<.001

Table 2. Frequencies of Negative Words in O'Connor's Five Texts

	Other Words	Total Negatives	Totals
Geranium	23,392	346 (14.57 per thousand)	23,738
Wise Blood	51,182	770 (14.82 per thousand)	51,952
Good Man is Hard to Find	74,040	1,023 (13.62 per thousand)	75,063
Violent Bear It Away	58,683	720 (12.12 per thousand)	59,403
Everything That Rises Must Converge	82,076	1,127 (13.54 per thousand)	83,203
Totals	289,373	3,986	293,359

$\chi^2 = 17.189$, p>.001

texts (short story collections or novels) represented in table 1, spanning a period of seventeen years, at least in publication years, we should consider the possibility that O'Connor's use of negation changed, either by increase or decrease, in those seventeen odd years.

Consider, then, table 2, which contains the figures for analytic negatives and other-word counts for each of the five O'Connor texts.

The difference in frequencies among the five major O'Connor texts is not significant to the .001 level. With p=.002, the differences reach the .01 level. I have set the alpha level for this study relatively high (at .001, with only one in a thousand chances that the results are due to chance) because I wanted to examine trends of difference that were unquestionably different. If I had finessed the alpha at .01, I would feel obligated to track down differences that are actually too subtle for the intentions of this study. Even with the alpha level set at .001, O'Connor is consistent enough in her use of analytic negation that the highest scoring and lowest scoring texts fall within 2.7 analytic negatives per thousand words. Compare this statistically insignificant (with alpha at .001) figure to the 4.33 statistically significant difference between per thousand negatives in the O'Connor and Brown texts.

One of the possible causes of the difference in concentration of analytic negation in the Brown general-fiction corpus vs. O'Connor's texts could be a difference in the concentrations of dialogue and narration. Tottie found in a sample of the Survey of English Usage at University College London that expressions of negation were twice as frequent per thousand words in her spoken sample as in her written sample. Tottie attributes the difference in concentration to, at least in part, "the amount of direct interaction that takes place between sender and receiver."[16] Thus, the lack of direct interaction between writer and reader leads to a lesser degree of negation of propositions than that which occurs in spoken language, where the interlocutors are typically directly engaged in dialogue and consequently have reason and opportunity to negate suppositions frequently. In table 3, I compare the frequencies of total words in dialogue and total words in narrative in the Brown general-fiction corpus and the O'Connor stories.

The difference is significant to the .001 level. The percentage of words in the Brown texts that are in narrative is 85.32 while that in the O'Connor texts is only 77.25. The percentage of words in the O'Connor stories that are in dialogue is 22.75 while that in the Brown texts is only 14.68. Thus, the greater percentage of dialogue could contribute to the higher negation in O'Connor.

Furthermore, if we compare the frequencies of analytic negation and other ("non-negative") words in narrative—rather than dialogue—in the

Table 3. Frequencies of Words in Dialogue and Narrative

	Brown	O'Connor	Totals
Narrative	49,587 *(85.32%)*	226,632 *(77.25%)*	276,219
Dialogue	8,533 *(14.68%)*	66,727 *(22.75%)*	75,260
Totals	58,120	293,359	351,479

$\chi^2 = 1874.190$, $p < .001$

two sets of texts, we find that there is not a significant difference, as is revealed in table 4.

The difference in frequency is not significant (p=.249). The ratio of negatives in the Brown narratives is 7.4 per thousand words while the ratio of negatives in the O'Connor narratives is not significantly higher, at 7.9 per thousand words. Because the differences in frequencies of negation in narrative do not account for the differences in overall frequencies of negation between the two corpora, I will not consider negation in narrative further in the quantitative section of this chapter.

If the difference in analytic negation were due simply to a higher ratio of words in dialogue in the O'Connor texts, we would not expect a significant

Table 4. Frequencies of Negative and Non-Negative Words in Narrative

Narrative Words	Brown	O'Connor	Totals
Non-Negative	49,216	224,819	274,035
Negative	371 *(7.4 per thousand)*	1,813 *(7.9 per thousand)*	2,184
Totals	49,587	226,632	276,219

$\chi^2=1.32$, p>.001

Table 5. Frequencies of Negative and Non-Negative Words in Dialogue

Dialogue Words	Brown	O'Connor	Totals
Non-Negative	8,366	64,554	72,920
Negative	167 *(19.57 per thousand)*	2,173 *(32.56 per thousand)*	2,340
Totals	8,533	66,727	75,260

$\chi^2=41.975$, p<.001

difference in the ratio of analytic negation to total words in dialogue in the two sets of texts. In table 5, I compare the ratios of analytic *not*'s and *n't*'s to non-negative words in dialogue in the Brown and O'Connor texts.

The difference in ratio is significant to the .001 level. The ratio of negatives to words in dialogue in the Brown texts is 19.57 negatives per thousand other words while the ratio in the O'Connor texts is 32.56 negatives per thousand other words. Thus, regardless of the greater concentration of dialogue in O'Connor's fiction than in the Brown general-fiction corpus, the verbs in O'Connor's dialogue are negated significantly more frequently than the verbs in the Brown dialogue.

My model thus far argues that there is an inexact correlation between number of words in dialogue and numbers of analytic negation. If the ratios of negation to total words in dialogue are different in the Brown and O'Connor texts, then there cannot be an exact correlation of, say, twenty negatives per thousand words of dialogue across both the Brown general-fiction corpus and the O'Connor stories and novels. To say that there is no exact correlation is not to say that there is no correlation. Thus, the Spearman correlation figure for all twenty-nine Brown excerpts and all twenty-seven O'Connor stories and novels is $\rho = .851$, $p < .001$.

However, correlation is not causation. That is, some third feature could be operating to produce both high concentrations of dialogue and high frequencies of negation simultaneously. Furthermore, a rate of dialogue negation in O'Connor that is 1.66 times the rate of dialogue negation in the Brown texts suggests either that concentration of words in dialogue is not the whole statistical story or that there is a stylistic feature to O'Connor's frequency of negation in dialogue.

Another possible cause of the difference in concentration of analytic negation in the Brown general-fiction corpus vs. the O'Connor stories could be a difference in the dialogism of the texts. I operationalize dialogism as frequency of speaker change. For the purposes of this study, frequency of speaker change equals total number of speaker changes in the story minus one, the very first, when the first speaker begins.

Consider the following brief example, an extract from a conversational passage—quoted with most of the narration deleted—from "The Life You Save May Be Your Own," in which there are four speaker changes:

> "Good evening," the old woman said. . . .
>
> "Lady," he said in a firm nasal voice, "I'd give a fortune to live where I could see me a sun do that every evening."

Table 6. Frequencies of Speaker Changes and Total Words in Dialogue

	Brown	O'Connor	Totals
Dialogue Words	8,533	66,727	75,260
Speaker Changes	438 *(51.33 per thousand)*	3,396 *(50.89 per thousand)*	3,834

$\chi^2 = .019$, p>.001

"Does it every evening," the old woman said and sat back down. . . .
"You ladies drive?" he asked.

"That car ain't run in fifteen year," the old woman said. "The day my husband died, it quit running." (*GM*, 54–55)

Note that the first utterance is not counted as a speaker change.

As the number of speaker changes goes up, one might expect the frequency of negation to increase as well. However, O'Connor is in general no more dialogic than the average author of the Brown general-fiction corpus, as is revealed in table 6.

Speaker changes are abstract changes of speaker, above the level of individual words. Thus, there is no overlap among cells in table 6 to compromise statistical validity. The difference in frequencies is non-significant (p=.890). The ratio of speaker-changes to words in dialogue in the Brown texts is 51.33 changes per thousand words while the ratio in the O'Connor texts is 50.89 changes per thousand words.

Thus, it cannot be degrees of dialogism that determine the significantly different frequencies of negation in the dialogue of the Brown general-fiction corpus and O'Connor's texts. As one would expect and as table 7 demonstrates, there is a significant difference in the ratios of negation to speaker changes in the two corpora.

The difference is significant to the .001 level. The ratio of negatives to speaker changes in the Brown general-fiction corpus is 38.12 negatives per hundred speaker changes while the ratio in the O'Connor short stories and novels is 63.98 negatives per hundred speaker changes.

It appears, then, that O'Connor's frequent analytic negation in dialogue is, in itself, stylistic, that is, a deviation from the norm of American literature in O'Connor's time as that norm is measured by the Brown general-fiction

Table 7. Frequencies of Negation and Speaker Changes in Dialogue

	Brown	O'Connor	Totals
Speaker Changes	438	3,396	3,834
Negation	167 *(38.12 per hundred)*	2,173 *(63.98 per hundred)*	2,340

$\chi^2=29.736$, p<.001

corpus. Thus, relatively frequent analytic negation in dialogue helps define O'Connor's unique literary voice. O'Connor is more negative in dialogue than the average writer in the Brown corpus even if one considers the potentially predictive effects of the concentration of dialogue and dialogism in her texts.

In chapter 5, I turn to a qualitative accounting of the use of analytic negation in O'Connor's dialogue. Besides its conclusions regarding the quantitative distribution of negation in the Brown and O'Connor texts, this chapter has shown that negation is integral to not only the quest for the non-self in O'Connor's fiction but also the construction of a viable O'Connoresque narrative. Chapter 5 will show that analytic negation in dialogue has varied and specific roles in the construction of background in O'Connor's fiction.

Chapter 5

The Explicit—Suggested Suppositional Continuum

> *"I thank Gawd,"* the white-trash woman said fervently, *"I ain't a lunatic."*
>
> —Flannery O'Connor (*ERMC*, 209)

Dialogic negation is the site in O'Connor's texts for many of the struggles that her characters have with faith and belief as well as with one another over any number of different issues. In some works, such as *Wise Blood*, negation as theme occupies practically the entire narrative. *Wise Blood* simply presents Hazel Motes's progressively more absurd confrontations with the suppositions of faith that he so consistently attempts to deny. Consider the following passage, in which Haze discusses theology with the woman who has "a bold game-hen expression and small eyes pointed directly on him."

> "If you've been redeemed," he said, "*I wouldn't want to be.*" Then he turned his head to the window. He saw his pale reflection with the dark empty space outside coming through it. A boxcar roared past, chopping the empty space in two, and one of the women laughed.
>
> "Do you think I believe in Jesus?" he said, leaning toward her and speaking almost as if he were breathless. "Well, *I wouldn't* even if He existed. Even if He was on this train."
>
> "Who said you had to?" she asked in a poisonous Eastern voice. (*WB,* 16)

There are two *not* (*n't*) negations in this passage, each italicized. Both deny what Haze cannot ultimately deny—his belief in Jesus as the savior of souls such as his. The first negation ("If you've been redeemed . . . I wouldn't want to be") responds to a supposition that whatever the "game-hen" woman has done Haze would want to do as well. The second denial is even more forceful since Haze argues that he wouldn't believe in Jesus even if

He existed, even if He were on the very train that Haze and the woman are on. The suppositions that Haze uses to deny his belief in Christ are indicative of the depth of his self delusions—one, that faith is social; two, that it is empirically based. As O'Connor writes to Louise Abbot concerning, among other things, faith, "Whatever you do anyway, remember that these things are mysteries and that if they were such that we could understand them, they wouldn't be worth understanding. A God you understood would be less than yourself. . . . Don't expect faith to clear things up for you" (*HB*, 354). Incidentally, Haze seems at least peripherally aware of the problem of denying the existence of Jesus, whose existence he presupposes in using the name *Jesus*, even in his blasphemy, as he explains later to the boy at the filling station where he has his car serviced: "He said he had only a few days ago believed in blasphemy as the way to salvation, but that you couldn't even believe in that because then you were believing in something to blaspheme" (*WB*, 206).

The key to the pragmatic force of negation lies in the game-hen woman's question on the train, "Who said you had to?" The woman responds to the implicit pragmatic force of a negative—that the hearers/readers suppose or believe the contrary. The import of the woman's question is that no one supposes that Haze has to believe in Jesus, even if she were redeemed and even if Jesus himself were on the train. The linguistic issue that the woman's question raises is the nature or origin of suppositions. This chapter examines two widely known supposition typologies and shows how both oral narrative and O'Connor's literary narratives support the addition of another category of supposition to those typologies—what I and Chris Newton have called "the suggested supposition" and what Paul Werth has referred to as "negative accommodation."[1]

Gunnel Tottie's and T. Givón's Supposition Typologies

Neither T. Givón nor any of the other linguists referred to in chapter 4 argue naïvely that behind every negative statement there is an assumed positive. In its weakest and probably most defensible form, Givón's hypothesis is that the hearer of a negative will be "familiar with the corresponding affirmative proposition." That familiarity, Givón argues, may come from a variety of sources: "explicitly in the preceding discourse," "specific knowledge about the hearer's state of affairs or state of mind," and "generic culturally-shared information."[2] Another well-known typology of negatives is that of Gunnel Tottie, as follows:

Rejections (including Refusals)

Denials   (a) Explicit
            (b) Implicit[3]

Tottie intends this typology to name types of negation, but it may be understood as a typology of supposition as well since the negatives are classified in part on the basis of the types of suppositions that they respond to. Because "all grammars leak," all typologies, which are secondary accounts of those leaky grammars (the structures of languages themselves), leak at least twice as fast.[4] However, Givón's and Tottie's typologies account for all but the most "implicit" of negative suppositions in O'Connor, those that I categorize as suggested. Those most suggested of suppositions demonstrate the fundamentally interactive nature of supposition creation.

The following examples invented by Tottie illustrate, respectively, rejection and refusal:

1. a. Would you care for some scotch?
    b. No thanks, I don't drink.
2. a. Come and play ball with me.
    b. No, I don't want to.

In (1), the speaker in (b) rejects an offer from the speaker in (a). In (2), the speaker in (b) refuses to perform an act suggested by the speaker in (a). The following examples invented by Tottie illustrate, respectively, explicit denial and implicit denial:

3. a. John is married.
    b. John isn't (married).
4. a. John's wife is a teacher.
    b. John isn't even married.[5]

These examples are rather clear-cut as intuitive examples of explicit and implicit denial. In (3) the speaker in (a) explicitly asserts that John is married, and the speaker in (b) denies this explicit assertion. In (4) the speaker in (a) presupposes, through the possessive construction ("John's wife"), that

John is married, and the speaker in (b) denies this implicit (presupposed) assertion. Note from this example that it is possible for a presupposition to become a supposition through negation. The presuppositional structure in (4a) is nice and tidy because it provides through the possessive construction an "implicit" indicator of presupposition and supposition.

The overlap between Givón's suppositions that occur "explicitly in the preceding discourse" and Tottie's "explicit" denials is unproblematic. Consider the following passage from O'Connor's "The Artificial Nigger," in which Nelson and Mr. Head begin to realize that they are lost in the city, surrounded by the blacks that they fear:

> Before long they began to pass rows of stores with colored customers in them but *they didn't pause at the entrances of these.* Black eyes in black faces were watching them from every direction. "Yes," Mr. Head said, "this is where you were born—right here with all these niggers."
>
> Nelson scowled. "*I think you done got us lost,*" he said.
>
> Mr. Head swung around sharply and looked for the dome. It was nowhere in sight. "*I ain't got us lost either,*" he said. "*You're just tired of walking.*"
>
> "*I ain't tired,* I'm hungry," Nelson said. "Give me a biscuit."
>
> They discovered then that they had lost the lunch. (*GM,* 117)

In this passage, we have two negatives that respond to propositions that occur explicitly in the preceding discourse. First, Nelson accuses his grandfather of getting them lost in the city. Mr. Head denies this with "I ain't got us lost either." Then, he in turn accuses Nelson of being tired of walking. Nelson denies this with "I ain't tired, I'm hungry." These examples, two occurring together, represent the ubiquitous negation of suppositions that occur explicitly in the text. But there is another subtler example of explicit negation illustrated here. The narrator comments that Mr. Head and Nelson "didn't pause at the entrances of" the stores "with colored customers in them." That they did not pause at these entrances is only narratable because of the following earlier narration: "As they walked along, Nelson began to distinguish details and take note of the store windows, jammed with every kind of equipment—hardware, drygoods, chicken feed, liquor. . . . They walked slowly and stopped and stood at the entrances so he could see what went on in each place but they did not go into any of them" (*GM,* 114).[6] Thus, a full three pages early, O'Connor prepares us for the negative "didn't pause at the entrances" with "They walked slowly and stopped and stood at the entrances."

Givón's second source of background expectation is "specific knowledge about the hearer's state of affairs or state of mind." This category overlaps in part with Tottie's "implicit" category. Implicit knowledge occurs as several specific types. Consider the following rather obvious examples from O'Connor's "The Enduring Chill," in which Asbury's mother first tells him that the illness he thought he was dying from is undulant fever:

> "Asbury," she said, "you have undulant fever. It'll keep coming back but *it won't kill you!*" Her smile was as bright and intense as a lightbulb without a shade. "I'm so relieved," she said.
>
> Asbury sat up slowly, his face expressionless; then he fell back down again.
>
> Block leaned over him and smiled. "*You ain't going to die,*" he said with deep satisfaction. (*ERMC,* 113)

The first negative responds to Asbury's state of mind. He has been convinced for quite some time that he is dying, and in fact, he asserts several times that he is dying. But nowhere in the text does anyone assert previously that undulant fever will kill a person. Asbury is simply convinced that whatever he has will kill him. Thus, if he has undulant fever, it will kill him. The second negative, from Asbury's doctor, does respond to several *ad nauseam* explicit textual assertions from Asbury that he will die.

In yet another type of negative that responds to the hearer's implicit state of mind, the speaker responds to his own state of mind, and thus through the negative we hear the dialogue that occurs in the speaker's mind, although we may only hear half of it, as in the following passage from *Wise Blood*:

> [Enoch] thought of how he had had to spend all his money on drapes and gilt when he could have bought him a shirt and a phosphorescent tie. It'll be something against the law, he said. It's always something against the law. *I ain't going to do it*, he said, and stopped. He had stopped in front of a movie house where there was a large illustration of a monster stuffing a young woman into an incinerator.
>
> *I ain't going in no picture show like that*, he said, giving it a nervous look. I'm going home. *I ain't going to wait around in no picture show. I ain't got the money*

to buy a ticket, he said, taking out his purse again. *I ain't even going to count thisyer change.*

It ain't but forty-three cent here, he said, *that ain't enough.* A sign said the price of a ticket for adults was forty-five cents, balcony, thirty-five. *I ain't going to sit in no balcony*, he said, buying a thirty-five cent ticket.

I ain't going in, he said.

Two doors flew open and he found himself moving down a long red foyer. . . . *I ain't going to look at it*, he said furiously. . . .

The first picture was about a scientist named The Eye who performed operations by remote control. You would wake up in the morning and find a slit in your chest or head or stomach and something you couldn't do without would be gone. (*WB*, 137–38)

In order to understand the "dialogue" in the passage above, one must recall the geography of Enoch's brain: "Enoch's brain was divided into two parts. The part in communication with his blood did the figuring but it never said anything in words. The other part was stocked up with all kinds of words and phrases" (*WB*, 87). The side that we hear from above is the side that was stocked up with all kinds of words and phrases. His wise blood provides all the implicit suppositions.

What is perhaps one of the most sinister passages in *The Violent Bear It Away* relies on the interpersonal power (shared knowledge) of suppositions that are implicitly in the hearer's mind. The woman at the front desk of the Cherokee Lodge, in whose lake Tarwater will drown his retarded cousin, takes an instant dislike to Tarwater and senses his intent. She speaks first in the following:

"Whatever devil's work you mean to do, *don't do it here*."

[Tarwater] continued to look down at her. "*You can't just say NO*," he said. "You got to do NO. You got to show it. You got to show you mean it by doing it. You got to show *you're not going to do one thing* by doing another. You got to make an end of it. One way or another."

"*Don't you do nothing here*," she said, wondering what he would do here. (*VBA*, 156–57)

The woman's first negative, which begins the quotation, responds to whatever supposition she imagines Tarwater to have in his head. The same is true of her second negative, which closes the quotation. Tarwater's negatives,

like Enoch's above, are in part responses to the implicit obsessive suppositions of his own mind, specifically first that he could just say no to his great
uncle's charge that he baptize his idiot cousin and second that he will after
all fulfill his destiny to do so.

The following example from "The Enduring Chill" is also of the type in
which the speaker of the negative responds to assumptions about the state
of mind of the hearer; yet it is more complex, demonstrating in part the
impossibility of maintaining airtight boundaries between suppositional
categories since the passage involves both the hearer's state of mind and
culturally shared information. In this example, the two black farm workers
that Asbury "befriends" in his condescending, self-centered way have come
to say goodbye to him. Actually, he has simply "sent" for them so that they
can "commune" together in one last smoke:

> Asbury's head was so heavy he could not think what he had been going to
> do. "I'm dying," he said.
>> Both their grins became gelid. "You looks fine," Randall said. . . .
>> "I speck you might have a little cold," Randall said after a time.
>> "I takes a little turpentine and sugar when I has a cold," Morgan said.
>> "Shut your mouth," Randall said, turning on him.
>> "Shut your own mouth," Morgan said. "I know what I takes."
>> "*He don't take what you take*," Randall growled.
>> "Mother!" Asbury called in a shaking voice.
>> His mother stood up. "Mister Asbury has had company long enough now,"
> she called. (*ERMC,* 110–12)

The subservience demonstrated by Randall and Morgan is ironic in the face
of "Mister Asbury's" self-righteous will to befriend them. Randall's "He
don't take what you take" can only mean that he assumes that Morgan
assumes that Asbury might want to take a little turpentine and sugar, not
realizing the gulf that separates white and black health care at that time. That
socioeconomic gulf is a further ironic comment on Asbury's "liberalness."
He has tried and failed once to write "a play about Negroes" (*ERMC,* 87).

Givón's third source of a background expectation is "generic culturally-
shared information," which would fit within Tottie's "implicit" category as
well. It is difficult to imagine a diagnostic to demonstrate a dramatic difference between culturally-shared information and what the speaker imagines
about the state of the hearer's mind. However, one might argue that the

more culturally salient material could be put in a separate category. In the following passage from "Judgement Day," the "Negro" actor who lives next to Tanner and his daughter in New York has finally had enough of Tanner's assuming that he is a black man of the sort that Tanner had known in Georgia. The man particularly does not like to be called "Preacher," Tanner's condescending term of address for blacks that he wants to "butter up":

> The Negro stopped and gripped the banister rail. A tremor racked him from his head to his crotch. Then he began to come forward slowly. When he was close enough he lunged and grasped Tanner by both shoulders. "*I don't take no crap*," he whispered, "*off no wool-hat red-neck son-of-a-bitch peckerwood old bastard like you*." He caught his breath. And then his voice came out in the sound of an exasperation so profound that it rocked on the verge of a laugh. It was high and piercing and weak. "*And I'm not no preacher! I'm not even no Christian. I don't believe that crap. There ain't no Jesus and there ain't no God*." (*ERMC*, 263)

This passage contains examples of all three sources of background information—that which is explicit, that which is presumed to be in the hearer's mind, and that which is culturally-shared information. The first negative clause—"I don't take no crap"—could be argued to be in response to what the black actor believes is implicitly in Tanner's mind, given that Tanner has revealed himself more than once to the man to be an unrepentant racist. The second negative clause—"And I'm not no preacher!"—is a reaction to Tanner's explicitly addressing the black man as "Preacher" several times. The final four negative clauses in the last three sentences are all responses to cultural assumptions. Tanner did not call him a Christian, nor accuse him of believing "that crap," nor assert that Jesus and God exist, although all of those suppositions follow in fundamentalist Christian culture if one is a "preacher."

To find a negative that responds purely to cultural assumptions, one has to find relatively decontextualized speech. And that, outside of linguistics books and articles, is a very hard creature to find. Consider, then, Givón's textbook examples in (5), in which is demonstrated, again, that both positives and negatives may have suppositions, in these cases, culturally based suppositions:

5. a. There was once a man who *didn't* have a head.
   b. ?There was once a man who had a head.

c. ?There was once a man who *didn't* look like a frog.
d. There was once a man who looked like a frog.

As Givón comments, (5a) and (5d) are "felicitous" because they break culturally shared norms. We live in a world in which we can suppose that men have heads so that if one saw or heard of one without one, it would be reportable in (5a) to claim knowledge of him. Most men, we suppose, also don't look like frogs, so if we run across one that does, we might felicitously report knowledge of him as in (5d). On the other hand, (5b) is pragmatically odd because it reports on the norm. And (5c) is odd because it assumes a background that is demonstrably odd, i.e., one that we would not culturally suppose—that most men look like frogs.[7] Although intuitively revealing, each of the sentences in (5), whether marked by the "pragmatically odd" question mark or not, is very unrealistic.

There is one clear passage of responses to almost purely cultural suppositions in "A Good Man Is Hard to Find." And the suppositions are almost purely decontextualized. Just before The Misfit orders Hiram and Bobby Lee to start dragging the members of the grandmother's family off into the woods to murder them, there is an awkward lull in the conversation:

> [The Misfit] looked at the six of them huddled together in front of him and he seemed to be embarrassed as if he couldn't think of anything to say. "*Ain't a cloud in the sky,*" he remarked, looking up at it. "*Don't see no sun but don't see no cloud neither.*"
>
> "Yes, it's a beautiful day," said the grandmother. "Listen," she said, "you shouldn't call yourself The Misfit because I know you're a good man at heart. I can just look at you and tell."
>
> "Hush!" Bailey yelled. (*GM,* 22–23)

There has been no mention between The Misfit's gang and the family of the weather until this passage. Thus, the negatives cannot be responses to an explicitly present textual affirmative; neither can they be responses to what The Misfit is thinking the family might be thinking. Imagine the ludicrous affirmative assumptions: "They are thinking that there is a cloud in the sky or that we can the sun." Instead, The Misfit's negatives are part of his phatic talk, simply designed to wile away the time until he begins the systematic murder of the entire family. The negatives are possible not because of previous mention, not because The Misfit assumes a specific state of mind in the grandmother's family, but only because (1) it is culturally acceptable to talk about the weather in socially uncomfortable settings as well as almost any other type of setting and (2) everyone knows (supposes) that there are usually clouds and/or a sun in a summer sky.

The Suggested Supposition

Implicit supposition and culturally shared supposition are extraordinarily flexible categories. However, Tottie classes in the same group with implicit denials some constructions which are arguably not of the same class as any that we have examined thus far. Consider the following example from Tottie, which comes ultimately from the text *Chinese Art: Recent Discoveries:*

> The Carbon[14] method is being used in several research centres, and many more results may be expected. *At the time of writing, the thermoluminescence technique for dating pottery had not yet been used in China.*

Tottie explains this example by way of what she calls, rather loosely, presupposition. She argues that the author himself might have expected that the latest techniques for dating pottery were used in China and then expects that the reader too will expect that. Thus, Tottie argues, the author "cooperates" by denying the implicit expectation.[8] First, I would not call the supposition expressed by the negation presupposition for the reasons outlined in chapter 4. Second, there is no reason to assume that the reader would think or find it even interesting to think that the latest techniques for dating pottery were used in China. I also do not think that this supposition is part of any culturally shared background between the writer and readers of the text. Instead, I would argue that the italicized negation in the passage above suggests its own supposition. Thus, I label the supposition in this type of denial a "suggested supposition." Werth seems to have the same phenomenon in mind in his "negative accommodation."[9] Note that I label the supposition, rather than the negation, in my typology with the labels "implicit," "explicit," or "suggested," since it is the suppositions themselves rather than the negatives, that lie at various epistemological depths of the text. (In analysis, I sometimes refer to the "textual," "implicit," "explicit," or "suggestive" negative, emphasizing the responsive and creative nature of negative forms.) The supposition and its denial are created at the same moment.

For my purposes here in elaborating yet another typology (one that encompasses the suggested supposition), the sources of suppositions are only two: mention in the text either explicitly or implicitly, which I will call "textual," and suggestion within the negative itself, which I will call "suggested." Mention in the text comes from the dialogic interaction of the characters, as in the following excerpt from "A Good Man Is Hard to Find," in which the grandmother attempts to motivate The Misfit to pray, this after she knows that The Misfit's gang has already murdered her son and her grandson and thus fears and expects that she will soon die herself:

> "If you would pray," the old lady said, "Jesus would help you."
> "That's right," The Misfit said.
> "Well then, why don't you pray?" she asked trembling with delight suddenly.
> "*I don't want no hep*," he said. "I'm doing all right by myself." (*GM,* 26)

We here see a good example of the real-life difficulty of the distinction between Tottie's implicit and explicit mention. The italicized negative could be categorized either as a rejection of an explicit offer of help, which was mentioned before in the text when the grandmother says explicitly that Jesus would help The Misfit if he prayed, or as a denial of an implicit claim, based on the inference that one who is offered help needs it. In Givón's and Tottie's terms, the explicit interpretation would be just that: explicit. However, the implicit interpretation would be that of a guess about the hearer's state of mind. Incidentally, it appears that Tottie's "explicit" negative is a minority category: only 15% of the 427 conversational negatives that Tottie categorizes are in reaction to explicit claims or offers.[10]

In part a simplification and in part a complication of Givón's and Tottie's typologies, my working typology is as follows:

Suppositions
1. Textual
    a) Explicit
    b) Implicit
2. Suggested

I maintain a heuristic distinction between explicit and implicit suppositions, however difficult or even impossible it may be to operationalize that distinction. Note that Tottie's rejections (and refusals) are simply rolled in with denials in my typology because it categorizes not the negatives themselves but the suppositions for the negatives. If the text mentions the supposition, either explicitly or implicitly through presupposition or entailment, I categorize the supposition as textual, i.e., as part of the textual interaction of the characters. If, on the other hand, the text does not either explicitly mention or implicitly presuppose or entail the supposition which is negated but, instead, first mentions the supposition in the negative itself, I categorize the supposition as suggested, whether that supposition is based on cultural knowledge or what is imagined about the state of the hearer's mind, or not. As we will see, determining the difference between a suggested supposition based on cultural assumptions or hearer-based assumptions and a purely nonce supposition is sometimes very difficult. Laura Hidalgo Downing recognizes a similar difficulty in determining such a difference in a discussion of Werth's "negative accommodation." One specific problem in determining what Werth fully intends by the term "negative accommodation" is, as Downing suggests, that he "does not provide sufficient illustrations of the phenomenon" in that he discusses at length only one episode from *A Passage to India*. My point here is not to determine the fine-grained analysis of the origins of suggested suppositions since I believe that those origins lie not only in the frame (roughly, cultural) knowledge that Downing explores but also in the deductions driven by the "general principles of co-operation, informativeness, and coherence" that Werth mentions.[11] Instead, in this chapter I seek simply to demonstrate in full the existence and use of suggested suppositions in O'Connor's fiction for the following reasons: the "normal" understanding of supposition in the negative literature is that the supposition must be there in the background for the negative to be felicitous, the phrase "in the background" is multiply ambiguous, and suggested suppositions are useful in the analysis of problematic suppositional knowledge in O'Connor's fiction.

In order to demonstrate the existence of the category of nonce suggested suppositions in narrative, I would like first to review their occurrence in natural oral narrative:

> Tom: and I said, uh, "I prayed to get me a good buck, a nice big one."
> . . . I said, "He was so pretty, I ju—, *I really didn't wanna shoot him.*" I said, "I felt so bad about it." I said, "Then he trotted off

out there and turned around and looked at me." And I said,
"Well, you foolish thing. You done the wrong thing."

Heather: You deserve to die.

Tom: So, I shot him.

Heather: *Don't need any stupid deer.*

The supposition for the first of the negatives in the passage ("I really didn't wanna shoot him") is textual and implicit, first because Tom earlier says that he prayed to get a good buck and second because his wanting the buck on a hunting trip entails his wanting to shoot it. I will explicitly define *entailment* in chapter 6, where such definitions are important. For now, we can simply understand the verb *entail* to be synonymous with *imply*. The second of the negatives in this passage ("Don't need any stupid deer") "responds" to a nonce suggested supposition. Heather's negative is interesting because it cannot have been a response to a pre-existing expectation, cultural or otherwise, that we need stupid deer wandering around in the woods. Instead, her suggested supposition is comic. An absurd nonce supposition is at once suggested and then defeated in the same utterance. Speakers must at least follow H. Paul Grice's relevance maxim in the construction of suggested suppositions.[12] After all, it would clearly be uncooperative for Heather to have said, "Don't need any compact cars"; however, to say that she adheres to the relevance maxim does not say that she responds to a supposition that is already there in the background that we need stupid deer wandering around in the woods.

The boundary between culture- and hearer-based suggested suppositions and nonce suggested suppositions is, by the nature of language itself, porous; i.e., that boundary "leaks."[13] So, for example, consider the following passage from "The Enduring Chill." Asbury has for a couple of weeks been trying to convince Morgan and Randall to drink raw, unpasteurized milk with him from his mother's dairy barn. It is the unpasteurized milk from which Asbury contracts undulant fever. Asbury overhears their conversation:

A few afternoons later when [Asbury] was standing outside the milk house about to go in, he heard Morgan ask, "Howcome you let him drink all that milk every day?"

"What he do is him," Randall said. "What I do is me."

"Howcome he talks so ugly about his ma?"

"*She ain't whup him enough when he was little*," Randall said.

The insufferableness of life at home had overcome him and he had returned to New York two days early. (*ERMC*, 98)

The difference between the privileged, spoiled, white Asbury and the non-privileged, black farm workers Morgan and Randall is highlighted ironically here in the conversation between the two blacks that Asbury self-servingly tries to bring into his solitary circle. Randall says, "What he do is him. . . . What I do is me." The supposition of "She ain't whup him enough when he was little" is subtly ambiguous between a nonce suggested supposition and a culturally based suggested supposition. That is, it is impossible to tell whether Randall is simply joking or whether he and Morgan share a cultural assumption that children should be whipped and whipped often.

The Use of Suggested Suppositions

I believe that the one super-strategy for the use of suggested supposition, in O'Connor's fiction at least, is to presume shared problematic knowledge between the speaker and hearer for the purpose of reducing the social distance, in Penelope Brown and Stephen Levinson's sense, between the interlocutors.[14] In reducing that distance, for whatever motivation itself and however successful it may be, the characters who suggest the suppositions reveal a great deal about their own minds.

In "A Good Man Is Hard to Find," the grandmother and Red Sam, the owner of the gas station/barbecue shop/dance hall that the doomed family visit, share their disappointment in the modern world. Note that their sharing is a face-protecting politeness device. The grandmother and Red Sam are in fact displaying their alikeness in order to make themselves and one another feel socially cohesive in the context of being, in fact, strangers to one another. And although Red Sam did not witness the incident, June Star has also just embarrassed the grandmother and everyone else who was present by telling Red Sam's wife that she "wouldn't live in a broken-down place like this for a million bucks!"

[Red Sam's] khaki trousers reached just to his hip bones and his stomach hung over them like a sack of meal swaying under his shirt. He came over and sat down at a table nearby and let out a combination sigh and yodel. "*You can't win*," he said. "*You can't win*," and he wiped his sweating red face off with a gray handkerchief. "*These days you don't know who to trust*," he said. "*Ain't that the truth?*"

"*People are certainly not nice like they used to be*," said the grandmother. (*GM*, 14–15)

Red Sam's "You can't win" contains a suggested supposition, given that this is the first conversational interaction he has had with the family. Even though suggested, the supposition relies on what Red can reasonably assume is legitimately culturally phatic, i.e., that so-called trust in one's fellow human beings will triumph, or more generally that one can "win." Red Sam feels particularly sorry for himself here for having allowed some customers to cheat him when he let them charge their gas, even though they were complete strangers. He is quick to build on his first suggested supposition with a related suggested supposition that "you" should know who to trust these days.[15] Finally, the grandmother chimes in with her own phatic negative, suggesting a supposition of a recent prelapsarian world in which people were nice and one knew whom to trust and a trusting nature was rewarded.

Any serious references to an unfallen world would reasonably make mention of the social consequences of the Fall. Consider, for example, the following dialogue from "A Good Man Is Hard to Find," which occurs as the grandmother's family drives toward Florida for their vacation.

. . . and they all turned and looked at the little Negro out of the back window. He waved. "*He didn't have any britches on*," June Star said.

"*He probably didn't have any*," the grandmother explained. "*Little niggers in the country don't have things like we do.*" (*GM*, 12)

June Star's negation responds to a straightforward culturally based suggested supposition—that people, including the child that she sees, wear "britches." The grandmother responds to June Star's supposition with a negation of another suggested supposition—that he owns britches but just isn't wearing them. Again, one might assume culturally that all children have at least one pair of pants. She then builds on that supposition to suggest and then negate another more general supposition—that rural blacks have the same material goods that whites have. Whether this last supposition is cultural or nonce is, of course, dependent on audience. Given June Star's awareness of the socioeconomic shortcomings of Red Sam's restaurant, it is not clear that she would assume that black country children would have the same things that she and her family have. In this ambiguity, then, the grandmother's attempt to provide gentle counsel to her granddaughter through suggested supposition is evident. Ironically, that counsel probably falls on cynical and all-too-knowing ears. By means of her characters' dialogue, then, O'Connor avoids didactic assertion that such and such ought to be the case but isn't. Instead, her characters negate the ideal unfallen world and thus suggest or respond to the suppositions of that unfallen world.

Finally, at the end of "A Good Man Is Hard to Find," just before he kills the grandmother, the suppositions of The Misfit's negatives are quite serious, revealing his flawed understanding of a fallen world:

> "I said long ago, you get you a signature and sign everything you do and keep a copy of it. Then you'll know what you done and you can hold up the crime to the punishment and see do they match and in the end you'll have something to prove *you ain't been treated right*. I call myself The Misfit," he said, "because *I can't make what all I done wrong fit what all I gone through in punishment*." (*GM*, 27–28)

The suggested supposition that lies behind The Misfit's first negative is that life is fair. The suggested supposition that lies behind his second negative is more particularly that the punishment ought to fit the crime. Only in a prelapsarian world, minus original sin, can one imagine the world that The Misfit suggestively supposes in his complaints. And, again, whether the suppositions are cultural or nonce depends on the audience. Most experienced readers of O'Connor would never suppose that her fictional world is anything approaching "fair" or "equitable" in the balance of crime (sin) and punishment. Whether intended or not, The Misfit's self-revelations here are one part of the assault on the grandmother's self-absorption so that eventually she sees The Misfit as one of her own children and expresses that charity, for which he shoots her.

Thus far, we have seen the use of suggested supposition to reveal as much about the speaker's mind as to register suggested suppositions of the hearer's mind. Suggested supposition may also be used more purely to manipulate the hearer. Suggestion of greater knowledge of the state of the mind of the hearer is, of course, a favorite trope in the Christian sermon. Consider the beginning of Reverend Bevel Summers' homily in "The River":

> "Maybe I know why you come," he said in the twangy voice, "*maybe I don't.*
>
> "*If you ain't come for Jesus, you ain't come for me.* If you just come to see can you leave your pain in the river, *you ain't come for Jesus. You can't leave your pain in the river,*" he said. (*GM,* 40)

After he finished his sermon, he "lifted his arms quickly and began to repeat all that he had said before about the River and the Kingdom of Christ" (*GM,* 43). The first negative is textual since it responds to "Maybe I know why you come." The second, third, and fourth negatives are all culture- and/or hearer-based suggestive, since people coming to a river-side religious service can be presumed to have come for Jesus and for the preacher himself. And, finally, the fifth negative is textually explicit, given that it responds to "If you just come to see can you leave your pain in the river." All of these negatives, whether suggestive or not, indicate that negatives may be used for manipulative (i.e., rhetorical) purposes.

In "A Circle in the Fire," Sally Virginia uses a nonce suggestive negative in her battle with her mother, Mrs. Cope, who wants to control her, for an even more straightforwardly manipulative purpose—to persuade her mother to leave her alone. The following passage begins with Mrs. Cope's upbraiding Sally Virginia for the way she is dressed, in a cowboy costume:

> Mrs. Cope watched her with a tragic look. "Why do you have to look like an idiot?" she asked. "Suppose company were to come? When are you going to grow up? What's going to become of you? I look at you and I want to cry! Sometimes you look like you might belong to Mrs. Pritchard!"
>
> "Leave me be," the child said in a high irritated voice. "Leave me be. Just leave me be. *I ain't you,*" and she went off to the woods as if she were stalking out an enemy, her head thrust forward and each hand gripped on a gun. (*GM,* 150)

Sally Virginia's parting shot—"I ain't you"—is a very clever negation since the nonce suggested supposition is "Sally Virginia is Mrs. Cope," indirectly accusing Mrs. Cope of attempting to destroy her daughter's individuality, which indeed she does try to do several times in the story. And even more interestingly, this passage shows that suggested supposition may be used ironically to increase social distance rather than decrease it. Sally Virginia suggests a supposition in her mother's mind—that they are the same—only simultaneously to negate that supposition, thereby creating social distance, i.e., telling her mother that she is her own person.[16]

I will conclude this chapter with an analysis of ironic supposition and presupposition manipulation in "The Life You Save May Be Your Own." These examples demonstrate the real complexity that results when supposition and presupposition intertwine. Consider, then, the following passage, in which Mr. Shiftlet, the drifter, sidesteps Lucynell Crater's (the Senior's) question about his origins:

> "Where you come from, Mr. Shiftlet?"
>
> *He didn't answer.* He reached into his pocket and brought out a sack of tobacco and a package of cigarette papers and rolled himself a cigarette. . . .
>
> He flipped away the dead match and blew a stream of gray into the evening. A sly look came over his face. "Lady," he said, "nowadays, people'll do anything anyways. I can tell you my name is Tom T. Shiftlet and I come from Tarwater, Tennessee, but you never have seen me before: how you know *I ain't lying*? How you know *my name ain't Aaron Sparks*, lady, and I come from Singleberry, Georgia, or how you know *it's not George Speeds* and I come from Lucy, Alabama, or how you know *I ain't Thompson Bright from Toolafalls, Mississippi*?"
>
> "*I don't know nothing about you*," the old woman muttered, irked. (*GM*, 56)

The first negative in this passage—"He didn't answer"—is fairly straight-forwardly textually implicit, although as narrative it is directed at the narratee rather than another character. If one character asks a question of another, the narratee has the reasonable expectation that the questioned character will answer. So, the first negative registers the defeat of an implicit expectation on the part of the reader.

The second negative—in "how you know I ain't lying"—is intensely complicated by presupposition. Consider the following examples:

6. a. I ain't lying.

   b. You know I ain't lying.

In (6a) we have the negative that serves as the pragmatic foundation of the question "how you know I ain't lying," foundational because it is the most deeply imbedded clause in sentence (6b), thus, the most back-grounded clause in sentence (6b), which is the declarative form of Shiftlet's interrogative "how you know I ain't lying?" The supposition for (6a)—that Shiftlet is lying—is textually implicit since he has evaded Crater's question in answering not that he is from Tarwater, Tennessee, but that he "can" tell her that he is Tom T. Shiftlet and that he is from Tarwater, Tennessee, even though she has never seen him before. Example (7), since it is the simple negative of (6b), ought to demonstrate the presupposed nature of the complement clause to the factive verb *know*—"I ain't lying."

7. You don't know I ain't lying.

Instead (7) hints that "I ain't lying" is not necessarily presupposed in either (6b) or (7), as is demonstrated by the examples in (8):

8. a. You don't know I ain't lying, but he does.
    b. You don't know I ain't lying, so you had better protect yourself.

In (8a), the presupposition that "I ain't lying" is supported by the second clause, which with a third-person pronominal subject guarantees the presupposition of its elided clause. However, in (8b), the purpose clause defeats the presupposition by implying that the hearer might be threatened in some way by the speaker's possible lies. Now, all of these very particular contextual modifications of presupposition are allowed by the choice of the verb *know*, which is here ambiguous between the meaning "be aware of," which is presuppositional (factive), and the meanings "have adequate evidence for" or "be certain of," neither of which is presuppositional (factive). If we substitute *realize* for *know* in (6b), the complement is unquestionably presupposed since *realize* is synonymous with the "be aware of" meaning of *know*. Note that if *realize* is substituted for *know* in (8b), as in (9), the sense of the warning in the purpose clause changes:

9. You don't realize I ain't lying, so you had better protect yourself.

In (9), the warning is that you should protect yourself against your own ignorance of what is uncontestably presupposed and true (i.e., "I ain't lying").

If we return to Shiftlet's first question, repeated in (10), we have to add one more layer of complexity to a complete analysis:

10. "How you know I ain't lying?"

Content questions of the sort that begin with *how, when, where, why,* etc. will presuppose their propositional content, except of course for the missing content asked for in the wh-word. Thus, in (10), it is presupposed that you "know" that "I ain't lying." If this presupposition is indeed not present in a particular context (i.e., if "you" don't have adequate evidence for "my" not lying), as it is indeed not present when Shiftlet asks this question of Lucynell Crater, one of the few responses possible is, "I *don't* know you aren't lying." But Shiftlet doesn't give her the chance to answer. In rapid fire, he asks the questions in (11), (12), and (13):

11. "How you know my name ain't Aaron Sparks, lady, and I come from Singleberry, Georgia"
12. "how you know it's not George Speeds and I come from Lucy, Alabama"
13. "how you know I ain't Thompson Bright from Toolafalls, Mississippi"

In each of these questions, there are presuppositions built upon the suggested suppositions of the negatives. And this layering is even more complex than that in (10) since the negatives are built on nonce suggested suppositions. Let us examine the suppositions and presuppositions that must lie behind each of these questions by analyzing just the first set in (11). The most deeply embedded assumptions are the suggested suppositions "He is Aaron Sparks, and he is from Singleberry, Georgia," which are clearly neither textually explicit nor implicit suppositions; neither are they culture- or hearer-based suggested suppositions. They are, instead, suggested by Shiftlet on a nonce basis. Then, the next higher assumption is the presupposition that he isn't Aaron Sparks from Singleberry, Georgia, which of course rests on the ambiguously factive or non-factive verb *know*. Then, the suggested supposition and presupposition are presupposed within the wh-question. All of these dubious suppositions and presuppositions are sleights designed to skirt the question that Lucynell Crater asks of Shiftlet: "Where you come from, Mr. Shiftlet?" Note Shiftlet's immediate response: "He didn't answer. He reached into his pocket and brought out a sack of tobacco and a package of cigarette papers and rolled himself a cigarette." Thus, para-doxically, Shiftlet uses inappropriate signals of greater knowledge of his hearer, in the forms of problematic suppositions and presuppositions, in order to avoid the transmission of knowledge. Lucynell Crater's ultimate response to Shiftlet's abuse is the following: "'I don't know nothing about you,' the old woman muttered, irked." In the end, Shiftlet escapes with the car, if not the wife, of his dreams.

As we have seen several times in this chapter, suggested supposition can represent suspect, fake, or problematic background knowledge; chapter 6 begins our exploration of the differences between implicational and pre-suppositional complements to the verb *see*, a verb that records the receipt and processing of knowledge by what is perhaps our most trusted sense.

Chapter 6

Seeing the Background

Very slowly, his expression changed as if [Bevel] were gradually
seeing appear what he didn't know he'd been looking for.
—Flannery O'Connor (*GM*, 50)

O'Connor's Misfit is an obsessive visual literalist, and that obsession drives everything from his theology to his interactional style: if he had been there when Christ raised the dead, he would have known that Jesus was who he said he was because he would have seen the miracle of raising the dead occur, and he corrects the grandmother when she says that their car turned over twice: "Oncet. . . . We seen it happen" (*GM*, 21). He tells the grandmother that the only reason he was convicted of a crime was that "they had the papers on me," although he was never shown his papers. His "proof" to the grandmother both that he didn't kill his own father, as the "head-doctor at the penitentiary" said he did, and that his father really died of influenza is for her to go "see" for herself his father's grave in the Mount Hopewell Baptist churchyard. On the basis of his own experience, he advises her that the best practice is to "get you a signature and sign everything you do and keep a copy of it. Then you'll know what you done and you can hold up the crime to the punishment and see do they match and in the end you'll have something to prove you ain't been treated right" (*GM*, 26–28). For The Misfit, to see is to believe—and to know. After he shoots the grandmother, he removes his glasses to clean them. The narrator tells us, "Without his glasses, The Misfit's eyes were red-rimmed and pale and defenseless-looking" (*GM*, 29). His reliance on spectacles, similar to that by Hulga Hopewell in "Good Country People," highlights his reliance on literal rather than spiritual vision. At least one of The Misfit's problems is that he sees obsessively and literally because he hasn't accepted the grace of God that would allow him to see correctly and spiritually. As O'Connor says, "Belief, in my own case anyway, is the engine that makes perception operate" (*MM*, 109).

In part, it is metaphorical seeing—that is, spiritual and cognitive seeing—that marks Hazel Motes and separates him from other characters in *Wise Blood*. Haze is throughout the novel described as if he were capable more of spiritual sight than of physical sight, which probably dooms his denial of Christ and God's grace to failure. Near the beginning of *Wise Blood*, the narrator tells us that Haze's eyes capture Mrs. Hitchcock's attention more than any of his other features: "Their settings were so deep that they seemed, to her, almost like passages leading somewhere and she leaned halfway across the space that separated the two seats, trying to see into them" (*WB*, 10–11). In the middle of the novel, Sabbath Lily tells her father why she likes Haze's eyes; she senses their spiritual hunger: "They don't look like they see what he's looking at but they keep on looking" (*WB*, 109). Even before Haze begins his obsessive denial of his redemption, he is hinted to be on the edge of experiencing a great revelation: "His second night in Taulkinham, Hazel Motes walked along down town close to the store fronts but not looking in them. The black sky was underpinned with long silver streaks that looked like scaffolding and depth on depth behind it were thousands of stars that all seemed to be moving very slowly as if they were about some vast construction work that involved the whole order of the universe and would take all time to complete. No one was paying any attention to the sky. The stores in Taulkinham stayed open on Thursday nights so that people could have an extra opportunity to see what was for sale" (*WB*, 37). Although Haze is most likely not observing this miracle in the skies, it is absolutely clear that the residents of Taulkinham don't see it. Haze is described here in the liminal position that he occupies—rejecting both heaven and hell, but potentially able to see the miracle unfolding in the sky. At the end of the novel, after his self-blinding, Haze explains that he walks with rocks in his shoes "to pay." His landlady, Mrs. Flood, responds as follows:

> "But what have you got to show that you're paying for?" she persisted.
> "Mind your business," he said rudely. "You can't see."
> The landlady continued to chew very slowly. "Do you think, Mr. Motes," she said hoarsely, "that when you're dead, you're blind?"
> "I hope so," he said after a minute.
> "Why?" she asked, staring at him.
> After a while he said, "If there's no bottom in your eyes, they hold more."
> The landlady stared for a long time, seeing nothing at all. (*WB*, 222)

Haze understands that if you can't literally see that you can "see" more. Mrs. Flood has a purely non-spiritual understanding of sight: "He could have been dead and get all he got out of life but the exercise. He might as well be one of them monks, she thought, he might as well be in a monkery. She didn't understand it. She didn't like the thought that something was being put over her head. She liked the clear light of day. She liked to see things" (*WB*, 218). Mrs. Flood is a type in O'Connor, a type that is obsessed with clarity of rational vision, no matter how incapable of that rationality she might be. That character type is also blind to spiritual vision, even when it sits in the presence of Christian grace. At the very end of *Wise Blood*, Mrs. Flood repeats Mrs. Hitchcock's obsession with Haze's eyes, now burned out with lime: "The outline of a skull was plain under his skin and the deep burned eye sockets seemed to lead into the dark tunnel where he had disappeared. She leaned closer and closer to his face, looking deep into them, trying to see how she had been cheated or what had cheated her, but she couldn't see anything. She shut her eyes and saw the pin point of light but so far away that she could not hold it steady in her mind. She felt as if she were blocked at the entrance of something. She sat staring with her eyes shut, into his eyes, and felt as if she had finally got to the beginning of something she couldn't begin, and she saw him moving farther and farther away, farther and farther into the darkness until he was the pin point of light" (*WB*, 231–32). Both Hitchcock and Flood are blocked by literal sight from the acute spiritual vision that Haze purchases with the sacrifice of his eyesight. Seeing and not seeing, claiming to have seen and claiming not to have seen all are important revelatory and revealing acts in most of O'Connor's fiction.

There are O'Connor works such as "A Good Man Is Hard to Find," "Good Country People," "Revelation," and of course *Wise Blood*, in which both literal vision and spiritual vision form hubs for the generation of metaphor, symbol, and character motivation. But even many less visuo-centric stories have threads of concerns with vision, particularly of the intellectual and spiritual sort, running through them. "The Comforts of Home," for example, narrates the common "intellectual child"/"protecting mother" O'Connor theme, with the child, Thomas, actively resisting his mother's urge to spread her charity to the care of Star Drake (Sarah Ham), the "nimpermaniac." Thomas observes of Star that she had a look "that suggested blindness but it was the blindness of those who don't know that they cannot see" (*ERMC*, 126). The narrator's observation of what Thomas observes pins the irony directly on him. Again in O'Connor, the intellectual fails to see correctly. After Thomas arranges for Sheriff Farebrother to investigate Star's theft of Thomas's pistol, he has a moment of near insight: "Had he delivered his mother over to the sheriff—to be a butt for the man's tongue? Was he betraying her to get rid of the little slut? He saw at once *that this was not the case.* He was doing what he was doing for her own good" (*ERMC,* 138). Thomas's flight from the truth about himself is delivered in an ironic complement to the verb *see.* The story ends with Farebrother walking in immediately after Thomas accidentally shoots his own mother instead of Star, whom he intended to kill. Farebrother "saw the facts as if they were already in print: the fellow had intended all along to kill his mother and pin it on the girl." But then he has "further insights" and "sees" more deeply: "Over her body, the killer and the slut were about to collapse into each other's arms. The sheriff knew a nasty bit when he saw it" (*ERMC,* 141–42). O'Connor's exploration of false seeing rarely reaches the same comical heights.

The prevalence of sight imagery and literal verbs of sight in O'Connor's fiction has been commented on frequently in the critical literature.[1] Patrick Shaw, for example, explores "the complex pattern of ironic false seeing and misconceptions that bedevil the dramatis personae of *The Violent Bear It Away.*" William E. H. Meyer Jr., recognizing the affinity of O'Connor for Hawthorne, is perhaps most forceful with his assertion that "with the exception of *Moby-Dick,* no American novels are so obsessed with the mere fact of *seeing* and *being seen*—with a kind of super voyeurism or super exhibitionism and a kind of super fear of exposure—as are *Wise Blood* and *The Scarlet Letter.*" Laura Kennelly argues that Hazel Motes's "visual errors" and "reliance on vision" are part of O'Connor's metaphorical dramatization of "vision's inherent deceitfulness." Miles Orvell comments on the importance of literal vision in the reception of grace in several of O'Connor's works and concludes, "O'Connor's first principle is thus rooted in the perception of the world and not in some disembodied cogito: rather, video ergo sum."[2] Another strong visionist tradition in O'Connor criticism explores the linkage between religious revelation and sacramental imagery.[3] M. Bernetta Quinn's comments are typical, except for the attention to etymology, of this school of criticism: "Miss O'Connor identifies with her special talent two very closely related words: *vision* and *revelation. Vision,* from the past participle *visus,* refers to a mental representation of external objects as in a religious revelation or dream. Such might be any transfiguration of the material world as found in Miss O'Connor's work. *Revelation*, a key term in her fiction, is the title of a short story published the spring before she died. Considered as an *unveiling* (*re* [back] & *velum* [veil]), it means to make visible, to show."[4] Most critics make at least passing reference to Quinn's concern—that vision, of an analogical sort, and spiritual revelation are practically one and the same in O'Connor's fictional world. But no one has yet investigated the quantitative or qualitative stylistics of any of the *see* verbs and imagery and how those stylistics reflect O'Connor's concerns with knowledge. As the following passage from *Mystery and Manners* indicates, there is a close connection between knowledge (as it manifests itself in judgment) and vision in O'Connor's poetics: "For the writer of fiction, everything has its testing point in the eye, and the eye is an organ that eventually involves the whole personality, and as much of the world as can be got into it. It involves judgment. Judgment is something that begins in the act of vision, and when it does not, or when it becomes separated from vision, then a confusion exists in the mind which transfers itself to the story" (*MM,* 91). Even though O'Connor speaks here of the writer's relation to vision and judgment, she might just as well have been speaking of her characters.

This chapter of *Narrating Knowledge* is mostly concerned with the quantitative, semantic, and pragmatic patterns of the verb *see* and phrasal and clausal complements to the verb *see*. My rather lengthy introduction to these patterns is necessary background for three reasons. First, we must understand the basic semantic structures of sense verbs in English in order to understand the special status of vision verbs. Second, I must present initial data to demonstrate quantitatively that verbs of the *see* class are stylistically important in O'Connor's fiction. Third, we need to understand the unmarked semantic and pragmatic patterns of complements to the verb *see* in particular to understand the literary challenges to those prototypical patterns in O'Connor's fiction.

Vision in English

Before we turn to a quantitative analysis of seeing in the O'Connor and Brown texts, we will first explore the special place of vision in the English language. Consider table 8, which is a blend of tables in Adrienne Lehrer's "Polysemy, Conventionality, and the Structure of the Lexicon" and Randolph Quirk et al.'s *Comprehensive Grammar of the English Language*, plus a few of my own modifications.[5]

Table 8. Verbs of Perception

Subject Role	Experiencer	Executor	Stimulus
Subject Agentivity	Non-Agentive	Agentive	Non-Agentive
	see	look at	look
	hear	listen to	sound
	feel	feel	feel
	smell	smell	smell
	taste	taste	taste

There are two variables of verb semantics represented in table 8: semantic role of subject and agentivity of subject. Role of subject has three values: *experiencer*, a perceptor of a state or event; *executor*, a performer of an event; and *stimulus*, something, human or otherwise, perceived. Agentivity of subject has two values: *agentive*, a controlling, intentional subject; and *non-agentive*, a non-controlling, non-intentional subject. These semantics are non-isomorphic since experiencer and stimulus are non-agentive while executor is agentive. Consider the following examples of the three types of subject role and agentivity values:

Experiencer Subject, Non-Agentive Subject

1. a. I saw the happy lawyer sitting in his new automobile.
   b. ?I intentionally saw the happy lawyer sitting in his new automobile.

Executor Subject, Agentive Subject

2. a. I looked at the lawyer sitting in his new automobile.
   b. I intentionally looked at the happy lawyer sitting in his new automobile.

Stimulus Subject, Non-Agentive Subject

3. a. The lawyer looked happy to me sitting in his new automobile.
   b. ?The lawyer intentionally looked happy to me sitting in his new automobile.

The question marks before sentences indicate semantically odd sentences. In (1a) the experiencer subject "I" non-agentively sees the happy lawyer. One way that we know that the experiencer subject is non-agentive is that it sounds intuitively wrong to add the agentive adverb *intentionally*, as in (1b).[6] The examples in (2) demonstrate that the verb *look at* may be used with an agentive executor subject. As (2b) shows, *look at* may occur with the agentive adverb *intentionally*. I use the form *look at* to demonstrate the general patterns of a number of different forms such as *look up*, *look down*, *look out*, *look through*, *look on*, and *look in*, all of which have in common an agentive executor subject. Finally, (3b) shows that the verb *look*, at least in the construction provided in (3b), is non-agentive; it may not occur with *intentionally*. It is important to point out the obvious but most important point here: *see*, *look at*, and *look* are all lexically different. Although closely related semantically, the three verbs take different forms to express three different variable combinations for semantic role and agentivity of subject.

Note from the following examples that the verb *hear* and members of its lexical class behave the same way as *see* and members of its lexical class:

Experiencer Subject, Non-Agentive Subject

4. a. I heard the lawyer practicing her opening argument.
    b. ?I intentionally heard the lawyer practicing her opening argument.

Executor Subject, Agentive Subject

5. a. I listened to the lawyer practicing her opening argument.
    b. I intentionally listened to the lawyer practicing her opening argument.

Stimulus Subject, Non-Agentive Subject

6. a. The lawyer sounded persuasive to me in her opening argument.
    b. ?The lawyer intentionally sounded persuasive to me in her opening argument.

Examples (1)–(6) demonstrate that speakers of English have lexically different items to express three different types of subjects (for role and agentivity) in the lexical classes for *see* (*see*, *look at*, and *look*) and *hear* (*hear*, *listen to*, and *sound*).

Note from the example of *feel* below that English does not lexically differentiate the verbs *feel, smell,* and *taste* for the three types of subjects; that is, these three verbs are polysemous (they do not have different lexical forms for the three types of subjects):

Experiencer Subject, Non-Agentive Subject

7. a. I felt the mild earthquake yesterday.
    b. ?I intentionally felt the mild earthquake yesterday.

Executor Subject, Agentive Subject

8. a. I felt the smooth finish on his car.
    b. I intentionally felt the smooth finish on his car.

Stimulus Subject, Non-Agentive Subject

9. a. The new finish on his car felt smooth to me.
    b. ?The new finish on his car intentionally felt smooth to me.

Readers might create their own examples and then check their own intuitions for the verbs *smell* and *taste*. It appears, then, at least on the basis of lexical differentiation that *see* and *hear* are more important than *feel, smell,* and *taste*. The question now is just what that differentiation signifies. Lehrer speculates, "The fact that human beings rely on vision and hearing for most of the information about the world may account for the lexical differentiation found in these [and other] perception verbs."[7]

Sight is certainly the most obvious sense of rationality since we so commonly say that we see when we mean that we understand. The only other sense that has a relatively direct metaphoric connection to rationality is hearing, since we can say, "I hear you" or "I hear where you're coming from," meaning "I agree with you or understand your premises." Even so, sight is more centrally rational than hearing. We can say, "I saw that Liz was in love with Peter" and mean "I concluded that Liz was in love with Peter." But when we say, "I heard that Liz was in love with Peter," we must necessarily mean that somewhere we literally heard someone say something to the effect that Liz was in love with Peter. As Stephen Tyler illustrates with the example in (10), sight is the sense whose lexicon we use to talk even about the other four senses:

	felt
	tasted
10. I just wanted to see what it	smelled like.
	sounded

Tyler argues that this "hegemony of the visual . . . is based on a profound misunderstanding of the evolution and functioning of the human sensorium." Tyler is, of course, not alone in his criticism of the centrality of vision metaphors in our intellectual life.[8] Richard Rorty refers to this vision skew as "the domination of the mind of the West by ocular metaphors." However, other serious thinkers on the mind and language find the visual metaphor natural. For example, Wallace Chafe writes, "Consciousness is like vision. The similarities are probably not accidental, since the eye is anatomically an extension of the brain, and since for most of us vision is so fundamental a part of conscious experience." Lehrer also argues, "Vision is perhaps the most important sense for humans, and if that is so, it is not surprising that the verb for visual perception, *see*, would generalize (if any verb should) to perception in general."[9] Essentially, what we have here in this split between my representative postmodern anthropologist, literary critic, and philosopher, who all criticize visual metaphors in our cognitive life, and the two linguists, who seek to explain the metaphors, is a representation of the difference between those who prescribe and those who describe. No matter how visuo-centric English is, that centeredness in the visual is simply, descriptively, the way it is.

Sense Verbs in Brown and O'Connor

O'Connor writes in one of her essays on the craft of fiction, "The first and most obvious characteristic of fiction is that it deals with reality through what can be seen, heard, smelt, tasted, and touched" (*MM*, 91). We will consider then, each in turn, the frequency distributions in the Brown general-fiction corpus and in O'Connor's texts of the five lexical classes of verbs analyzed in the last section. The verb classes represent the lexical items for each of the three types of subjects covered above. Thus in table 9, the *see* class represents tokens of *see, look at,* and *look* along with their specific tense and aspectual realizations, such as *seeing, looked at,* and *looks.*

The difference in frequencies of occurrence of verbs of the *see* class in Brown and O'Connor is significant to the .001 level. These verbs occur on

Table 9. Frequencies of *see* Class Verbs

Total Words	Brown	O'Connor	Totals
Other Words	57,840	290,869	348,709
See *Class*: *see, look at, look*	280 *(4.8 per thousand)*	2,490 *(8.4 per thousand)*	2,770
Totals	58,120	293,359	351,479

$\chi^2=83.107, p<.001$

average 4.8 tokens per thousand words in the Brown general-fiction corpus; they occur in O'Connor's texts at 8.4 tokens per thousand words.

The *hear* class in table 10 represents tokens of *hear, listen to,* and *sound* along with their specific tense and aspect realizations, such as *hearing, listened to,* and *sounds.*

The difference in distributions of the *hear* class in Brown and O'Connor is not significant to the .001 level (p=.370). The frequencies are almost identical, with 1.5 occurrences per thousand words in the Brown general-fiction corpus and 1.7 per thousand in O'Connor. Thus, in spite of the ability of *hear* verbs to encode acquisition of knowledge, and in spite of O'Connor's interest in knowledge, she apparently did not stylistically exploit the *hear* class of verbs for that purpose. Consider the following passage, in which Haze challenges Asa Hawks to "see" whether he "can see" him throw away his religious tracts:

> "I'll take them up there and throw them over into the bushes!" Haze shouted. "You be watching and *see can you see.*"
> "I can see more than you!" the blind man yelled, laughing. "You got eyes and see not, ears and hear not, but you'll have to see some time." (*WB,* 54)

Hawks, who failed in his attempt to blind himself and simply pretends to be blind, mentions two (sight, hearing) of the four senses (sight, hearing, smell, touch) mentioned in Psalm 115, to which he alludes, but it is only sight that he promises Haze will have to endure one day, a promise that is ironic in the light of Haze's successful self-blinding.

Table 10. Frequencies of *hear* Class Verbs

Total Words	Brown	O'Connor	Totals
Other Words	58,028	292,842	350,870
Hear class: hear, listen to, sound	92 *(1.5 per thousand)*	517 *(1.7 per thousand)*	609
Totals	58,120	293,359	351,479

χ^2=.802, p>.001

Table 11. Frequencies of *feel* and *smell* Class Verbs

Total Words	Brown	O'Connor	Totals
Other Words	58,027	292,938	350,965
Feel class	85 *(1.4 per thousand)*	382 *(1.3 per thousand)*	467
Smell class	8 *(.137 per thousand)*	39 *(.132 per thousand)*	47
Totals	58,120	293,359	351,479

χ^2=.948, p>.001

In table 11, the *feel* class and *smell* class represent tokens of *feel* and *smell* along with their specific tense and aspect realizations, such as *feeling, smelled,* and *feels.*

The differences in frequency distributions of the *feel* and *smell* classes of verbs are not significant to the .001 level in Brown and O'Connor (p=.623). Again, the proportions are almost identical for each case: for *feel* 1.4 per thousand in Brown and 1.3 per thousand in O'Connor; for *smell* .137 per thousand in Brown and .132 per thousand in O'Connor.

The *taste* class is too low in frequency to test statistically: the Brown general-fiction corpus has only three tokens, and the O'Connor texts have only one!

O'Connor is well-known as a writer that both appeals to the senses and frequently claims in her expository prose to aim for that effect in her fiction. As for use of the five major classes of sense verbs—*see, hear, feel, smell,* and *taste*—there is thus far evidence only that she exploits the frequency of the *see* class. Furthermore, if sheer frequency is any measure of importance, the verb *see* is the most important sense verb in O'Connor since at 1248 tokens it is the most frequent of any of the sense verbs. For this quantitative reason and for the sake of thorough exploration of its patterns, I will limit my discussion of visual verbs for the most part to *see*.

In the next section, we turn to a theoretical description of the pragmatic and semantic qualities of verbal complements, presupposition, and implication.

The Form and Semantics of Syntactic Integration of Verb Complements

First, I explore some intuitional data to establish some formal distinctions in types of complements to the verb *see*. There are three types of nonfinite (nontensed) complements to the verb *see*:

Bare Stem

11. a. Bill saw *Liz leave.*
    b. *Liz leave.

Present Participial

12. a. Bill saw *Liz leaving.*
    b. *Liz leaving.

Past Participial

13. a. Bill saw *Liz stopped for a traffic violation.*
    b. *Liz [semantic PATIENT] stopped for a traffic violation.

A verbal complement in English is a phrase or a clause with a verb in it, whether the verb is tensed (as in a clause) or not tensed (as in a phrase); the complement is subordinated to a matrix clause as the grammatical object of

Figure 6. Formal Integration

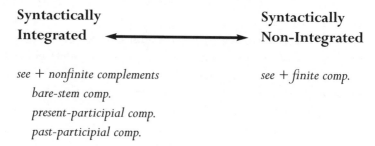

the main verb. A finite (tensed) complement will have one of the three tenses—past, present, or future—while a nonfinite (nontensed) complement has none of those tenses but may occur with the aspects progressive and/or perfect. The italicized complement in (11a) is known as the bare-stem complement since its verb has absolutely no added morphology such as tense or aspect. The italicized complement in (12a) is known as the present-participial complement since its verb contains the *-ing* form that is used for the present participial, or for the progressive aspect. And the italicized complement in (13a) is known as the past-participial complement since its verb has the *-ed/-en* form that is used for the past participial, or for the perfective aspect. As I pointed out in chapter 1, despite the traditional labels, the "present" participial and the "past" participial are without tense. Note that in (13b) I have labeled the subject "Liz" for its semantic role as *patient*, that is, the participant that undergoes the action of the event rather than *executor*, the participant that performs the event. In other words, (13a) and (13b) show that Liz was stopped, not that Liz stopped. One obvious sign of the tight syntactic integration of these verb complements with the matrix clause is that they may not stand grammatically by themselves, as is illustrated in the grammatically incorrect asterisked (b) examples in (11) through (13).[10]

As the following examples demonstrate, finite complements to the verb *see* behave very differently from the nontensed complements:

14. a. Bill saw *that Liz left*.
    b. Liz left.
15. a. Bill saw *that Liz was leaving*.
    b. Liz was leaving.
16. a. Bill saw *that Liz was stopped for a traffic violation*.
    b. Liz was stopped for a traffic violation.

Compare (14), (15), and (16) with (11), (12), and (13), respectively. Through the simple deletion of the subordinator, each of the complements in (14) through (16) can occur as a grammatical sentence. The structural difference, besides the subordinator, between (11) through (13) and (14) through (16) is the presence of tense in (14) through (16), in these cases, past tense. A finite complement, because it contains tense, is more syntactically and semantically independent of the matrix clause than nonfinite complements.[11] Figure 6 illustrates the relationship between complement type and syntactic integration.

Second, I explore some intuitional data to establish a few semantic distinctions in types of complements to the verb *see*. Notice that the nonfinite complements, represented categorically below by the present participial, generally indicate a direct physical observation of the action of the complement (17a) while the finite complement may be understood either as a direct physical observation (18b) or as an indirect cognition (18c).[12] Example (18a), then, is ambiguous between a direct physical observation and an indirect cognition:

17. a. Bill saw *Liz leaving* (as she was walking out the door) and said good bye.
    b. ?Bill saw *Liz leaving* from the fact that her car was packed.
18. a. Bill saw *that Liz was leaving* and said goodbye.
    b. Bill saw *that Liz was leaving* as she was walking out the door and said goodbye.
    c. Bill saw *that Liz was leaving* from the fact that her car was packed.

Example (17b) is semantically ill formed because the italicized participial complement signals direct observation while the prepositional phrase, "from the fact that her car was packed," signals that the observation was indirect. Robert Kirsner and Sandra Thompson, as well as T. Givón separately, point out that nonfinite complements to *see* "communicate basic physical perception while [finite complements to *see*] involve *interpretation* as well." One of the important issues in this chapter and the next is the nature of the interpretation involved in an example like (18a). It is possible to interpret the complement in (18a) as encoding direct perception or indirect cognition or some mixture of the two, partially because the adverbial clause "as she was walking out the door," which is optional in (17a) even for the direct perception reading, is absent in (18a). Note that in (18b), where

Figure 7. Formal and Semantic Integration

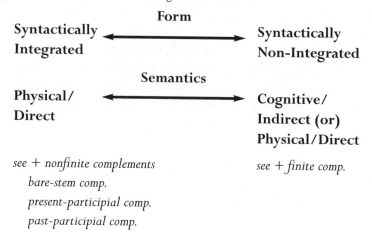

the adverbial clause appears, the reading that is probable is a direct perception. Example (18c) is equally likely to be interpreted as referring to an indirect cognition because of the same prepositional phrase that makes (17b)
semantically ill formed. Kirsner and Thompson argue further, "The contrast
between direct perception and deductions from something perceived is,
like other linguistic contrasts[,] a matter of degree."[13] I will argue in chapter
7 that these degrees of difference are vital to defining O'Connor's style.

Again, *hear* works very similarly to *see.* Consider how the examples in
(19) and (20) parallel those in (17) and (18):

19. a. Bill heard *Liz leaving* (as she was walking out the door) and went
to say goodbye.
b. ?Bill heard *Liz leaving* through an e-mail message from Jim.
20. a. Bill heard *that Liz was leaving* and went to say goodbye.
b. Bill heard *that Liz was leaving* as she was walking out the door and
went to say goodbye.
c. Bill heard *that Liz was leaving* through an e-mail message from Jim.

As with *see, hear* allows a physically direct interpretation of a nonfinite complement, as in (19a), but not a cognitive, or indirect, interpretation of a nonfinite complement, as in (19b).[14] Note that just as in (17a), the adverbial "as
she was walking out the door" is optional in deriving the physically direct
reading in (19a). Just like *see, hear* allows either an ambiguous physically
direct/cognitively indirect interpretation of a finite complement, as in (20a),

or a physically direct interpretation of a finite complement, as in (20b), or a cognitively indirect interpretation of a finite complement, as in (20c).

Many verbs that do take nonfinite complements do not allow the use of finite complements for the very reason that they may not have a cognitive interpretation. Givón points out, for example, that manipulation verbs (e.g., *make, tell, order, help, ask*) along with modality verbs (e.g., *want, begin, finish, try*), have the strongest syntactic integration of verbs that take complements.[15] Consider (21) and (22):

21. a. Bill made *Liz write the letter.*
    b. *Bill made *that Liz wrote the letter.*
22. a. Bill helped *Liz write the letter.*
    b. *Bill helped *that Liz wrote the letter.*

In (21a) and (22a), the bare-stem complements are grammatical because the manipulation verbs *make* and *help* demand syntactic integration, reflecting their directness. Compare (17a) and (19a). In (21b) and (22b), the finite complements are ungrammatical because the matrix verbs demand more syntactic integration than the finite complements provide. Compare (18a) and (20a). Figure 7 illustrates the interaction of syntactic integration with physical / cognitive semantics.

There is an iconic relationship between form and meaning illustrated in figure 7 whose significance is easy to overlook.[16] That which is formally syntactically integrated (i.e., nonfinite complements with matrix clauses) is semantically integrated if we understand that which is physical to be more direct than that which is cognitive. Conversely, that which is formally less syntactically integrated (i.e., finite complements with matrix clauses) is semantically less integrated by the same reasoning since finite complements may be interpreted as either physically direct or cognitively indirect, again depending on the context. This ambiguity makes all of this sound suspiciously less like semantics and more like pragmatics, a suggestion that we will explore in chapter 7.

Next, let's consider some intuitional data to establish the pragmatic similarity between various types of complements to the verb *see*:

	Figure	Ground
23. a.	Bill saw	*Liz leave.*
b.	He did?	
c.	?She did?	

	Figure	*Ground*
24.a.	Bill saw	*Liz leaving.*
b.	He did?	
c.	?She did?	
25.a.	Bill saw	*Liz left at the altar.*
b.	He did?	
c.	?She was?	
26.a.	Bill saw	*that Liz left.*
b.	He did?	
c.	?She did?	

Examples (23) through (26) demonstrate, at least intuitively, that nonfinite complements and finite complements have in common a pragmatic backgrounding, as is revealed in the intuitive preference to question the proposition of the matrix clause (the b-examples) rather than that of the complement (the c-examples).[17] What is foregrounded in each example is the act of seeing, whether it is physical (in 23–26) or, perhaps, cognitive (in 26). Note, again, that (26), with a finite complement, can be interpreted as either a physical or cognitive perception. We will see in chapter 7 that O'Connor's choice to foreground the act of seeing, whether physical or cognitive, rather than what is seen has profound consequences for both the interpretation and the structure of her fiction.

Presupposition vs. Implication

Before we determine the pragmatic differences between nonfinite and finite complements, we first must introduce the differences between presuppositional seeing and implicational seeing. Although very similar, presupposition and entailment (or, as I refer to the latter in this book, implication) may be distinguished. Consider the following definition of entailment (implication) from Stephen Levinson's *Pragmatics*:

> A *semantically entails* B (written A | |- B) iff [if and only if] every situation that makes A true, makes B true (or: in all worlds in which A is true, B is true)[18]

Implication helps us to define many linguistic relationships, for example hyponymy, in which a hypernym—perhaps the name of a car company like *Mazda*—logically includes many hyponyms—perhaps the names of particular models of car that Mazda makes, such as *Miata, 626, Millenia, MPV.* Thus, consider example (27):

27. My car is a Miata.

From statement (27), we can infer statements (28) and (29):

28. My car is a Mazda.
29. I have a car.

If (27) is true in any world, statements (28) and (29) are true in that world as well. But, only sentence (28) is considered an implication of sentence (27). Notice that if (27) is false (that is, if my car is not a Miata), sentence (28) may be true or false but sentence (29) must still be true. There is, thus, a high degree of "semantic" integration between the matrix verb and the complement when the complement is implicative; that is, if sentence (27) is false, implication (28) is destroyed. Implication is usually considered a semantic relationship, as in Terence Parsons' *Events in the Semantics of English*, although as Kirsner and Thompson and George Lakoff show clearly, implication is pragmatic rather than semantic.[19] We will explore the issue of pragmatics vs. semantics in depth in chapter 7.

Sentence (29) is not an implication but instead a presupposition of sentence (27). Consider a paraphrase of P. F. Strawson's view of presupposition:

A statement A presupposes another statement B when
(a) if A is true, then B is true
(b) if A is false, then B is true[20]

Note that this definition is centered on truth value, which is typical of Strawson's view that presupposition is what allows a statement to have a truth value. If, for example, in the statement of (27), I do not have a car in the first place, the truth value of (27) vanishes. It is neither true nor false because one cannot go out into the parking lot and match ownership to the model. Presupposition is more independent than implication of the polarity of the matrix verb because presupposition survives negation, as is indicated in the definition of presupposition above and as is proven by (30):

30. My car is not a Miata.

Again, in (30), the implication of (27), that my car is a Mazda (see 28) vanishes, but the presupposition that I have a car (see 29) remains. As Levinson puts it, "In short, negation alters a sentence's entailments [implications], but it leaves the presuppositions untouched."[21] That presupposition survives negation is one of the clearest indications that presuppositions are backgrounded to such an extreme degree that unless they are "marked" they are practically "invisible."

Implication and presupposition are intertwined with the forms of verbal complements. Note the following examples, where >=implicates, ~>= does not implicate, Q=question, and R=response:

31. Q: Did Bill see *Liz leave?*
    R: Yes, (Bill saw Liz leave).   >   Liz left.
32. a. Bill saw *Liz leave.*   >   Liz left.
    b. ?Bill saw Liz leave, but she didn't leave.

As (31) shows, if the respondent answers the question with the proposition "Bill saw Liz leave" (implicitly with "yes," or explicitly with "Bill saw Liz leave"), the implication is that Liz, indeed, left. Implication explains the oddity of (32b), where the first clause implicates that Liz left, but the second denies that implication.[22] Thus, if Bill saw Liz leave, she necessarily left. And if she didn't leave, Bill couldn't have seen her leave.

All nonfinite complements to *see* work in the same way as the bare-stem complement in (31) and (32). Note the identical pattern of the following present-participial complements.

33. Q: Did Bill see *Liz leaving?*
    R: Yes, (Bill saw Liz leaving).   >   Liz was leaving.
34. a. Bill saw *Liz leaving.*   >   Liz was leaving.
    b. ?Bill saw Liz leaving, but she wasn't leaving.

Note the identical pattern of the following past-participial complements:

35. Q: Did Bill see *Liz taken to jail?*
    R: Yes, (Bill saw Liz taken to jail).   >   Liz was taken to jail.
36. a. Bill saw *Liz taken to jail.*   >   Liz was taken to jail.
    b. ?Bill saw Liz taken to jail, but she wasn't taken to jail.

All nonfinite complements are more tightly integrated formally and semantically with the matrix verb *see* than are the finite complements. Remember that one of the tests for semantic integration is direct perception vs. indirect cognition in the complement. Another test for semantic integration is the effect of negation on the truth of the complement. That is, negation in the matrix clause will or will not affect the truth of complements, depending upon their syntactic integration. The truth of relatively non-integrated presuppositional complements will not be affected by negation, while the truth of relatively integrated implicational complements will be affected. Note in (37) and (38) that negation of the matrix verb destroys the implication of the nonfinite bare-stem complement.

37. Q: Did Bill see *Liz leave*?
    R: No, (Bill didn't see Liz leave). ~>Liz left. ~>Liz didn't leave.
38. a. Bill didn't see *Liz leave*.   ~>Liz left. ~>Liz didn't leave.
    b. Bill didn't see Liz leave, so she's here somewhere.
    c. Bill didn't see Liz leave, but I did.

In (37), if the respondent replies to the question with the proposition "Bill didn't see Liz leave" (implicitly with "no," or explicitly with "Bill didn't see Liz leave"), there is no implication, one way or the other that Liz left. The lack of an implication is repeated in (38a) and proven in (38b) and (38c). As the second clause in (38b) shows, if Bill didn't see Liz leave, she could still conceivably be on the premises. But as the second clause in (38c) also shows, if Bill didn't see Liz leave, she might still have left.

Different types of complements to different types of implicative verbs will behave differently under negation:

39. a. Liz managed to leave.   >   Liz left.
    b. Liz didn't manage to leave.   >   Liz didn't leave.
    c. ?Liz managed to leave, but she didn't leave.
    d. ?Liz didn't manage to leave, but she left.

As Lauri Karttunen points out, constructions such as those in (39) show that negation of implicative verbs with infinitive complements implicate the negation of the complement. If Liz didn't manage to leave, she necessarily didn't leave. Thus, (39c) and (39d) are semantically unacceptable because the second clauses contradict the value of the complement, either positive or negative. See Levinson's *Pragmatics* as well.[23]

Presupposition is also intimately involved in the production and management of knowledge in clausal complements. Again, in presupposition, the truth of the presupposed proposition is simply taken for granted whether or not the main verb is negated. Thus, both implication and presupposition are forms of background knowledge, but the relationship of the complement to the matrix verb is different in each. Note the following examples, where >>=presupposes and~>>= does not presuppose:

Figure 8. Formal, Semantic, and Pragmatic Integration

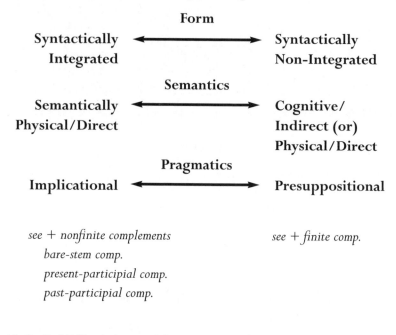

40. Q: Did Bill see *that Liz left*?
    R: Yes, (Bill saw that Liz left)   >>   Liz left.
41. a. Bill saw *that Liz left*.   >>   Liz left.
    b. ?Bill saw that Liz left, but she didn't leave.

As (40) and (41) show, finite complements to the verb *see* in a positive pre-suppose the truth of the complement. Note that (41b) is incoherent in the same way that (32b) is incoherent. If Bill saw that Liz left, she must necessarily have left. When *see* occurs with a finite complement, it functions as a factive verb, like *realize*.

Not all finite complements are presupposed. Nonfactive verbs, such as *believe*, do not presuppose their finite complements, as one sees in (42).

42. a. Bill believed *that Liz left*.   ~>> Liz left.
    b. Bill believed that Liz left, but she didn't leave.

Note that it is not incoherent to contradict in the second independent clause of (42b) the finite complement of *believe* in the first independent clause.

Recall that presuppositions remain constant under negation, meaning that negation of the matrix verb does not destroy the presupposition. Thus, there is a lesser degree of semantic/pragmatic integration between the matrix clause and a presuppositional finite complement clause than there is between the matrix clause and an implicational nonfinite complement. Remember also from (37) and (38) that negation of the verb *see* destroys the implication of the nonfinite complement, thus indicating a high degree of integration between the matrix verb *see* and the nonfinite complement. If Bill didn't see Liz leave, she may or may not have left. Contrast the behavior of the negated verb *see* with a presuppositional finite complement in (43):

43. a. Bill didn't see *that Liz left*.   >>   Liz left
    b. ?Bill didn't see that Liz left, so she's here somewhere.
    c. Bill didn't see that Liz left, but I did.

The sentences in (43) demonstrate that negation does not destroy the presupposition in a finite complement to the verb *see*. Note that (43b) is incoherent since it denies in the second independent clause the proposition of the presupposed subordinate clause in the first independent clause. Example (43c) is coherent because both independent clauses presuppose the same dependent finite clause, which is elided in the second independent clause.

Figure 8 illustrates the interactions among syntactic integration, semantic integration, and pragmatic integration of *see* and various forms of its phrasal and clausal complements.

As Givón argues, "What emerges from the study of the syntax of complementation, perhaps more clearly than in any other area of grammar, is the profoundly **non-arbitrary** nature of the coding relation between grammar and meaning."[24] Thus, on the left hand side of the continua in figure 8, we have the tightly bound nature of syntactic integration, semantic directness, and pragmatic implication, while on the right hand side, we have the loosely bound nature of syntactic non-integration, semantic directness/indirectness, and pragmatic presupposition. The iconic relationship between form and semantics that was explored in figure 7 is elaborated in figure 8 by the addition of the pragmatics of implication and presupposition.

In chapter 7, we turn to a quantitative analysis of *see* complements in O'Connor's texts and in the Brown general-fiction corpus. I will also present a detailed and qualitative examination of complements to the verb *see* in O'Connor's fiction. There we will see that literature provides the natural context for the blurring of the pragmatic and semantic distinctions between implication and presupposition, thus justifying the implicit claim of figure 8 that implication is pragmatic rather than semantic.

Chapter 7

The Cognitive—Physical
Complement Continuum

> *"We are all damned," [Hulga Hopewell] said, "but some of us
> have taken off our blindfolds and see that there's nothing to see.
> It's a kind of salvation."*
>
> —Flannery O'Connor (*GM,* 191)

At the end of chapter 6, we left nonfinite complements and finite complements to the verb *see* on opposite sides of the continua of form, semantics,
and pragmatics. Nonfinites are implicational; finites are presuppositional.
Nonfinites are perceptually physical; finites can be perceptually physical or
cognitive. We know that one of the differences between implication and
presupposition is the effect of the polarity value—positive or negative—of
the matrix clause on the complement clause, whether implicational or presuppositional. Presuppositional clauses are assumed to be true whether the
matrix clause is positive or negative. Implicational phrases, or at least the
ones we have examined thus far in *Narrating Knowledge*, are assumed to be
true only when the matrix clause is positive. In chapter 3, we saw that the
truth of some presuppositions may, in fact, be highly questionable. In this
chapter, we will see that both presuppositions and implications are similarly
susceptible to contextual defeat of their truth. In this chapter, we will also
see that the physical perception in both finite complements and nonfinite
complements to the verb *see* may be shaded by cognitive content. Thus, this
chapter will both question the semantic and pragmatic characterizations of
the complements that I made in chapter 6 and demonstrate how O'Connor's texts bend those characterizations for literary effect. However, none
of these issues is of obvious importance unless we realize the overwhelming
importance of the verb *see* in particular and of the various syntactic complements to that verb in O'Connor's fiction, so in this chapter we will consider two final quantitative patterns.

The prototypical ending for an O'Connor story that exposes false pride, knowledge, and intellect might be that of "Good Country People," with Hulga stranded in the hayloft as Manley Pointer makes off with her glasses and her artificial leg, which, as O'Connor explains to those who are hard of hearing, Hulga "took care of . . . as someone else would his soul, in private and almost with her own eyes turned away" (*GM*, 192). Hulga Hopewell, born Joy Hopewell, might serve as a poster child for the visually centered West since she (1) uses a great number of *see* verbs and (2) is an unemployed Ph.D. in philosophy who sits around all day "on her neck in a deep chair, reading." As her mother says of her highly degreed daughter, Hulga has "gone through" school (*GM*, 175–76). One of the narrative touches that places Hulga's ocular centeredness in relief is her mother's opposite and just as pronounced orality. Mrs. Hopewell has her "favorite sayings": e.g., "Nothing is perfect"; "that is life"; "well, other people have their opinions too." Hulga's fierce visual nature is violently shaken by her mother's orality: when her mother delivers her oral gems, "in a tone of gentle insistence as if no one held them but her," Hulga "would stare just a little to the side of her, her eyes icy blue, with the look of someone who has achieved blindness by an act of will and means to keep it" (*GM*, 171). Hulga's "blindness" is ironic, of course, since she is intellectually driven and thus spiritually blinded by her reliance solely on Western ocular metaphors for knowledge. She asks her mother angrily, "Do you ever look inside and see what you are *not*?" (*GM*, 176, italics in original), which is the very question she might better be asking herself.

The arc of the "Good Country People" follows the ironic presentation of Hulga's haughty pretentions to knowledge through to the abrupt stripping away of those pretentions after her violations by Manley Pointer, the itinerant Bible salesman. When imagining her seduction of Manley, "She . . . started thinking of it as a great joke and then she [began] to see profound implications in it" (*GM*, 184). During her/his seduction, she tells Manley, "I don't have illusions. I'm one of those people who see *through* to nothing" (italics in original). Presumably she is recalling her Heidegger here. She tells him, "We are all damned . . . but some of us have taken off our blindfolds and see *that there's nothing to see*. It's a kind of salvation" (*GM*, 191). All of these intellectually tinged *see* verbs from Hulga, especially the last one with the presupposition "that there's nothing to see," drip with O'Connor's characteristic irony. Hulga tells Manley that, in effect, she is one who knows that there is nothing to know. But even that pretension to negative knowledge will be stripped away when she is forced to learn to see all over again, without her leg, without her glasses, without the false pride that makes her think that she is better and smarter than everyone around her, especially the supposedly naïve Manley Pointer. As Manley completes his seduction of her (robbing her of her intellectual and emotional crutches), her vision is reduced to perceptually implicational complements: Hulga "saw *him grab the leg* and then she saw *it for an instant slanted forlornly across the inside of the suitcase with a Bible at either side of its opposite ends*" (*GM,* 195).

The examples above from "Good Country People" seem, then, to support the generalization that finite complements to *see* can be cognitive and nonfinite complements are physically perceptual. However, consider the elements of interpretation involved in Hulga's nonfinite implicational perception of Manley walking across a meadow after he leaves her stranded in the hayloft, without her glasses: "When she turned her churning face toward the opening, she saw *his blue figure struggling successfully over the green speckled lake*" (*GM,* 195). Of course, Hulga sees incorrectly here. That is, she misinterprets the images in spite of their being narrated in a nonfinite implicational participial complement. That Hulga's misinterpretation of the landscape is genuine is indicated earlier, just after Manley takes her glasses from her face and slips them into his pocket: "She looked away from him off into the hollow sky and then down at a black ridge and then down farther into what appeared to be two green swelling lakes. She didn't realize he had taken her glasses but this landscape could not seem exceptional to her for she seldom paid any close attention to her surroundings" (*GM,* 190–91). In a sense, Hulga must begin again in life. She will crawl before she walks again, and she will learn as well to see again, starting from the basis of the impressionistic images that are literally misinterpretations of the world but which are truer than her usual presuppositional cognitive interpretations of her surroundings. Again, this chapter will examine the literary basis for critiquing the truth as well as the physical/cognitive content of both presuppositional and implicational complements to the verb *see.*

In the following section, we will consider the quantitative distributions of *see* and of different types of complements to the verb *see.*

The Quantitative Data on **See**

Chapter 6 demonstrated that the *see* class of verbs—including *see, look at,* and *look*—occurs significantly more frequently in the O'Connor texts than in the Brown general-fiction corpus. There are at least two more related quantitative issues that can be investigated in the Brown and O'Connor texts: proportion of *see* tokens themselves and proportion of various types of complements to the verb *see*.

Table 12 indicates that the difference in the frequencies of *see* tokens in the Brown vs. O'Connor texts is significant to the .001 level.

In the Brown general-fiction corpus, 2.7 tokens of *see* occur for every thousand words, while the rate in the O'Connor texts is 4.2 per thousand words.

The stylistic impact of this statistical significance could easily be overlooked without pausing to consider the qualitative effect of simply the sheer concentration of the verb *see* in O'Connor's texts, regardless of type of complement. The following, for example, is Ruby Turpin's vision near the end of the story "Revelation":

> A visionary light settled in her eyes. (1) *She saw the streak as a vast swinging bridge extending upward from the earth through a field of living fire.* Upon it a vast horde of souls were rumbling toward heaven. There were whole companies of white-trash, clean for the first time in their lives, and bands of black niggers in white robes, and battalions of freaks and lunatics shouting and clapping and leaping like frogs. And bringing up the end of the procession was a tribe of people whom she recognized at once as those who, like herself and Claud, had always had a little of everything and the God-given wit to use it right. She leaned forward to observe them closer. They were marching behind the others with great dignity, accountable as they had

Table 12. Frequencies of *see* Tokens

Total Words	Brown	O'Connor	Totals
Tokens other than *see*	57,961	292,111	350,072
See tokens	159 *(2.7 per thousand)*	1,248 *(4.2 per thousand)*	1,407
Totals	58,120	293,359	351,479

$\chi^2 = 27.673$, p<.001

always been for good order and common sense and respectable behavior. They alone were on key. (2) *Yet she could see by their shocked and altered faces that even their virtues were being burned away*. She lowered her hands and gripped the rail of the hog pen, her eyes small but fixed unblinkingly on what lay ahead. In a moment the vision faded but she remained where she was, immobile. (*ERMC*, 217–18)

Ruby's revelation, in which the top rail is put on bottom and the bottom on top, is bracketed internally by the verb *see*. The quoted passage begins with an announcement from the narrator that a vision is about to appear to Ruby, hinting that Ruby's long-awaited revelation is soon to come. The passage continues with the clause in (1) with *see* as the main verb, but each of the images in the following sentences is framed by this clause and thus is implicitly seen as well by Ruby. She "sees" that all the classes of people that she knows herself to be superior to not only enter heaven but do so before her. Finally in the sentence marked (2) the narrator uses a finite, presupposed complement clause to *see* to present the paradoxical fact that the fierce and burning heat of God's revelatory fire will burn away the "virtues" of even his most self-righteous of disciples. Thus, the effect of these tokens of *see*, as well as the common effect of the high frequency of *see* tokens in general in O'Connor's fiction, is to frame action and thoughts through characters themselves as focalizers rather than through the narrator. Two terms for this narrational device, which is very close in structure and function to free indirect discourse, are "substitutionary perception" and "narrated perception."[1] One of the general results of focalizing in the passage above through a character like Ruby rather than the narrator is that the narrator can avoid having "to claim" words like *white-trash* and *nigger* as well as the vision in general. It is Ruby Turpin, not the narrator or the narratee, who "sees" the "white-trash" and the "bands of black niggers." However, it is not only O'Connor's hard-headed characters who are given the gift of focalizing sight. In "Good Country People," O'Connor creates a nondescript focalizer in order to generalize observations that she makes about Mrs. Freeman. O'Connor's narrator remarks that Mrs. Freeman has three facial expressions in her dealings with people: neutral, forward, and reverse, just like a "heavy truck." The narrator comments that Mrs. Freeman rarely used the reverse expression "because it was not often necessary for her to retract a statement, but when she did, her face came to a complete stop, there was an almost imperceptible movement of her black eyes, during which they seemed to be receding, and then the observer would see *that Mrs. Freeman, though she might stand there as real as several grain sacks thrown on top of each other, was no longer there in spirit*" (*GM,* 169). This generalized "observer" has the effect of at least potentially making the narratee the focalizer. The finite complement to the verb *see* is presuppositional in this passage, indicating that the narrator and narratee share that background knowledge. A great variety of characters in O'Connor's fictional world focalize the narration at one time or another through the act of seeing, even the famous O'Connor peacocks, as in "The Displaced Person": "The peacock stopped just behind [Mrs. Shortley], his tail—glittering green-gold and blue in the sunlight— lifted just enough so that it would not touch the ground. It flowed out on either side like a floating train and his head on the long blue reed-like neck was drawn back as if his attention were fixed in the distance on something no one else could *see*" (*GM,* 197).

The frequent focalization through the use of *see* in O'Connor's fiction is, then, one of the techniques in modern fiction that make possible what O'Connor calls "the disappearance" of the author. In O'Connor's fiction, the narrator never literally *sees*. O'Connor has no first-person narration, except that produced occasionally within a third-person narration by one of her characters. O'Connor writes in one of her essays that the Victorian novelists "were always coming in, explaining and psychologizing about their characters. But along about the time of Henry James, the author began to tell his story in a different way. He began to let it come through the minds and *eyes* of the characters themselves, and he sat behind the scenes, apparently disinterested. By the time we get to James Joyce, the author is nowhere to be found in the book. The reader is on his own, floundering around in the thoughts of various unsavory characters" (*MM,* 74). That O'Connor uses significantly more *see* tokens than the authors of the Brown general-fiction corpus as a group demonstrates simply that there is more than one way to get rid of the author. But it also demonstrates that O'Connor chose as one of her premier devices for doing so the use of a sight verb that allows both physical and cognitive perception.

O'Connor believed fiercely in a poetics of knowledge through the five senses: "I think we have to begin thinking about stories at a much more fundamental level, so I want to talk about one quality of fiction which I think is its least common denominator—the fact that it is concrete—and about a few of the qualities that follow from this. . . . The beginning of human knowledge is through the senses, and the fiction writer begins where human perception begins. He appeals through the senses, and you cannot appeal to the senses with abstractions" (*MM*, 67). Probably the most obvious result of O'Connor's poetics of knowledge through the senses is her unwavering concentration on physical description, as in Mrs. McIntyre's remembrance of the death of the displaced person Mr. Guizac: "She heard the brake on the large tractor slip and, looking up, she saw it move forward, calculating its own path. Later she remembered that she had seen the Negro jump silently out of the way. . . . She had felt her eyes and Mr. Shortley's eyes and the Negro's eyes come together in one look that froze them in collusion forever, and she had heard the little noise the Pole made as the tractor wheel broke his backbone" (*GM*, 249–50). The sense of hearing frames this scene, in which Mrs. McIntyre first in real time hears the brake slip and second in remembered time, that is, in her imagination or memory, hears Mr. Guizac's back break. It is another sense—vision—that seals the three of them, McIntyre, Shortley, and the Negro, in collusion in the murder of Guizac.

The following are examples from O'Connor's texts, one each of the types of complements to *see* in which we are interested:

Finite Complement

1. he saw now *that his true depravity had been hidden from him lest it cause him despair.* (*GM*, 129)

Present Participial Complement

2. There he saw *a pale ghost-like face scowling at him beneath the brim of a pale ghost-like hat.* (*GM*, 107)

Past Participial Complement

3. he saw *half of the moon five feet away in his shaving mirror, paused as if it were waiting for his permission to enter.* (*GM*, 102)

Bare-stem Complement

4. She saw *a pick-up truck stop at the gate and let off three boys who started walking up the pink dirt road.* (*GM*, 134)

The finite complement in (1) is, of course, part of a cognitive generalization, one of those made, or received, by Mr. Head at the end of "The Artificial

Nigger." All three of the nonfinite complements in (2) through (4) are concrete—(2) and (3) from "The Artificial Nigger" and (4) from "A Circle in the Fire."

One might reason that because O'Connor was committed to the senses as the origin of knowledge the concrete nonfinite physical complements to the verb *see* would predominate in her fiction, as in the intuitive example "He saw him baptize the child." Or given O'Connor's concerns with the fallibility of human reasoning, we might just as well expect more ironic finite complements to the verb *see* than the other more predictably nonfinite concrete types, as in the intuitive example "He saw now that his mission was to baptize the child." In short, in the absence of empirical evidence, one might be tempted to support either prediction.

Table 13 shows the distributions of the four types of complements to *see* in the Brown general-fiction corpus and the O'Connor texts.

The difference in the distribution of the four types of complements to *see* in the Brown and O'Connor texts is not significant to the .001 level (p=.539).[2] If we include the noun-phrase complements and the adverbial complements, the distribution remains statistically non-significant (χ^2=2.450, p=.784). Thus, despite the greater concentration of complements to the verb *see* in O'Connor's texts, the distribution, or proportion, of the different types of complements within the Brown general-fiction

Table 13. Distributions of Types of Complements to *see*

	Brown	O'Connor	Totals
Finite	24 *(36.9%)*	233 *(43.3%)*	257
Bare Stem	11 *(16.9%)*	107 *(19.8%)*	118
Past Participial	8 *(12.3%)*	54 *(10.0%)*	62
Present Participial	22 *(33.8%)*	144 *(26.7%)*	166
Totals	65	538	603

χ^2=2.162, p>.001

corpus and the O'Connor texts is statistically the same. Whatever stylistic concerns led O'Connor to use very high frequencies of *see* complements did not lead her to use various types of those complements in different proportions than the "average" American fiction writer of her time as represented by the Brown general-fiction corpus. The fact that types of complements to the verb *see* are equally distributed along with the fact that the concentration of *see* verbs is unequally distributed in the Brown and O'Connor texts suggests that all four types of complements to the verb *see* are statistically significant in O'Connor's writing. That is, high and statistically equivalent frequencies of both finite and nonfinite complements mark O'Connor's style. In the next section, I resume my analysis of the presuppositional/implicational divide.

Pragmatics vs. Semantics: The Intuitional Data

As I indicated in chapter 6, implication is traditionally considered a semantic phenomenon, that is, one not determined by contextual (pragmatic) factors. One strong argument that presupposition, on the other hand, is a pragmatic phenomenon is that it is contextually "defeasible."[3] That is, the presupposition can be canceled by pragmatic factors, such as the "person"—first, second, or third—of the subject of the matrix verb:

5. a. You realize that Bill is sick.   >> Bill is sick.
    b. You don't realize that Bill is sick.   >> Bill is sick.
6. a. Liz realizes that Bill is sick.   >> Bill is sick.
    b. Liz doesn't realize that Bill is sick. >> Bill is sick.
7. a. I realize that Bill is sick.   >> Bill is sick.
    b. I don't realize that Bill is sick.   ~>> Bill is sick.

When the subject of a factive verb is second or third person, if no other special circumstances occur, the finite complement is presupposed, as is shown in (5) and (6). But if the subject of the factive verb is first person, the finite complement is assumed to be true only in the positive, as in (7a). If the factive verb is negated, the presupposition is canceled, as in (7b), since a speaker cannot presuppose that of which he or she denies any current knowledge.

The subtlety of the pragmatics of presupposition is partially revealed when we note that a simple shift to past tense restores the presupposition to (7b):

8. a. I realized that Bill was sick.   >> Bill was sick.
    b. I didn't realize that Bill was sick.   >> Bill was sick.

Thus, while (7b) shows that a speaker cannot presuppose what s/he denies any current knowledge of, (8b) shows that s/he may presuppose what is now current knowledge and what s/he at one time did not know.

Again, it may have appeared from our examples in chapter 6 that implication is purely semantic, i.e., not dependent on contextual factors. Thus, consider the following:

9. a. Bill saw Liz leave.   > Liz left.
    b. Bill saw Liz leaving.   > Liz was leaving.
    c. Bill saw the house painted.   > The house was painted.

It would seem incontrovertible that if someone positively sees an event occur that that event necessarily, or implicationally, occurred. However, it is perhaps a sign of an overzealous quest for rigorous semantic rules such as implication in linguistics that Robert Kirsner and Sandra Thompson must point out what sounds, once it is pointed out, like a truism: "that people can perceive things which do not exist and events which do not take place." Lakoff makes the same point. Consider the following examples from Kirsner and Thompson:

10. The delirious patient saw the room spinning around him, but we know it wasn't spinning.
11. When the neurologist stimulated that particular area of her brain, Susan saw the light turn red even though it really did not.[4]

Example (10) does not implicate "the room was spinning around him," nor does (11) implicate "the light turned red" for the simple reason that the factivity of the complements is defeated, or canceled, within the sentences in which they occur. The patients may indeed have seen what they are claimed to have seen, but we know that the perceived events did not occur. Thus, just as presuppositions may be canceled on the basis of contextual factors such as person of the matrix-verb subject and tense, the implications of complements to positive matrix verbs may be canceled by means of contextual indications that the perceptions are not real. We may note, however, that absent negation it normally takes more linguistic effort to defeat implications than presuppositions. Examples (12) and (13) illustrate this fact:

12. a. Liz doesn't see that Bill is trying to help his neighbor.
       >>Bill is trying to help his neighbor.
    b. I don't see that Bill is trying to help his neighbor.
       ~>>Bill is trying to help his neighbor.
13. a. Liz saw Bill trying to help his neighbor.
       >Bill was trying to help his neighbor.
    b. I saw Bill trying to help his neighbor.
       >Bill was trying to help his neighbor.
    c. Liz saw Bill trying to help his neighbor, but I know for a fact that
       Bill was just pretending to try to help.
       ~>Bill was trying to help his neighbor.

The differing tenses in (12) and (13) are irrelevant here. Examples (12a)
and (12b) show that all that is required to cancel a presupposition in a
finite complement clause is the change from a third-person subject to a
first-person subject of the matrix verb (i.e., a morphological change).
Examples (13a) and (13b) show that a simple change from third-person
subject to first-person subject does not cancel an implication. Instead, as
(13c) shows, the cancellation of the implication requires here a separate
clause indicating doubt about the epistemic certainty of the complement
to the verb *see*. We will see later in this chapter that doubt about epistemic certainty may be much subtler than is indicated in these intuitional
examples.

One question for linguistics would be why, in most cases, examples like
those in (13a) and (13b) seem unquestionably semantically implicative.
Kirsner and Thompson respond as follows: "The answer, we suggest, is
again a matter of pragmatics. Philosophic speculation about the 'reality' of
sense data has always been a luxury reserved for the very few. For the vast
majority, however, sense data are, in fact, 'all they have.'"[5] Another, parallel
but more grammatically minded, answer would make reference to the
continua of grammatical integration—formal, semantic, and pragmatic.
Nonfinite complements are not categorically more epistemically assured
(implicational) than finite complements (presuppositional). But because of
the scalar phenomena of both epistemic surety and grammatical integration, and because of the iconic links between epistemic surety and grammatical integration, there is greater pragmatic surety, though still less than
absolute, that the nonfinite "implicational" complement to *see* will be true

more frequently, in the absence of negation of the matrix verb, than the finite "presuppositional" complement to *see*.

Presupposition and Implication in O'Connor's Style

As we have seen, both implication and presupposition are important in O'Connor's exploration of the limitations and possibilities of human knowledge. In this section, we will consider the effect of the quality of the backgrounded implications and presuppositions on the foregrounded matrix clause with a *see* verb. Consider example (14), from "The Enduring Chill," in which Asbury is afflicted with what Brainard Cheney called a "green intellectual sickness," etiologically unrelated to his physical illness (*CFOBC,* 131). In (14), Asbury learns that he will live even though he has been convinced that he will die of his mysterious disease.

14. Asbury blanched and the last film of illusion was torn as if by a whirlwind from his eyes. He saw *that for the rest of his days, frail, racked, but enduring, he would live in the face of a purifying terror.* (*ERMC,* 114)

In the story, Asbury returns to his mother's country home from the city to die, he believes, of some mysterious tragic disease in a state of what he believes to be enlightened and intellectual atheism. Instead, Asbury is simply and plainly a son who is overbearingly rude to his loving and self-sacrificing mother, a brother who regularly insults his sister, a writer who can't write, and an intellectual who can't think. It finally comes to light that Asbury is afflicted with undulant fever, contracted from drinking unpasteurized milk in a childish fit of rebellion against his mother. He won't get well, but he neither will he die from the fever. Asbury will live after all, with his intellectualism and atheism exposed as the poses that they are. Father Finn, who Asbury hoped would be as "cynical" and "intelligent" as he is, turns out to be a rather standard, believing, catechism-citing Catholic priest; and he almost immediately senses Asbury's true problem. Asbury demonstrates no knowledge of the catechism, claims that "God is an idea created by man," and says that the Holy Ghost is "the last thing [he's] looking for." Father Finn responds as follows: "How can the Holy Ghost fill your soul when it's full of trash? . . . The Holy Ghost will not come until you see yourself as you are—a lazy ignorant conceited youth!" (*ERMC,* 106–7). After the revelation of his true self, narrated in (14), the Holy Ghost descends in the form of the fierce bird (the water stain) at the end of the story; the priest predicted correctly that Asbury had to see himself as he truly was. Thus, the foregrounded act of seeing in (14) is colored not only by the background of the finite complement, which we as readers now know to be true, but also by the knowledge on the part of the reader that Asbury is finally beginning to see himself clearly. Thus, it is possible for a flawed character to see (understand) correctly, given his or her experience of a revelation.

On the other hand, it is also possible, of course, for there to be an extreme disparity between what is presupposed in the finite complement to *see* and what is known on the part of the audience. Example (15) is from "A View of the Woods," the story of a child (Mary Fortune), her grandfather (Mr. Fortune), Mr. Fortune's murder of Mary Fortune, and Mr. Fortune's subsequent death by heart attack. In (15), Mr. Fortune "sees" that Mary Fortune's opposition to his selling land out from underneath her immediate family is due to his "mistake" in not beating her:

15. Then he saw, with the sudden vision that sometimes comes with delayed recognition, *that that had been his mistake.* . . . He saw *that the time had come, that he could no longer avoid whipping her.* (*ERMC,* 77)

We "know" that Mr. Fortune is incorrect in his visions since (1) Mr. Fortune has been shown to be an old fool and (2) his finite complements involve violence to a child. As the title of the story suggests, however, vision is a central issue of the story. Mary Fortune tells her grandfather seven times in the story that the reason she opposes selling the land so that the buyers can build a filling station on it is that "[w]e won't be able to see the woods across the road" (*ERMC,* 63). Her six siblings, in unison, complain the same. Mr. Fortune, however, has a different vision: "The Fortune place was in the country on a clay road that left the paved road fifteen miles away and he would never have been able to sell off any lots if it had not been for progress, which had always been his ally. He was not one of these old people who fight improvement, who object to everything new and cringe at every change. *He wanted to see a paved highway in front of his house with plenty of new-model cars on it, he wanted to see a supermarket store across the road from him, he wanted to see a gas station, a motel, a drive-in picture-show within easy distance.* . . . He was a man of advanced vision, even if he was seventy-nine years old" (*ERMC,* 57–58). Although the three *see* verbs in the long quotation above are not actually causative, they do contain an element of volitionality, imparted by all occurring inside an infinitive phrase that is the complement of the verb *wanted*. Thus, Mr. Fortune is a typical willful O'Connor character, one who is eventually shown that he cannot escape the woods. After he kills his granddaughter, he has his heart attack and his final vision: "[His heart] expanded so fast that the old man felt as if he were being pulled after it through the woods, felt as if he were running as fast as he could with the ugly pines toward the lake. He perceived that there would be a little opening there, a little place where he could escape and leave the woods behind him. . . . On both sides of him he saw that the gaunt trees had thickened into mysterious dark files that were marching across the water and away into the distance" (*ERMC*, 80–81).

Examples (14) and (15) illustrate the extremes of the reader's likely acceptance or rejection of the truth of literary finite complements to the verb *see*. Many times, the truth is not so obvious, as is illustrated in (16), from "Revelation." In (16), Ruby Turpin has just entered the small, crowded doctor's waiting room:

16. Her little bright black eyes took in all the patients as she sized up the seating situation. There was one vacant chair and a place on the sofa occupied by a blond child in a dirty blue romper who should have been told to move over and make room for the lady. He was five or six, but Mrs. Turpin saw at once *that no one was going to tell him to move over.* (*ERMC,* 191)

Unlike (14), in which we are sure that the presupposed complement to *see* is true, and unlike (15), in which we are sure that the presupposed complement is false, in (16) we are not entirely sure. It could very well be the case that no one will tell him to move over; on the other hand, it could just as well be the case that Mrs. Turpin has unjustly "sized up" the fellow patients in the room. In fact "the pleasant lady" does indirectly tell him to move when she says, "Maybe the little boy would move over" (*ERMC,* 192). The boy does not move, and no one else encourages him to. So, Ruby was in part right and in part wrong. The ambiguity here is typical of this story, just as I have argued elsewhere about the ambiguity of free indirect discourse in this story.[6]

Each of the examples in (14), (15), and (16) contains a finite complement, but the truth of nonfinite complements to positive matrix verbs may be questionable as well, as we know from the last section. Consider the following lengthy passage from "The Displaced Person":

The priest came frequently to see the Guizacs and he would always stop in and visit Mrs. McIntyre too and they would walk around the place and she would point out her improvements and listen to his rattling talk. It suddenly came to Mrs. Shortley that he was trying to persuade her to bring another Polish family onto the place. With two of them here, there would be almost nothing spoken but Polish! The Negroes would be gone and there would be the two families against Mr. Shortley and herself! She began to *imagine* a war of words, to see (1) *the Polish words and the English words coming at each other, stalking forward, not sentences, just words, gabble gabble gabble, flung out high and shrill and stalking forward and then grappling with each other.* She saw (2) *the Polish words, dirty and all-knowing and unreformed, flinging mud on the clean English words until everything was equally dirty.* She saw (3) *them all piled up in a room, all the dead dirty words, theirs and hers too, piled up like the naked bodies in the newsreel.* God save me! she cried silently, from the stinking power of Satan! And she started from that day to read her Bible with a new attention. She [pored] over the Apocalypse and began to quote from the Prophets and before long she had come to a deeper understanding of her existence. She saw plainly (4) *that the meaning of the world was a mystery that had been planned* and she was not surprised to suspect that she had a special part in the plan because she was strong. She saw (5) *that the Lord God Almighty had created the strong people to do what had to be done* and she felt that she would be ready when she was called. Right now she felt that her business was to watch the priest. (*GM*, 216–17)

Each of the complements to the verb *see* is numbered (1) through (5). A problematic question for this study is the location of epistemic doubt and certainty. Both finite and nonfinite complements to *see* can be questionable although finites are, at least, intuitively, more problematic than nonfinites since finites are more cognitive than the more concrete nonfinites. The passage that is quoted above is not unusual in O'Connor in reversing the intuitive expected epistemic certainty of complements to *see*. Although complements (1) through (3) are all nonfinites, and thus should be implicational (beyond doubt as to their truth), their truth is called into question by the italicized infinitive verb *imagine*. Note that the entire first complement in (1) is an appositive to the phrase "to imagine a war of words." The second (2) and third (3) complements are further developments of the first complement, as is revealed by their being complements to the verb *see*, the matrix verb of the first complement in (1). Note, on the other hand, that the finite complements in (4) and (5) are without question, within O'Connor's faith, true. The reversal of contexts in which we assume likelihood of truth and falsity is part of O'Connor's challenge to human rationality in the face of the mystery of God's will and plan. That is, one can know true things by way of revelatory, but literally untrue, visions and even bigots like Mrs. Shortley can "know" God's will and mystery.

The foreground in each of the examples in (14), (15), and (16), and the long quotation from "The Displaced Person" is the act of seeing. The first level of background to the act of seeing is the complement itself. Thus, an unquestionably false complement will shade the act of seeing with false knowledge, while an unquestionably true complement will show the act of seeing to be accurate. But the truth of the complements is frequently in turn determined by the larger background of the tone, or attitude of the narratee toward the character and the character's finite complement. Thus, a partial schematic might be as in figure 9.

Figure 9 minimally illustrates the true multilevel nature of foreground and background. The tone of the narratee is not the absolute foundation, of course. It, too, is determined by a number of issues and forms, such as the word *imagine* in the long quotation from "The Displaced Person," feelings of racial and social superiority in (16), child abuse in (15), and the interaction of violence and Christian grace in (14). Thus, the tone of the narratee would in a fuller, but still necessarily incomplete "diagram," be enclosed by other textual or contextual backgrounds.

Figure 9. Multilevel Foreground and Background

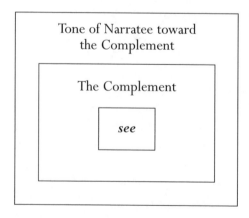

At this point, an analysis of implication and presupposition has helped us to show (1) how O'Connor's fiction presents characters who see spiritually both physically and mentally, (2) how the "truth" of the implications or presuppositions is dependent on the background of the narratee's attitude towards the character and the complement, and (3) how the "truth" of seeing is dependent on the quality of the complement. I must, then, conclude along with Kirsner and Thompson that the truth of implications, like that of presuppositions, is pragmatic, i.e., at least in part determined by "contextual" factors. Thus, one of the few semantic factors remaining standing from our intuitive introduction to implicational vs. presuppositional complements to the verb *see* is the perceptual difference of implicationals being physical and presuppositionals being cognitive and/or physical.

We already know that the physical/cognitive distinction is blurred in finite complements. In the following example, from "Greenleaf," Mrs. May sees a bull racing toward her, just before it gores her:

17. She looked back and saw *that the bull, his head lowered, was racing toward her*. (*ERMC,* 52)

Consider an alternative present participial nonfinite complement in (18):

18. She look back and saw *the bull, his head lowered, racing toward her.*

I would argue that the difference between (17) and (18) is exactly that which is suggested in chapter 6. That is, the finite in (17) is presuppositional and relatively more cognitive even though it has a physical component, while the nonfinite in (18) is implicational and relatively more physical. Context demonstrates the cognitive nature of the finite complement in sentence (17): "In a few minutes something emerged from the tree line, a black heavy shadow that tossed its head several times and then bounded forward. *After a second she saw it was the bull.* He was crossing the pasture toward her at a slow gallop, a gay almost rocking gait as if he were overjoyed to find her again. She looked beyond him to see if Mr. Greenleaf was coming out of the woods too but he was not. 'Here he is, Mr. Greenleaf!' she called and looked on the other side of the pasture to see if he could be coming out there but he was not in sight. *She looked back and saw that the bull, his head lowered, was racing toward her.* She remained perfectly still, not in fright, but in a freezing unbelief" (*ERMC,* 52). Note that Mrs. May is preoccupied with looking for Mr. Greenleaf when she looks back and sees, or rather, recognizes the bull.

Mrs. May, like many of O'Connor's characters, is hardheaded and thinks she is much smarter and more competent than she really is. Thus, the cognitive flavor of her physical perception in the finite complement of (17) is suggestive of her alienation from her own limitations. Before I comment further on the presuppositional nature of sentence (17), let us consider the first italicized sentence in the long quotation above, repeated in (19):

19. After a second she saw *it was the bull.*

Sentence (19) cannot be transformed into a nonfinite complement, but instead only into a simple transitive clause, as in (20):

20. After a second she saw *the bull.*

The difference between (19) and (20) is essentially the difference between (17) and (18). That is, (19) is more cognitive than the physically perceptual (20). In the long quotation above, Mrs. May does not initially recognize the bull because she is distracted and bored waiting for Mr. Greenleaf to return. However, the reader already knows that the heavy black shadow is the bull; thus, the narrator presents the information in a presupposed finite clause. The presupposition of sentence (19) suggests presupposition in sentence (17) as well. Thus, the finite complement in (19) hints not only at Mrs. May's alienated cognition but also at a conspiratorial presupposition between the narrator and reader that they already know that the bull is racing towards Mrs. May to kill her. One of the most common patterns in the endings for O'Connor's stories is that her characters "see" or realize a truth just before they die or just after the death of another: the grandmother in "A Good Man Is Hard to Find," Mrs. McIntyre in "The Displaced Person," Mr. Fortune in "A View of the Woods," Sheppard in "The Lame Shall Enter First," Julian in "Everything That Rises Must Converge," and here, Mrs. May in "Greenleaf."

Examples like those in (17) and (19), that is, finite complements that present intellectualized physical perception are common in O'Connor. Consider from "The Enduring Chill" part of Asbury's dream of his burial:

21. He had failed his god, Art, but he had been a faithful servant and Art was sending him Death. He had seen *this* from the first with a kind of mystical clarity. He went to sleep thinking of the peaceful spot in the family burying ground where he would soon lie, and after a while he saw *that his body was being borne slowly toward it while his mother and Mary George*

watched without interest from their chairs on the porch. As the bier was carried across the dam, they could look up and see *the procession reflected upside down in the pond.* (*ERMC,* 103)

First note that even though the first *see* in (21) is simply transitive with the pronoun *this* as an object, the pronoun *this* is coreferential with the entire first sentence of the quotation. Thus, the cognition that Asbury sees "with a kind of mystical clarity" is just another product of his pretentious and pathetic intellectualism. Note that the second *see* verb has a finite complement, even though the complement could just as easily be written in the form of a nonfinite, as in (22):

22. He saw his body being borne slowly toward it while his mother and Mary George watched without interest from their chairs on the porch.

Just as with the finite complements in (17) and (19), the finite complement in (21) serves to flavor Asbury's perception with intellectualism. He is, after all, dreaming, not actually perceiving anything. And note finally that in the last sentence of (21), the complement to the verb *see* is nonfinite, reflecting the non-cognitive flavoring of Asbury's mother and sister's, rather than his own, perceptions.

Thus far, although the detailed treatment of literary examples may be new, what I have shown about the blend of cognition and physical perception in finite complements is not surprising, given the possibility of just such a blend demonstrated in chapter 6. That same chapter claimed through the use of intuitional data to show that nonfinite complements are purely physically perceptual. However, like finite complements, nonfinite complements may also suggest a blend of cognition and physical perception, as readers might have noticed already in the long quotation earlier in this chapter from "The Displaced Person." There we read that Mrs. Shortley saw, for example, "the Polish words, dirty and all-knowing and unreformed, flinging mud on the clean English words until everything was equally dirty" (*GM,* 217). Mrs. Shortley's xenophobia has no boundaries. She hates the language as well as the people, and that hatred colors her nonfinite perceptions. The nonfinite cognitively flavored complements in (23) occur in "Everything That Rises Must Converge":

23. His eyes were narrowed and through the indignation he had generated, he saw *his mother across the aisle, purple-faced, shrunken to the dwarf-like*

> proportions of her moral nature, sitting like a mummy beneath the ridiculous ban-
> ner of her hat. (*ERMC*, 15)

I have pointed out earlier in this chapter the fallacious nature of much material presented in nonfinite complements to the verb *see* (e.g., anyone seeing
hallucinations is not perceived to be "seeing" implicational propositions). In
(23), Julian is reported as seeing his mother, but the past participial and
present participial are not wholly physical perceptions. Nonfinite complements are "normally" physically direct, but here as in many other nonfinite
complements like those in the earlier long quotation from "The Displaced
Person," there is a strongly subjective and cognitive content. Thus, Julian—
one of O'Connor's many self-righteous "intellectuals" and "liberals"—
harshly judges his mother's "dwarf-like" attitudes towards blacks and her
appearance "like a mummy beneath the ridiculous banner of her hat." Note
that the subjective and cognitive nature of the nonfinite complements in
(23) lies not in the nonfinite verbs themselves—*faced*, *shrunken*, *sitting*—but
instead in the modificational material (i.e., the background to the participials), here in the modifier *purple* and mainly in the prepositional phrases: "to
the dwarf-like proportions of her moral nature," "like a mummy," and
"beneath the ridiculous banner of her hat." An even more complex example,
from *The Violent Bear It Away*, follows in (24):

24. He saw them dark grey, *shadowed with knowledge*, and the knowledge
    moved like tree reflections in a pond where far below the surface shad-
    ows a snake may glide and disappear. (*VBA*, 56)

In (24), Young Tarwater imagines the eyes of his uncle Rayber. Again, the cognitive content of the participial *shadowed* is buried in the prepositional phrase
"with knowledge." The word *knowledge* is then elaborated in a simile in which
images of sin and knowledge glide like snakes among the reflections of tree
limbs deep below the surface of the water. Patterns such as these, in which
syntactic material serves as background to the participial verbs, which in
turn serve as background to the verb *see*, demonstrate both the multileveled
nature of foregrounding and backgrounding and one mechanism that allows
nonfinite complements to be colored by cognitive content.

The levels of foregrounding and backgrounding sketched in figure 9 and
argued for in the examples in (23) and (24) are not simply interpretive
tropes. For example, O'Connor's famous "as if" construction is frequently
the adverbial background not to the verb *see* but instead to the nonfinite

complements that are in turn background to the verb *see*, as in the following examples:[7]

25. Then she saw *a heavy form some distance away, paused as if observing her.* (*ERMC*, 47)
26. In a few minutes they saw *a car some distance away on top of a hill, coming slowly as if the occupants were watching them.* (*GM*, 20)
27. he saw *half of the moon five feet away in his shaving mirror, paused as if it were waiting for his permission to enter.* (*GM*, 102)

O'Connor's "as if" construction is in its essence cognitive because it registers an interpretation of an event or state as a quasi simile. The event or state is hypothetically likened to another event or state. Thus, in (25), Mrs. May in "Greenleaf" sees the bull that is to kill her and interprets his pausing as taking an opportunity to watch her. In (26), the family in "A Good Man Is Hard to Find" sees the car carrying The Misfit and his gang, who are to kill them all, approaching and interprets the car's pace to be the result of the occupants going slow to watch them. And in (27), Mr. Head in "The Artificial Nigger" interprets the moon's hesitation as politeness. Again, these quasi similes modify the participial rather than the verb *see*.

This chapter has demonstrated that most of the intuitive distinctions between finite and nonfinite complements are compromised in the arena of O'Connor's literary texts. Those compromises reveal the thematic complexity of vision and knowledge in O'Connor's world. The final chapter of *Narrating Knowledge* will address some issues of scope and thoroughness of analysis in stylistics and will briefly treat some of the historical issues in the interaction of literary theory, linguistics, and stylistics.

Chapter 8

History and Conclusions

> *The meaning of a story should go on expanding for the reader*
> *the more he thinks about it, but meaning cannot be captured in*
> *an interpretation.*
>
> —Flannery O'Connor (*HB*, 437)

This concluding chapter serves two functions. First, it briefly situates *Narrating Knowledge* within the history of the interaction of linguistics and literature in America. As part of the historical context for the book, I will show that probably the most promising development for stylistics in the post-structuralist interaction of linguistics and literary theory is the common interest in what both ordinary language and literary language can tell us about the nature of both literature and language themselves. The chapter ends with a discussion of some further stylistic work that could be done on O'Connor's work, even in the areas of negation and vision, thus demonstrating that *Narrating Knowledge* tackles only a small chunk of the enormous amount of work that can be done in a linguistic analysis of O'Connor's fiction.

History

In order to appreciate what has been attempted in *Narrating Knowledge* (as well as what has not), readers perhaps need to be reminded of some of the issues that have been involved in the history of the interaction between linguistic and literary theory in the United States. From the beginning of the establishment of the study of English literature as a university discipline in the late nineteenth century, one of the abiding questions in the never-ending quest to define and delimit literary studies has been, "What are we going to do with linguistics, or English philology?" In 1886, James Morgan Hart, Professor of Modern Languages and Literature at the University of Cincinnati, asks in the pages of a new journal, *Transactions of the Modern Language Association of America*, what is historically the central and most recurrent question of literary studies: "What does *not* rightfully pertain to English Literature?" (italics in original). Hart argues that this "main question resolves itself into three: What are we to do with Logic, with Rhetoric, with English Philology (Anglo Saxon and Early English)?" Logic was irretrievably claimed by mathematics, philosophy, and science, as Hart himself saw happening at the time. Rhetoric all but withered away, except for its atrophied but profitable form in composition classes, although it has in recent years made a strong professional comeback. The guest that just wouldn't go away has been philology, or its modern offspring, linguistics. Thus, early on in the history of literary studies, literary critics and professors defined themselves at least in part negatively by saying what they were not. Now, if literary study is not logic, rhetoric, or philology, then what is it, or what was it? For Hart it was, variously, the study of life, feelings, thought, and how to read. Specifically, "The proper object of literary study, in one word, is to train us to *read*, to grasp an author's personality in all its bearings" (italics in original).[1] The personality of the author would itself, along with rhetoric, logic, and linguistics, form part of the negative definition of literary studies for the New Critics in a later generation of literary theorists.

In 1925, some thirty-nine years after Hart, Leonard Bloomfield busily set about building his own fence when he attempted to justify the establishment of the Linguistic Society of America to the "layman" in another new journal, *Language*. Reading Bloomfield's essay, one gets the feeling that Bloomfield adopted the strategic fictional lay audience rather than make clear what he was actually doing—preaching to the choir: "Let it not be taken invidiously, if we say, in particular, that linguistics cannot be properly viewed as a subsidiary discipline to the study of literature, or paired with it as 'the linguistic side' of philology, or even placed in any close connection with the study of fine arts, of which literary history and criticism form a part." Bloomfield's mission in this lead article in the first issue of what was to become the most important journal in American linguistics was at least in part to convince linguists to battle the belief both in the general public and in the academic community that "a student of language is merely a kind of crow-baited student of literature." Bloomfield's textbook *Language* has next to nothing to say about literature other than that it "consists of beautiful or otherwise notable utterances."[2] In spite of the exemplars of Edward Sapir's literary book reviews and chapter "Language and Literature" in his own 1921 book *Language*, the loudest and most enduring voices in the days of the establishment of literary studies and linguistics as independent disciplines, at least in the United States, had this much in common: they wanted nothing at all to do with each other.[3]

There have been notable periodic attempts to break down the barriers between linguistics and literary study. In 1958, at the Indiana University "Conference on Style," Roman Jakobson's now famous "Closing Statement: Linguistics and Poetics" itself closed with a statement that today sounds a bit naïve, even if we read it in the context of the heady interdisciplinary hopes of the 1950s and 1960s. After blaming literary critics' lack of faith in "the competence of linguistics to embrace the field of poetics" on "the poetic incompetence of some bigoted linguists," Jakobson closes with, "All of us here, however, definitely realize that a linguist deaf to the poetic function of language and a literary scholar indifferent to linguistic problems and unconversant with linguistic methods are equally flagrant anachronisms."[4] Jakobson's statement itself is probably understood as anachronistic by most contemporary readers.

In spite of Jakobson's call and the willingness of some literary critics to embrace the methods not only of American structuralist and generative grammar but even of French structuralism, there has been strong resistance in the American literary community to the intrusion of linguistic scientism into the humanities shrine. Barbara Herrnstein Smith is typical of some of the more strident post-structuralists in her caricature of linguistic method and terminology as "noxious jargon." Because both stylistics and literary structuralism were allied with the science of linguistics, critiques of them, not surprisingly, sound very much alike. Smith is a little more creative than most but consequently less intelligible when she calls for structuralism to break free of linguistics. In his famous "What Is Stylistics and Why Are They Saying Such Terrible Things about It?" Stanley Fish similarly reflects the literary outrage over the intrusion of the science of linguistics into literary studies when he argues that stylistics is part of the general "impulse to escape from the flux and variability of the human situation to the security and stability of a timeless formalism."[5]

Perhaps the best modern examples of an importation of "literary" concerns in linguistics are a result not of a direct borrowing of literary theory but instead a shared interest in post-structuralism. For example, many post-structuralist functionalist linguists question the value of investigating any so-called autonomous grammar—i.e., one which is autonomous from social determination, particularly in the form of social (conversational) interaction. Roy Harris puts the case most succinctly when he argues that "languages presuppose communication," rather than, as in the structuralist view, "communication presupposes languages." For example, the notion of communicative competence in structuralist pragmatics usually assumes a stable base of Saussurian langue or Chomskian linguistic competence on which to build knowledge of how to use language in particular social contexts. On the other hand, Harris calls for a linguistics based on the premise that whatever language structure there may be exists as a result of social context and communication.[6] Many American linguists have investigated much the same thesis using different approaches and terminology, e.g., Paul Hopper's "emergent grammar," or T. Givón's "syntacticization" of discourse, or John Du Bois's "ecology of grammar," or Wallace Chafe's "flow of consciousness." Although Du Bois stresses that the responsibility for the shape of a language is shared equally by discourse constraints and the relatively fixed structure of the language, all of these post-structuralist linguists, and others like them, share with post-structuralist literary theorists, like Fish, and philosophers, like Richard Rorty, the theoretical orientation that, as Hopper expresses it, "grammar [or literary meaning, or philosophical consensus] . . . must be viewed as a real-time, social phenomenon, and therefore is temporal; its structure is always deferred, always in a process but never arriving, and therefore emergent." In reference to what Hopper suggests is one of the primary goals of the field of emergent grammar— to study the strategies that writers and speakers tend to use again and again to construct texts—Michael Toolan comments that the goal is "remarkably akin to what some stylisticians already do." He writes, "At the level of individual texts or individual authors, this has long been a goal of stylistic analyses."[7]

One of the more interesting and revealing suggestions resulting from the general merger of concerns of post-structuralist literary theory and functional linguistics is put forward by Christopher Norris, who argues that the linguistic investigation of ordinary language is disappointingly narrow because linguists' preconceptions of ordinary language are impoverished. Norris contends that linguists should turn to literature for data since there one sees a linguistic creativity that is much more reflective of human language than the closed-system creativity that Chomsky, among others, looks for in "ordinary" language.[8] My approach to linguistics in *Narrating Knowledge* shows the influence of post-structuralism to the degree that my analyses reflect the change in the allowable database that Norris calls for. In the last twenty-five years, the object of study in mainstream linguistics has expanded from intuitional data to include both naturally occurring oral data and written, or even literary, language. The expansion of the database, or in the case of corpus linguistics, the return to more traditional data sources, has importantly foregrounded the influence of genre and context on both linguistic form and meaning. The attention to naturally occurring oral language has already had a far-reaching influence that is by now probably beginning to be taken for granted. For example, Barbara Fox and Sandra Thompson have only as recently as 1987 and 1990 radically revised Edward Keenan and Bernard Comrie's hypotheses about the structure and function of relative clauses, primarily through analysis of naturally occurring English oral conversation. On the basis of written texts, Keenan had concluded in 1975 that the ease with which subjects are relativized (compared to other grammatical relations) reflects a cognitive subject primacy. In 1987, Fox first showed that in naturally occurring oral conversation, there is no such subject primacy at least with regard to relativization strategies. Subjects of intransitive verbs and objects of transitive verbs were equally likely to be relativized upon. Relativization on subjects of transitive verbs, common in written language, is exceedingly rare in oral conversation. Fox in her 1987 paper and Fox and Thompson in their paper show that relativizations on subjects of intransitives and objects of transitives are well-motivated by the discourse demands of characterization of new discourse referents and identification of new discourse referents, respectively. Adding data from both first-person and third-person literary narratives, Karen Milton and I show that distributions of various types of relativizations are due more to the discourse demands of genre than any "unmarked" or structurally favored type of relativization.[9]

Finally, there is rarely anything really new in post-structuralism that hasn't been at least foreshadowed, sometimes very strongly, by earlier literary movements. For example, post-structuralist diffusion of meaning is foreshadowed in the New Critical argument against the paraphrasability of meaning in literary language. The New Critics were not the first to argue the ordinary/literary language division, but they were the first to matter in twentieth-century America. Their argument, essentially the same as that of the Russian formalists, was that literary language is different from ordinary language in that it defamiliarizes, or makes strange, our ordinary, prosaic ways of understanding the world. Flannery O'Connor was raised as a writer on New Critical theory, primarily through Caroline Gordon. For example, in the following passage from one of her many talks on the craft of writing, O'Connor echoes the New Critical party line on paraphrasability: "When you can state the theme of a story, when you can separate it from the story itself, then you can be sure the story is not a very good one. . . . A story is a way to say something that can't be said any other way, and it takes every word in the story to say what the meaning is. . . . When anybody asks what a story is about, the only proper thing is to tell him to read the story" (*MM*, 96).

Conclusions

Two well-recognized problems in the contemporary quantitative study of literature in stylistics are that the meaning of particular forms is diffuse and the converse, that literary effect is spread in a diffuse manner through the text. The first point recognizes the impossibility of finding a specific unique meaning for any particular form, and the second point suggests the impossibility of explaining (or even paraphrasing) the full literary effect of any text. The bulk of each of the chapters in *Narrating Knowledge* on particular linguistic forms has shown that the stylistic meanings of presupposition, negation, and verb complementation are heavily context-dependent. First of all, the entire analysis has been framed by O'Connor's concerns with the limitations of human knowledge. Furthermore, the analyses of the specific forms in the texts were framed by William Labov's analysis of narrative structure, as was detailed in chapter 2. Specifically, all forms that were analyzed were departures from main narrative syntax as they serve as various types of evaluation to the main narrative. Note that regardless of the contextual determination of stylistic meaning or significance each examined form has a clear operational definition. Each form provides several types of background significance to the foregrounded narrative events. For example, chapter 3 developed a typology of the functions of presupposition in O'Connor's fiction. The statistical analyses of the distributions of negation, perceptual verbs, and verb complements in later chapters also demonstrate the fundamental contextual nature of stylistic variation. For example,

O'Connor's fictional dialogue is stylistically marked for relatively heavy analytic negation as is demonstrated by the comparison of her dialogue with her own narrative passages and with the Brown general-fiction corpus. Similarly, her fiction is marked for heavy concentration of *see* verbs, although statistical analysis shows that the types of complements to those *see* verbs are distributed in approximately the same proportions in the O'Connor texts and the Brown texts. Finally, the essential contextual nature of the significance of all of these patterns—presupposition, negation, and complements—has been revealed in how they may be mined for the endless complexity of O'Connor's explorations of reason and faith.

In support of the second point—that literary effect is spread in a diffuse manner through the text—one could argue the incontestable view that the stylistic quality of O'Connor's exploration of knowledge has not been exhausted by my analysis of presupposition, supposition, and implication. As Geoffrey Leech and Michael Short argue, there is no mesh "fine enough" to capture all of the linguistic features that "contribute to readers' feeling for differences of style."[10] Negation, presuppositional constructions in general, and complements to the verb *see* constitute a mesh through which a great deal, perhaps especially about the topic of knowledge in Flannery O'Connor's fiction, can slip past.

What characterizes O'Connor's style is obviously much more than the features of negation and vision; however, I have not exhausted even these topics in this book. For example, Gerald Prince has made a three-part distinction in negative events, that is, events that are not those occurring in the text. First, there is the *nonnarratable*, with several subtypes, one of which is that which "defies the powers of a particular narrator." Consider the following exchange, which occurs between The Misfit and the grandmother just after Bobby Lee and Hiram, The Misfit's compatriots, take the mother, the baby, and June Star off into the woods to murder them just as they murdered Bailey and John Wesley:

> There was a piercing scream from the woods, followed closely by a pistol report. "Does it seem right to you, lady, that one is punished a heap and another ain't punished at all?"
>
> "Jesus!" the old lady cried. "You've got good blood! I know you wouldn't shoot a lady! I know you come from nice people! Pray! Jesus, you ought not to shoot a lady. I'll give you all the money I've got!"

"Lady," The Misfit said, looking beyond her far into the woods, "there never was a body that give the undertaker a tip."

There were two more pistol reports and the grandmother raised her head like a parched old turkey hen crying for water. (*GM*, 28)

I estimate, given the natural rhythms of speech, that there are a good fifteen seconds between the first shot and the final two shots. We do not know who is murdered first and who second and third. And we do not know what happened in those terrible fifteen seconds, in which at least one or both of the mother and June Star had to look at the dead body or bodies (Bailey and John Wesley) of their family members. This information remains nonnarratable since the narrator is limited mostly to the grandmother's point of view.

Prince's second category is the *nonnarrated*, events that occur but that are not told about, at least initially, and perhaps for the duration of the narration, even though the narrator has the power to narrate them. I illustrated this pattern briefly in chapter 2 with the nonnarration of Enoch's passage downtown to the business district, where his wise blood wants him to be as he gradually accepts his duty to steal the museum mummy for Hazel. Another such example is the following, which does not narrate the actual crash of the family's car in "A Good Man Is Hard to Find":

The instant the valise moved, the newspaper top she had over the basket under it rose with a snarl and Pitty Sing, the cat, sprang onto Bailey's shoulder.

The children were thrown to the floor and their mother, clutching the baby, was thrown out the door onto the ground; the old lady was thrown into the front seat. The car turned over once and landed right-side-up in a gulch off the side of the road. (*GM*, 18–19)

The gap between Pitty Sing's springing onto Bailey's shoulder and the children's being thrown on the floor of the car is filled only by the reader's background knowledge of car-crash scripts. Prince's third category, the *disnarrated*, "covers all the events that *do not* happen but, nonetheless, are referred to (in a negative or hypothetical mode) by the narrative text" (italics in original).[11] The disnarrated is, by definition, the category that covers *not* negation, the subject of chapters 4 and 5. And, of course, those chapters are limited to the negative word *not* and its contraction; they cover none of the synthetic negations like *never, nor,* and *nothing* and none of the various others of Labov's comparators.

As an idea of the sort of further detail that one could squeeze from "vision" in Flannery O'Connor, given another chapter or two, consider O'Connor's "A Circle in the Fire," a story concerned with a farm matron (Mrs. Cope), her hired help (Mrs. Pritchard), her daughter (Sally Virginia), and three juvenile delinquents who set the woods on fire. The story is largely narrated with Sally Virginia as the focalizer, and her focalization is achieved almost entirely by references to what she is looking at and where she is when she is looking. The following sentence is the third of "A Circle in the Fire"; neither of the previous two sentences has even mentioned "the child": "She [Mrs. Pritchard] and the child's mother [Mrs. Cope] were underneath the window the child was looking down from" (*GM,* 130). This is an exceedingly odd sentence. First, the possessive construction "the child's" is cataphoric, meaning that one must look forward for its reference, and even then the nearest reference is simply "the child." Sally Virginia's name is mentioned only once in the story, by her mother. Thus, one ground-ing device for the referent "mother," the possessive construction, is sub-verted since we don't know who the child is yet. Then, a second grounding device is subverted—the relative clause that modifies "the window": "the child was looking down from." Normally at least one referent in a relative clause with two participants will be central in the awareness of the hearer because that referent serves as the grounding device for the head of the rela-tive clause.[12] However, the child's identity is still unknown at this point. Once established, however oddly, as the focalizer, Sally Virginia diligently provides the point of view for the remainder of the story. She is the one who first notices the arrival of the three boys: "The child could see over to where the dirt road joined the highway. She saw a pick-up truck stop at the gate and let off three boys who started walking up the pink dirt road" (*GM,* 134). The boys' first discussions with Mrs. Cope and Mrs. Pritchard are observed by Sally Virginia on one side of the house. Then, Mrs. Cope sends the boys to the other side of the house so that she can serve them sand-wiches: "The child moved from the right bedroom across the hall and over into the left bedroom and looked down on the other side of the house where there were three white lawn chairs and a red hammock strung between two hazelnut trees. . . . The three boys came around the corner of the house" (*GM,* 137). The deictic orientation of the verb form *came*, rather than *went*, signals that the narrator describes the scene and events from Sally Virginia's point of view. That is, we see what she sees, regardless of whether the narrator uses the verb *see* or any other verb of sight. One of the most remarkable scenes in O'Connor's texts for point of view occurs after the child hears "her mother and Mrs. Pritchard in a muted conference in the kitchen." O'Connor plays comically with the technique of limited perspective: "She got up and went out into the hall and leaned over the banisters. Mrs. Cope's and Mrs. Prichard's legs were facing each other in the back hall" (*GM,* 138).

"A Circle in the Fire" is a typical O'Connor story in its central theme of the loss of innocence and the subsequent entry into the world of sorrow. Sally Virginia is clearly not only the focalizer but also the central character in the coming-of-age thread. She watches, she sees, she looks, and she learns. Only once does she reveal herself to the three boys—when she sticks her head out of the upper window and makes an ugly face at them. When she, her mother, and Mrs. Pritchard drive down to the road, where the three juveniles sit throwing stones at the mailbox, O'Connor writes that Sally Virginia "had a furious outraged look on her face but she kept her head drawn back from the window so that they couldn't see her" (*GM,* 148). Sally Virginia sees the three boys running and swimming naked in the back pasture, but she remains unseen by them even as they set fire to the woods. Finally, in the last paragraph of the story, Sally Virginia's roles as focalizer and initiate into the sorrow of the world come together when she observes her mother watching her woods burn: "The child came to a stop beside her mother and stared up at her face as if she had never seen it before. It was the face of the new misery she felt, but on her mother it looked old and it looked as if it might have belonged to anybody, a Negro or a European or to Powell himself" (*GM,* 154). All of this fine detail was missed in my analysis of the verb *see* in chapters 6 and 7, and even this analysis, which has called on evidence not only from the verb *see* and other verbs of sight but also from deictic verb orientation and from literary context itself, has undoubtedly itself missed considerable detail related to the theme of knowing.

If there is any lesson to take away from any reading of O'Connor's fiction it is surely that we don't know quite as much as we might think we do. The measure of all literary analysis is not how much one manages to cover in the analysis nor how "objective" one is but instead how tight the focus of one's lens is and how thoroughly the focused area is explored. In other words, the goal is not knowing, but seeing, in all its cognitive and physical ambiguities.

Notes

Chapter 1

1. For a discussion of O'Connor's attempts to control the interpretation of her works, see James M. Mellard, "Flannery O'Connor's Others: Freud, Lacan, and the Unconscious," *American Literature* 61 (1989): 625–43.

2. Jane Carter Keller, "The Figures of the Empiricist and the Rationalist in the Fiction of Flannery O'Connor," *Arizona Quarterly* 28 (1972): 263–73; Jane Marston, "Epistemology and the Solipsistic Consciousness in Flannery O'Connor's 'Greenleaf,'" *Studies in Short Fiction* 21, no. 4 (1984): 375–82; John F. McCarthy, "Human Intelligence Versus Divine Truth: The Intellectual in Flannery O'Connor's Works," *English Journal* 55 (1966): 1143; John F. Desmond, *Risen Sons: Flannery O'Connor's Vision of History* (Athens: University of Georgia Press, 1987), 36; Carol Shloss, *Flannery O'Connor's Dark Comedies: The Limits of Inference* (Baton Rouge: Louisiana State University Press, 1980), 48; Edward Kessler, *Flannery O'Connor and the Language of Apocalypse* (Princeton: Princeton University Press, 1986), 75; Stephen C. Behrendt, "Knowledge and Innocence in Flannery O'Connor's 'The River,'" *Studies in American Fiction* 17, no. 2 (1989): 145, 147; Bob Dowell, "The Moment of Grace in the Fiction of Flannery O'Connor," *College English* 27 (1965): 236; Michael L. Schroeder, "Ruby Turpin, Job, and Mystery: Flannery O'Connor on the Question of Knowing," *Flannery O'Connor Bulletin* 21 (1992): 75–83; Zhong Ming, "Designed Shock and Grotesquerie: The Form of Flannery O'Connor's Fiction," *Flannery O'Connor Bulletin* 17 (1988): 51–61; Miles Orvell, *Invisible Parade: The Fiction of Flannery O'Connor* (Philadelphia: Temple University Press, 1972), 18; Frederick Asals, *Flannery O'Connor: The Imagination of Extremity* (Athens: University of Georgia Press, 1982), 214; Jeanne Campbell Reesman, "Women, Language, and the Grotesque in Flannery O'Connor and Eudora Welty," in *Flannery O'Connor: New Perspectives,* ed. Sura P. Rath and Mary Neff Shaw (Athens: University of Georgia Press, 1996), 38–56.

3. McCarthy, "Human Intelligence," 1143–48; Joyce Carol Oates, "The Visionary Art of Flannery O'Connor," *Southern Humanities Review* 7 (1973): 235–46; Richard H. Rupp, "Fact and Mystery: Flannery O'Connor," *Commonweal* 79 (1963): 304–7; Joseph Louis Zornado, "Flannery O'Connor: A Fiction of Unknowing" (Ph.D. diss., University of Connecticut, 1992).

4. For metaphor and simile, see David R. Mayer, "'Like Ticks off a Dog': Flannery O'Connor's 'As If,'" *Christianity and Literature* 33, no. 4 (1984): 17–34; Kessler,

Language of Apocalypse. For modes of speech presentation, see Dale Leslie Ludwig, "Controlled Distance: Internal Character Presentation in Flannery O'Connor's Short Stories" (Ph.D. diss., University of Illinois at Urbana-Champaign, 1988); Donald E. Hardy, "Free Indirect Discourse, Irony, and Empathy in Flannery O'Connor's 'Revelation,'" *Language and Literature* (San Antonio) 16 (1991): 37–53; Donald E. Hardy, "The Dialogic Repetition of Free Indirect Discourse in Oral and Literary Narrative," in *Repetition in Dialogue,* ed. Carla Bazzanella (Tübingen: Niemeyer, 1996), 90–103, 174–91. For onomastics, see Paul F. Ferguson, "Onomastic Revisions in Flannery O'Connor's *Wise Blood,*" *Literary Onomastics Studies* 13 (1986): 97–110; Emily Archer, "Naming in the Neighborhood of Being: O'Connor and Percy on Language," *Studies in the Literary Imagination* 20, no. 2 (1987): 97–108. For rhetorical exhortation, Laura B. Kennelly, "Exhortation in *Wise Blood:* Rhetorical Theory as an Approach to Flannery O'Connor," in *Flannery O'Connor: New Perspectives,* ed. Sura P. Rath and Mary Neff Shaw (Athens: University of Georgia Press, 1996), 152–68.

5. Shloss, *Dark Comedies,* 98, 108.

6. Tony McEnery and Andrew Wilson, *Corpus Linguistics* (Edinburgh: Edinburgh University Press, 1996), 4–10.

7. The following are the sources for the K subcorpus of the Brown Corpus, which is used in the quantitative analyses of chapters 4, 6, and 7.

> K01. Christopher Davis, *First Family* (New York: Coward McCann, 1961), 204–10.
>
> K02. Clayton C. Barbeau, *The Ikon* (New York: Coward McCann, 1961), 80–85.
>
> K03. Tristram Coffin, *Not to the Swift* (New York: W. W. Norton, 1961), 200–4.
>
> K04. W. E. B. DuBois, *Worlds of Color* (New York: Mainstream Publishers, 1961), 134–39.
>
> K05. David Stacton, *The Judges of the Secret Court* (New York: Pantheon Books, 1961), 50–56.
>
> K06. Louis Zara, *Dark Rider* (Cleveland, Ohio: World Publishing Company, 1961), 40–44.
>
> K07. Francis Pollini, *Night* (Boston: Houghton Mifflin Company, 1961), 246–52.
>
> K08. Guy Endore, *Voltaire! Voltaire!* (New York: Simon and Schuster, 1961), 96–100.
>
> K09. Howard Fast, *April Morning* (New York: Crown Publishers, 1961), 130–36.

K10. Glayds H. Barr, *The Master of Geneva* (New York: Holt, Rinehart and Winston, 1961), 152–57.

K11. Robert Penn Warren, *Wilderness* (New York: Random House, 1961), 162–70.

K12. Gerald Green, *The Heartless Light* (New York: Charles Scribner's Sons, 1961), 166–70.

K13. William Maxwell, *The Chateau* (New York: Alfred A. Knopf, 1961), 240–45.

K14. Irving Stone, *The Agony and the Ecstasy* (Garden City, N.Y.: Doubleday, 1961), 294–98.

K15. Ann Hebson, *The Lattimer Legend* (New York: The Macmillan Company, 1961), 190–95.

K16. Stephen Longstreet, *Eagles Where I Walk* (Garden City, N.Y.: Doubleday, 1961), 92–96.

K17. Leon Uris, *Mila 18* (New York: Doubleday, 1961), 324–29.

K18. John Dos Passos, *Midcentury* (Boston: Houghton Mifflin, 1961), 94–98.

K19. Robert L. Duncan, *The Voice of Strangers* (Garden City, N.Y.: Doubleday, 1961), 242–48.

K20. Guy Bolton, *The Olympians* (Cleveland, Ohio, and New York: World Publishing, 1961), 128–34.

K21. Bruce Palmer, "My Brother's Keeper," in *Many Are the Hearts* (New York: Simon & Schuster, 1961), 132–38.

K22. John Cheever, "The Brigadier and the Golf Widow," *New Yorker,* 11 November 1961, 53–54.

K23. Frieda Arkin, "The Light of the Sea," in *The Best American Short Stories,* ed. Martha Foley and David Burnett (Boston: Houghton Mifflin, 1961), 2–6.

K24. W. H. Gass, "The Pedersen Kid," in *The Best American Short Stories,* ed. Martha Foley and David Burnett (Boston: Houghton Mifflin, 1962), 110–15.

K25. Arthur Miller, "The Prophecy," in *The Best American Short Stories,* ed. Martha Foley and David Burnett (Boston: Houghton Mifflin, 1962), 258–62.

K26. Jane Gilmore Rushing, "Against the Moon," *Virginia Quarterly Review* 37, no. 3 (1961): 378–83.

K27. E. Lucas Myers, "The Vindication of Dr. Nestor," *Sewanee Review* 69, no. 2 (1961), 290–95.

K28. Sallie Bingham, "Moving Day," *Atlantic Monthly,* November 1961, 63–65.

K29. Marvin Schiller, "The Sheep's in the Meadow," *Antioch Review* 21, no. 3 (1961), 336–40.

8. For details on TACT, see Ian Lancashire et al., *Using TACT with Texts: A Guide to Text-Analysis Computing Tools* (New York: Modern Language Association of America, 1996); Eric Rochester, "New Tools for Analyzing Texts," *Language and Literature* (London) 10 (2001): 187–91.

9. Douglas Biber, Susan Conrad, and Randi Reppen, *Corpus Linguistics: Investigating Language Structure and Use* (Cambridge: Cambridge University Press, 1998), 255–56.

10. William Labov, "The Transformation of Experience in Narrative Syntax," in *Language in the Inner City: Studies in the Black English Vernacular* (Philadelphia: University of Pennsylvania Press, 1972), 354–96; William Labov and Joshua Waletzky, "Narrative Analysis: Oral Versions of Personal Experience," in *Essays on the Verbal and Visual Arts: Proceedings of the 1966 Annual Spring Meetings of the American Ethnological Society,* ed. June Helm (Seattle: University of Washington Press, 1967), 12–44.

Chapter 2

1. Ferdinand de Saussure, *Course in General Linguistics,* ed. Charles Bally, Albert Sechehaye, and Albert Reidlinger, trans. Wade Baskin (New York: Philosophical Library, 1959), 23–32; Edward Sapir, *Language: An Introduction to the Study of Speech* (New York: Harcourt, Brace and World, 1921), 19–20; Leonard Bloomfield, *Language* (New York: Holt, Rinehart and Winston, 1933), 282; Charles F. Hockett, "The Problem of Universals in Language," in *The View from Language: Selected Essays, 1948–1974* (Athens: University of Georgia Press, 1977), 174.

2. Monika Fludernik, *Towards a 'Natural' Narratology* (New York: Routledge, 1996), 57–60.

3. Eric A. Havelock, *Preface to Plato* (Cambridge: Harvard University Press, 1963); Walter J. Ong, *Orality and Literacy: The Technologizing of the Word* (London: Methuen, 1982); Eric A. Havelock, *The Muse Learns to Write: Reflections on Orality and Literacy from Antiquity to the Present* (New Haven: Yale University Press, 1986), 64.

4. Deborah Tannen, *Talking Voices: Repetition, Dialogue, and Imagery in Conversational Discourse* (Cambridge: Cambridge University Press, 1989); Barbara Johnstone, *Stories, Community, and Place: Narratives from Middle America* (Bloomington: Indiana University Press, 1990); Labov and Waletzky, "Narrative Analysis"; Labov, "Transformation of Experience"; Monika Fludernik, *The Fictions of Language and the Languages of Fiction: The Linguistic Representation of Speech and Consciousness* (London:

Routledge, 1993); Fludernik, *Towards a 'Natural' Narratology;* Suzanne Fleishman, *Tense and Narrativity: From Medieval Performance to Modern Fiction* (Austin: University of Texas Press, 1990).

5. William Labov, "The Transformation of Experience in Narrative Syntax," in *Language in the Inner City: Studies in the Black English Vernacular* (Philadelphia: University of Pennsylvania Press, 1972), 364. This and further references to Labov's book chapter "The Transformation of Experience in Narrative Syntax" are cited in the text with the abbreviation *LIC,* for *Language in the Inner City,* the book in which the chapter appears.

6. Gustav Freytag, *Freytag's Technique of the Drama: An Exposition of Dramatic Composition and Art,* trans. Elias J. MacEwan (Chicago: Griggs, 1895); Mary Louise Pratt, *Toward a Speech Act Theory of Literary Discourse* (Bloomington: Indiana University Press, 1977), 51.

7. I thank Tom Hardy and Heather Hardy for granting me permission to use this narrative in my book. I thank the narrators and students of my graduate and undergraduate courses in discourse analysis at Northern Illinois University for allowing me to use portions of other oral narratives scattered throughout this chapter.

8. John Crowe Ransom, *The World's Body* (Port Washington, N.Y.: Kennikat, 1938), 349; J. Hillis Miller, "Narrative," in *Critical Terms for Literary Study,* ed. Frank Lentricchia and Thomas McLaughlin (Chicago: University of Chicago Press, 1990), 72.

9. Pratt, *Literary Discourse;* Fludernik, *Towards a 'Natural' Narratology.*

10. Kessler, *Language of Apocalypse.*

11. Hardy, "Dialogic Repetition."

12. Marston, "Epistemology and the Solipsistic Consciousness," 376.

13. Kessler, *Language of Apocalypse,* 15.

14. Mayer, "Like Ticks off a Dog."

15. Barbara A. Fox, "The Noun Phrase Accessibility Hierarchy Reinterpreted: Subject Primacy or the Absolutive Hypothesis?" *Language* 63 (1987): 859; Barbara A. Fox and Sandra A. Thompson, "A Discourse Explanation of the Grammar of Relative Clauses in English Conversation," *Language* 66 (1990): 307; Donald E. Hardy and Karen Milton, "The Distribution and Function of Relative Clauses in Literature," *Pragmatics and Language Learning* 5 (1994): 253–54.

16. David J. Townsend and Thomas Gordon Bever, *Main and Subordinate Clauses: A Study in Figure and Ground* (Bloomington: Indiana University Linguistics Club, 1977); Leonard Talmy, "Figure and Ground in Complex Sentences," in *Universals of Human Language,* vol. 4, *Syntax,* ed. Joseph H. Greenberg, Charles A. Ferguson, and Edith A. Moravcsik (Stanford: Stanford University Press, 1978), 625–49; Steven

Wallace, "Figure and Ground: The Interrelationships of Linguistic Categories," in *Tense-Aspect: Between Semantics and Pragmatics,* ed. Paul J. Hopper (Amsterdam: John Benjamins, 1982), 201–23; Tanya Reinhart, "Principles of Gestalt Perception in the Temporal Organization of Narrative Texts," *Linguistics* 22 (1984): 779–809; Donald E. Hardy, "Figure and Ground in the Creek Auxiliary *Oom,*" *Word* 43, no. 2 (1992): 217–31.

17. Kurt Koffka, *Principles of Gestalt Psychology* (New York: Harcourt, Brace and World, 1935), 177ff.

18. Reinhart, "Principles of Gestalt Perception," 781; Seymour Chatman, *Story and Discourse: Narrative Structure in Fiction and Film* (Ithaca: Cornell University Press, 1978), 19–20; Shlomith Rimmon-Kenan, *Narrative Fiction: Contemporary Poetics* (London: Routledge, 1983), 6.

19. Reinhart, "Principles of Gestalt Perception," 787; Jean Jacques Weber, "The Foregound-Background Distinction: A Survey of Its Definitions and Applications," *Language and Literature* (San Antonio) 6 (1983): 1–15; Jan Mukarovsky, "Standard Language and Poetic Language," in *A Prague School Reader,* ed. Paul L. Garvin (Washington: Georgetown University Press, 1964), 18–19; Geoffrey N. Leech and Michael H. Short, *Style in Fiction: A Linguistic Introduction to English Fictional Prose* (London: Longman, 1981), 139; Willie van Peer, *Stylistics and Psychology: Investigations of Foregrounding* (London: Croom Helm, 1986); Labov, *LIC;* Paul Hopper, "Aspect and Foregrounding in Discourse," in *Discourse and Syntax,* vol. 12, ed. T. Givón, *Syntax and Semantics* (New York: Academic Press, 1979), 213–41; Paul Hopper and Sandra A. Thompson, "Transitivity in Grammar and Discourse," *Language* 56 (1980): 251–99; Robert E. Longacre, "A Spectrum and Profile Approach to Discourse Analysis," *Text* 1 (1981): 337–59.

20. For nonnarration, see Gerald Prince, "The Disnarrated," *Style* 22 (1988): 1–8.

21. Jon Lance Bacon, *Flannery O'Connor and Cold War Culture* (Cambridge: Cambridge University Press, 1993), 118–23.

22. Wallace, "Figure and Ground," 212.

23. William Faulker, *The Sound and the Fury* (New York: Modern Library, 1929), 1.

Chapter 3

1. Reinhart, "Principles of Gestalt Perception," 789.

2. Gottlob Frege, "On Sense and Reference," in *Translations from the Philosophical Writings of Gottlob Frege,* ed. Peter Geach and Max Black (Oxford: Blackwell, 1952), 56–78; Bertrand Russell, "On Denoting," *Mind* 14 (1905): 479–93; P. F. Strawson, *Introduction to Logical Theory* (London: Methuen, 1952); Robert C. Stalnaker,

"Pragmatic Presuppositions," in *Semantics and Philosophy,* ed. Milton K. Munitz and Peter K. Unger (New York: New York University Press, 1974), 197–214.

3. Stephen C. Levinson, *Pragmatics* (Cambridge: Cambridge University Press, 1983), 180–81; Stalnaker, "Pragmatic Presuppositions."

4. Donald E. Hardy, "Russell Edson's Humor: Absurdity in a Surreal World," *Studies in American Humor* 6 (1988): 93–100.

5. Levinson, *Pragmatics,* 181–84.

6. Ibid., 183–84.

7. Stalnaker, "Pragmatic Presuppositions"; T. Givón, "Logic vs. Pragmatics, with Human Language as the Referee: Toward an Empirically Viable Epistemology," *Journal of Pragmatics* 6 (1982): 98–101; Umberto Eco and Patrizia Violi, "Instructional Semantics for Presuppositions," *Semiotica* 64 (1987): 4.

8. Hopper and Thompson, "Transitivity in Grammar and Discourse."

9. Sandra A. Thompson, "'Subordination' and Narrative Event Structure," in *Coherence and Grounding in Discourse,* ed. Russell S. Tomlin (Amsterdam: John Benjamins, 1987), 435–53.

10. Stalnaker, "Pragmatic Presuppositions," 202; Givón, "Logic vs. Pragmatics," 101; Eco and Violi, "Instructional Semantics for Presuppositions," 9.

11. Roland Barthes, *S/Z,* trans. Richard Miller (New York: Hill and Wang, 1974); Donald E. Hardy, "Presupposition and the Coconspirator," *Style* 26 (1992): 2.

12. O'Connor used in her posthumously published letters the words *negro, colored,* and *nigger,* but *nigger* was reserved for one of three contexts. The first was in DD or ID quotation of someone whom she considered less than fully enlightened as when she quoted the book editor who gave a reason for not reviewing Brainard Cheney's *This Is Adam* that "it was about niggers" (*CFOBC,* 75). In a 1964 letter to "A," O'Connor comments that one of her hospital nurses "was a dead ringer for Mrs. Turpin. . . . She said she treated everybody alike whether it were a person with money or a black nigger" (*HB,* 569). The second context was in reference to characters in her fiction and their perceptions of blacks. O'Connor wrote to Ben Griffith about Nelson of "The Artificial Nigger," "he not only has never seen a nigger but he didn't know any women and I felt that such a black mountain of maternity would give him the required shock to start those black forms moving up from his unconscious" (*HB,* 78). The third was in her own voice to very close friends, as Barbara Wilkie Tedford has pointed out in "Flannery O'Connor and the Social Classes," *Southern Literary Journal* 13, no. 2 (1981): 28. O'Connor wrote to "A," "I might write a novella about life on the farm with plenty of niggers, poor white trash, and gentry of various kinds" (*HB,* 368). Sally Fitzgerald ("Introduction" to *HB,*

xvi–xvii) and Tedford ("Social Classes," 28) have both argued that in her actions with individuals, both black and white, O'Connor's racial attitudes were remarkably advanced for her time and place. And even though she did use the word *nigger* in her private life and letters and however muddled the distinction between the private and the public may be, it is clear from O'Connor's public self that she did not condone the use of the word or the racist attitudes that it represents and evokes.

13. Asals, *The Imagination of Extremity,* 117.

14. Robert H. Brinkmeyer, Jr., *The Art and Vision of Flannery O'Connor* (Baton Rouge: Louisiana State University Press, 1989), 73–83.

15. Shloss, *Dark Comedies,* 123.

16. Gerald Prince, "On Presupposition and Narrative Strategy," *Centrum* 1 (1973): 23–31; Roger Fowler, "The Referential Code and Narrative Authority," *Language and Style* 10 (1977): 129–61; Chatman, *Story and Discourse,* 209–11; Milton Chadwick Butler, "Factive Predicates and Narrative Point of View," *Texas Linguistic Forum* 13 (1979): 34–39; Jonathan Culler, *The Pursuit of Signs: Semiotics, Literature, Deconstruction* (Ithaca: Cornell University Press, 1981), 100–118; Leech and Short, *Style in Fiction,* 179–80, 213, 239; Helen Aristar Dry and Susan Kucinkas, "Ghostly Ambiguity: Presuppositional Constructions in *The Turn of the Screw,*" *Style* 25 (1991): 71–88; Hardy, "Presupposition and the Coconspirator."

Chapter 4

1. Gunnel Tottie, *Negation in English Speech and Writing: A Study in Variation* (New York: Academic Press, 1991), 17–18.

2. Pratt, *Literary Discourse,* 65–66; Prince, "The Disnarrated"; Harold F. Mosher, Jr., "The Narrated and Its Negatives: The Nonnarrated and the Disnarrated in Joyce's *Dubliners,*" *Style* 27 (1993): 407–27; Labov, *LIC.*

3. Maire Jaanus Kurrik, *Literature and Negation* (New York: Columbia University Press, 1979), ix, 207.

4. Zornado, "A Fiction of Unknowing"; Kimberly Greene Angle, "Flannery O'Connor's Literary Art: Spiritual Portraits in Negative Space," *Flannery O'Connor Bulletin* 23 (1994–95): 158–74.

5. J. F. Burrows, *Computation into Criticism: A Study of Jane Austen's Novels and an Experiment in Method* (Oxford: Clarendon Press, 1987); Greg Watson, *Doin' Mudrooroo: Elements of Style and Involvement in the Early Prose Fiction of Mudrooroo* (Joensuu, Finland: University of Joensuu, 1997), 102; Peter C. Wason, "The Processing of Positive and Negative Information," *Quarterly Journal of Experimental Psychology* 11 (1959): 92–107; Laura Hidalgo Downing, "Negation in Discourse: A Text World

Approach to Joseph Heller's *Catch-22*," *Language and Literature* (London) 9, no. 3 (2000): 215–39; Laura Hidalgo Downing, *Negation, Text Worlds, and Discourse: The Pragmatics of Fiction*, Advances in Discourse Processes, vol. 66, ed. Roy O. Freedle (Stamford, Conn. Ablex, 2000); Paul Werth, *Text Worlds: Representing Conceptual Space in Discourse* (London: Longman, 1999).

6. Joanne Halleran McMullen, *Writing against God: Language as Message in the Literature of Flannery O'Connor* (Macon, Ga.: Mercer University Press, 1996); George L. Dillon, *Language Processing and the Reading of Literature: Toward a Model of Comprehension* (Bloomington: Indiana University Press, 1978), 142; Stanley Fish, "What Is Stylistics and Why Are They Saying Such Terrible Things about It?" in *Is There a Text in This Class? The Authority of Interpretive Communities* (Cambridge: Harvard University Press, 1980), 68–96.

7. T. Givón, *English Grammar: A Function-Based Introduction*, vol. 1 (Amsterdam: John Benjamins, 1993), 189; Peter C. Wason, "The Contexts of Plausible Denial," *Journal of Verbal Learning and Verbal Behavior* 4 (1965): 7; Herbert H. Clark, "Semantics and Comprehension," in *Current Trends in Linguistics*, vol. 12, *Linguistics and Adjacent Arts and Sciences*, ed. Thomas A. Sebeok (The Hague: Mouton, 1974), 1312–13; Stella Vosniadou, "Drawing Inferences from Semantically Positive and Negative Implicative Predicates," *Journal of Psycholinguistic Research* 11 (1982): 80; Laurence R. Horn, *A Natural History of Negation* (Chicago: University of Chicago Press, 1989), 181–82; Tottie, *Negation in English Speech and Writing*, 19–29.

8. Horn, *A Natural History of Negation*, 199.

9. Geoffrey N. Leech, *Principles of Pragmatics* (London: Longman, 1983), 100–102; Horn, *A Natural History of Negation*, 198.

10. Clark, "Semantics and Comprehension," 1316.

11. Givón, *English Grammar*, vol. 1, 190; Eco and Violi, "Instructional Semantics for Presuppositions," 4; Hardy, "Presupposition and the Coconspirator."

12. Zornado, "A Fiction of Unknowing."

13. Martin Heidegger, "What Is Metaphysics?" trans. R. F. C. Hull and Alan Crick, in *Existence and Being* (Chicago: Henry Regnery Company, 1949), 329; Heidegger, *An Introduction to Metaphysics*, trans. Ralph Manheim (New Haven: Yale University Press, 1959), 1.

14. Barthes, *S/Z*, 75–76; Wolfgang Iser, *The Act of Reading: A Theory of Aesthetic Response* (Baltimore: Johns Hopkins University Press, 1976), 185–86.

15. Brian Abel Ragen, *A Wreck on the Road to Damascus: Innocence, Guilt, and Conversion in Flannery O'Connor* (Chicago: Loyola University Press, 1989).

16. Tottie, *Negation in English Speech and Writing*, 17–18.

Chapter 5

1. Donald E. Hardy and Chris Newton, "Why Is She So Negative? Negation and Knowledge in Flannery O'Connor's *A Good Man Is Hard to Find*," *Southwest Journal of Linguistics* 17, no. 2 (1998): 72. no. 2 (1998): 72. Werth, *Text Worlds,* 254. Newton and I actually refer to the "suggestive supposition," but I now prefer the participial form *suggested* since it reflects the supposition's status as created rather than creative.

2. Givón, *English Grammar,* vol. 1, 189.

3. Tottie, *Negation in English Speech and Writing,* 22.

4. Sapir, *Language,* 38.

5. Tottie, *Negation in English Speech and Writing,* 19–21.

6. Prince, "The Disnarrated," 1.

7. Givón, *English Grammar,* vol. 1, 189–90.

8. Tottie, *Negation in English Speech and Writing,* 26; M. Sullivan, *Chinese Art: Recent Discoveries* (London: Thames and Hudson, 1973).

9. Werth, *Text Worlds,* 254–57.

10. Tottie, *Negation in English Speech and Writing,* 35.

11. Downing, *Negation, Text Worlds, and Discourse,* 94; Werth, *Text Worlds,* 254.

12. H. Paul Grice, "Logic and Conversation," in *Pragmatics: A Reader,* ed. Steven Davis (Oxford: Oxford University Press, 1991), 308.

13. Sapir, *Language,* 38.

14. Penelope Brown and Stephen C. Levinson, *Politeness: Some Universals in Language Usage* (Cambridge: Cambridge University Press, 1987).

15. Red Sam's question "Ain't that the truth" is what Randolph Quirk, Sidney Greenbaum, Geoffrey Leech, and Jan Svartvik (*A Comprehensive Grammar of the English Language* [London: Longman, 1985], 825) term an "exclamatory question." Quirk et al. write, "The meaning, contrary to the appearance of the literal wording, is vigorously positive."

16. I show in another publication how presupposition manipulation is used for much the same purpose in a Hemingway story see Donald E. Hardy, "Politeness Strategies and the Face of Honesty in Hemingway's 'The Doctor and the Doctor's Wife,'" *Language and Style,* forthcoming.

Chapter 6

1. Mary Glenn Freeman, "Flannery O'Connor and the Quality of Sight: A Standard for Writing and Reading," *Flannery O'Connor Bulletin* 16 (1987): 26; Larue Love Sloan, "The Rhetoric of the Seer: Eye Imagery in Flannery O'Connor's 'Revelation,'" *Studies in Short Fiction* 25, no. 2 (1988): 136; James M. Mellard, "Framed in the Gaze: Haze, *Wise Blood,* and Lacanian Reading," in *New Essays on Wise Blood,* ed.

Michael Kreyling (Cambridge: Cambridge University Press, 1995), 53; Reesman, "Women, Language, and the Grotesque," 42, 46–47.

2. Patrick W. Shaw, "*The Violent Bear It Away* and the Irony of False Seeing," *Texas Review* 3, no. 2 (1982): 49; William E. H. Meyer, Jr., "Melville and O'Connor: The Hypervisual Crisis," *Stanford Literature Review* 4, no. 2 (1987), 220; Kennelly, "Exhortation in *Wise Blood*," 163–65; Orvell, *Invisible Parade,* 168.

3. Harold C. Gardiner, S.J., "Flannery O'Connor's Clarity of Vision," in *The Added Dimension: The Art and Mind of Flannery O'Connor,* ed. Melvin J. Friedman and Lewis A. Lawson (New York: Fordham University Press, 1966), 184–95; Clinton W. Trowbridge, "The Symbolic Vision of Flannery O'Connor: Patterns of Imagery in *The Violent Bear It Away,*" *Sewanee Review* 76 (1968), 298–318; Desmond, *Risen Sons,* 32–50.

4. M. Bernetta Quinn, O.S.F., "Flannery O'Connor, A Realist of Distances," in *The Added Dimension: The Art and Mind of Flannery O'Connor,* ed. Melvin J. Friedman and Lewis A. Lawson (New York: Fordham University Press, 1966), 157–58.

5. Adrienne Lehrer, "Polysemy, Conventionality, and the Structure of the Lexicon," *Cognitive Linguistics* 1–2 (1990): 223; Randolph Quirk, Sidney Greenbaum, Geoffrey Leech, and Jan Svartvik, *A Comprehensive Grammar of the English Language* (London: Longman, 1985), 205.

6. Similar diagnostic tests are used to determine agentivity in "The Role of Pragmatic Inference in Semantics: A Study of Sensory Verb Complements in English," Robert S. Kirsner and Sandra A. Thompson. *Glossa* 10 (1976): 225–31.

7. Lehrer, "Structure of the Lexicon," 224.

8. Stephen A. Tyler, *The Unspeakable: Discourse, Dialogue, and Rhetoric in the Postmodern World* (Madison: University of Wisconsin Press, 1987), 156, 150; Susan A. Handelman, *The Slayers of Moses: The Emergence of Rabbinic Interpretation in Modern Literary Theory* (Albany: State University of New York Press, 1982), 33–34; Ong, *Orality and Literacy,* 12–14.

9. Richard Rorty, *Philosophy and the Mirror of Nature* (Princeton: Princeton University Press, 1979), 13; Wallace Chafe, *Discourse, Consciousness, and Time: The Flow and Displacement of Conscious Experience in Speaking and Writing* (Chicago: University of Chicago Press, 1994), 53; Lehrer, "Structure of the Lexicon," 224.

10. Givón, *English Grammar,* vol. 2, 23–28.

11. Ibid.

12. Kirsner and Thompson, "Pragmatic Inference"; Givón, *English Grammar,* vol. 2, 14.

13. Kirsner and Thompson, "Pragmatic Inference," 206; Givón, *English Grammar,* vol. 2, 14.

14. Kirsner and Thompson, "Pragmatic Inference," 205–6.

15. Givón, *English Grammar*, vol. 2, 3.

16. Givón, *English Grammar*, vol. 2, 2.

17. For similar tests that demonstrate the grounding of relative clauses see Givón's *English Grammar*, vol. 2, 111.

18. Levinson, *Pragmatics*, 174.

19. Terence Parsons, *Events in the Semantics of English: A Study in Subatomic Semantics* (Cambridge: MIT Press, 1990), 15–17; Kirsner and Thompson, "Pragmatic Inference"; George Lakoff, *Women, Fire, and Dangerous Things: What Categories Reveal about the Mind* (Chicago: University of Chicago Press, 1987), 125–30.

20. Levinson, *Pragmatics*, 175–76. Strawson, *Introduction to Logical Theory*. I paraphrase Levinson's summary of Strawson here.

21. Levinson, *Pragmatics*, 178.

22. For demonstration of the same diagnostic tests, see Kirsner and Thompson "Pragmatic Inference," 211ff.

23. Lauri Karttunen, "Implicative Verbs," *Language* 47 (1971): 343; Levinson, *Pragmatics*, 178.

24. Givón, *English Grammar*, vol. 2, 24.

Chapter 7

1. Bernard Fehr, "Substitutionary Narration and Description: A Chapter in Stylistics," *English Studies* 20 (1938): 98; Fludernik, *The Fictions of Language*, 305–9.

2. The frequency counts of complements in Donald E. Hardy and David Durian's "The Stylistics of Syntactic Complements: Grammar and Seeing in Flannery O'Connor's Fiction" (*Style* 34 [2000]: 92–116) are different because in *Narrating Knowledge* I do not count each conjoined complement as a separate complement. Thus, each complement, no matter how many conjoined elements it might have, is counted as one complement. I believe that this practice improves the reliability of the frequency counts because of the ambiguity of embedding and conjoining in many complements. Although the differing methodology leads to different frequency counts, what is important is that in the results of both methodologies there is no significant statistical difference in the distributions of the different complement types in the Brown general-fiction corpus and the O'Connor texts.

3. Levinson, *Pragmatics*, 186–91.

4. Kirsner and Thompson, "Pragmatic Inference," 212; Lakoff, *Women, Fire, and Dangerous Things*, 125–30.

5. Kirsner and Thompson, "Pragmatic Inference," 213.

6. Hardy, "Free Indirect Discourse."

7. Mayer, "Flannery O'Connor's 'As If'"; Kessler, *Language of Apocalypse.*

Chapter 8

1. James Morgan Hart, "The College Course in English Literature: How It May Be Improved," *Transactions of the Modern Language Association of America* 1 (1886): 84–85.

2. Leonard Bloomfield, "Why a Linguistic Society?" *Language* 1 (1925): 4; Leonard Bloomfield, *Language,* 21–22.

3. Edward Sapir, *Selected Writings of Edward Sapir in Language, Culture, and Personality,* ed. David G. Mandelbaum (Berkeley: University of California Press, 1949); Sapir, *Language,* 221–31; see Stephen R. Anderson *Phonology in the Twentieth Century: Theories of Rules and Theories of Representations* (Chicago: University of Chicago Press, 1985), 220–21. Anderson catalogues reasons that explain why Bloomfield rather than Sapir had the more enduring influence on linguistics after World War II.

4. Roman Jakobson, "Closing Statement: Linguistics and Poetics," in *Style in Language,* ed. Thomas A. Sebeok (Cambridge: MIT Press, 1960), 377.

5. Barbara Herrnstein Smith, *On the Margins of Discourse: The Relation of Literature to Language* (Chicago: University of Chicago Press, 1978), 158, 176; Fish, "What Is Stylistics?" 71.

6. Roy Harris, "Communication and Language," in *The Foundations of Linguistic Theory: Selected Writings of Roy Harris,* ed. Nigel Love (London: Routledge, 1990), 148–49.

7. Paul Hopper, "Emergent Grammar," *Papers of the Annual Meeting of the Berkeley Linguistics Society* 13 (1987): 139–57; Hopper, "Emergent Grammar and the A Priori Grammar Postulate," in *Linguistics in Context: Connecting, Observation, and Understanding,* ed. Deborah Tannen (Norwood, N.J.: Ablex, 1988), 117–34; T. Givón, *On Understanding Grammar* (New York: Academic Press, 1979), 207–33; John W. Du Bois, "Competing Motivations," in *Iconicity in Syntax,* ed. John Haiman (Amsterdam: John Benjamins, 1985), 343–65; Chafe, *Discourse, Consciousness, and Time,* 41–50; Hopper, "Emergent Grammar," 141; Michael Toolan, *Total Speech: An Integrational Linguistic Approach to Language* (Durham: Duke University Press, 1996), 242.

8. Christopher Norris, "Theory of Language and the Language of Literature," *Journal of Literary Semantics* 7, no. 2 (1978): 90–98.

9. Fox, "The Noun Phrase Accessibility Hierarchy Reinterpreted"; Fox and Thompson, "A Discourse Explanation of the Grammar of Relative Clauses";

Edward Keenan, "Variation in Universal Grammar," in *Analyzing Variation in Language,* ed. Ralph Fasold and Roger Shuy (Washington, D.C.: Georgetown University Press, 1975), 136–48; Edward Keenan and Bernard Comrie, "Noun Phrase Accessibility and Universal Grammar," *Linguistic Inquiry* 8, no. 1 (1977): 63–99; Hardy and Milton, "The Distribution and Function of Relative Clauses."

10. Leech and Short, *Style in Fiction,* 46.

11. Prince, "The Disnarrated."

12. Fox, "The Noun Phrase Accessibility Hierarchy Reinterpreted"; Fox and Thompson, "A Discourse Explanation of the Grammar of Relative Clauses"; Hardy and Milton, "The Distribution and Function of Relative Clauses."

Bibliography

Anderson, Stephen R. *Phonology in the Twentieth Century: Theories of Rules and Theories of Representations.* Chicago: University of Chicago Press, 1985.

Angle, Kimberly Greene. "Flannery O'Connor's Literary Art: Spiritual Portraits in Negative Space." *Flannery O'Connor Bulletin* 23 (1994–95): 158–74.

Archer, Emily. "Naming in the Neighborhood of Being: O'Connor and Percy on Language." *Studies in the Literary Imagination* 20, no. 2 (1987): 97–108.

Asals, Frederick. *Flannery O'Connor: The Imagination of Extremity.* Athens: University of Georgia Press, 1982.

Bacon, Jon Lance. *Flannery O'Connor and Cold War Culture.* Cambridge: Cambridge University Press, 1993.

Barthes, Roland. *S/Z.* Translated by Richard Miller. New York: Hill and Wang, 1974.

Behrendt, Stephen C. "Knowledge and Innocence in Flannery O'Connor's 'The River.'" *Studies in American Fiction* 17, no. 2 (1989): 143–55.

Biber, Douglas, Susan Conrad, and Randi Reppen. *Corpus Linguistics: Investigating Language Structure and Use.* Cambridge: Cambridge University Press, 1998.

Bloomfield, Leonard. *Language.* New York: Holt, Rinehart and Winston, 1933.

—————. "Why a Linguistic Society?" *Language* 1 (1925): 1–5.

Brinkmeyer, Robert H., Jr., *The Art and Vision of Flannery O'Connor.* Baton Rouge: Louisiana State University Press, 1989.

Brown, Penelope, and Stephen C. Levinson. *Politeness: Some Universals in Language Usage.* Cambridge: Cambridge University Press, 1987.

Burrows, J. F. *Computation into Criticism: A Study of Jane Austen's Novels and an Experiment in Method.* Oxford: Clarendon Press, 1987.

Butler, Milton Chadwick. "Factive Predicates and Narrative Point of View." *Texas Linguistic Forum* 13 (1979): 34–39.

Chafe, Wallace. *Discourse, Consciousness, and Time: The Flow and Displacement of Conscious Experience in Speaking and Writing.* Chicago: University of Chicago Press, 1994.

Chatman, Seymour. *Story and Discourse: Narrative Structure in Fiction and Film.* Ithaca: Cornell University Press, 1978.

Clark, Herbert H. "Semantics and Comprehension." In *Current Trends in Linguistics,* vol. 12, *Linguistics and Adjacent Arts and Sciences,* edited by Thomas A. Sebeok, 1291–428. The Hague: Mouton, 1974.

Culler, Jonathan. *The Pursuit of Signs: Semiotics, Literature, Deconstruction.* Ithaca: Cornell University Press, 1981.

Desmond, John F. *Risen Sons: Flannery O'Connor's Vision of History.* Athens: University of Georgia Press, 1987.

Dillon, George L. *Language Processing and the Reading of Literature: Toward a Model of Comprehension.* Bloomington: Indiana University Press, 1978.

Dowell, Bob. "The Moment of Grace in the Fiction of Flannery O'Connor." *College English* 27 (1965): 235–39.

Downing, Laura Hidalgo. "Negation in Discourse: A Text World Approach to Joseph Heller's *Catch-22.*" *Language and Literature* (London) 9, no. 3 (2000): 215–39.

———. *Negation, Text Worlds, and Discourse: The Pragmatics of Fiction.* Advances in Discourse Processes, vol. 66, edited by Roy O. Freedle. Stamford, Conn.: Ablex, 2000.

Dry, Helen Aristar, and Susan Kucinkas. "Ghostly Ambiguity: Presuppositional Constructions in *The Turn of the Screw.*" *Style* 25 (1991): 71–88.

Du Bois, John W. "Competing Motivations." In *Iconicity in Syntax,* edited by John Haiman, 343–65. Amsterdam: John Benjamins, 1985.

Eco, Umberto, and Patrizia Violi. "Instructional Semantics for Presuppositions." *Semiotica* 64 (1987): 1–39.

Faulkner, William. *The Sound and the Fury.* New York: Modern Library, 1929.

Fehr, Bernard. "Substitutionary Narration and Description: A Chapter in Stylistics." *English Studies* 20 (1938): 97–107.

Ferguson, Paul F. "Onomastic Revisions in Flannery O'Connor's *Wise Blood.*" *Literary Onomastics Studies* 13 (1986): 97–110.

Fish, Stanley. "What Is Stylistics and Why Are They Saying Such Terrible Things about It?" In *Is There a Text in This Class? The Authority of Interpretive Communities,* 68–96. Cambridge: Harvard University Press, 1980.

Fitzgerald, Sally. Introduction to *The Habit of Being,* by Flannery O'Connor. New York: Vintage, 1980.

Fleischman, Suzanne. *Tense and Narrativity: From Medieval Performance to Modern Fiction.* Austin: University of Texas Press, 1990.

Fludernik, Monika. *The Fictions of Language and the Languages of Fiction: The Linguistic Representation of Speech and Consciousness.* London: Routledge, 1993.

———. *Towards a 'Natural' Narratology.* London: Routledge, 1996.

Fowler, Roger. "The Referential Code and Narrative Authority." *Language and Style* 10 (1977): 129–61.

Fox, Barbara A. "The Noun Phrase Accessibility Hierarchy Reinterpreted: Subject Primacy or the Absolutive Hypothesis?" *Language* 63 (1987): 856–70.

Fox, Barbara A., and Sandra A. Thompson. "A Discourse Explanation of the Grammar of Relative Clauses in English Conversation." *Language* 66 (1990): 297–316.

Freeman, Mary Glenn. "Flannery O'Connor and the Quality of Sight: A Standard for Writing and Reading." *Flannery O'Connor Bulletin* 16 (1987): 26–33.

Frege, Gottlob. "On Sense and Reference." In *Translations from the Philosophical Writings of Gottlob Frege,* edited by Peter Geach and Max Black, 56–78. Oxford: Blackwell, 1952.

Freytag, Gustav. *Freytag's Technique of the Drama: An Exposition of Dramatic Composition and Art.* Translated by Elias J. MacEwan. Chicago: Griggs, 1895.

Gardiner, Harold C., S.J. "Flannery O'Connor's Clarity of Vision." In *The Added Dimension: The Art and Mind of Flannery O'Connor,* edited by Melvin J. Friedman and Lewis A. Lawson, 184–95. New York: Fordham University Press, 1966.

Givón, T. *English Grammar: A Function-Based Introduction.* 2 vols. Amsterdam: John Benjamins, 1993.

———. "Logic vs. Pragmatics, with Human Language as the Referee: Toward an Empirically Viable Epistemology." *Journal of Pragmatics* 6 (1982): 81–133.

———. *On Understanding Grammar.* New York: Academic Press, 1979.

Grice, H. Paul. "Logic and Conversation." In *Pragmatics: A Reader,* edited by Steven Davis, 305–15. Oxford: Oxford University Press, 1991.

Handelman, Susan A. *The Slayers of Moses: The Emergence of Rabbinic Interpretation in Modern Literary Theory.* Albany: State University of New York Press, 1982.

Hardy, Donald E. "The Dialogic Repetition of Free Indirect Discourse in Oral and Literary Narrative." In *Repetition in Dialogue,* edited by Carla Bazzanella, 90–103, 174–91. Tübingen: Niemeyer, 1996.

———. "Figure and Ground in the Creek Auxiliary *Oom.*" *Word* 43, no. 2 (1992): 217–31.

———. "Free Indirect Discourse, Irony, and Empathy in Flannery O'Connor's 'Revelation.'" *Language and Literature* (San Antonio) 16 (1991): 37–53.

———. "Introduction: Tracing the Crosscurrents of Influence: Literary vs. Ordinary vs. Scientific Language." *Crosscurrents of Influence: Linguistics and Literary Theory,* edited by Donald E. Hardy. Special issue of *Language and Literature* (San Antonio) 17 (1992): 1–17.

———. "Linguistic and Literary Theory: The Dancer and the Dance." *Southwest Journal of Linguistics* 10, no. 2 (1991): 1–29.

————. "Narrating Knowledge: Presupposition and Background in Flannery O'Connor's Fiction." *Language and Literature* (London) 6 (1997): 29–41.

————. "Politeness Strategies and the Face of Honesty in Hemingway's 'The Doctor and the Doctor's Wife.'" *Language and Style,* forthcoming.

————. "Presupposition and the Coconspirator." *Style* 26 (1992): 1–11.

————. "Russell Edson's Humor: Absurdity in a Surreal World." *Studies in American Humor* 6 (1988): 93–100.

Hardy, Donald E., and David Durian. "The Stylistics of Syntactic Complements: Grammar and Seeing in Flannery O'Connor's Fiction." *Style* 34 (2000): 92–116.

Hardy, Donald E., and Karen Milton. "The Distribution and Function of Relative Clauses in Literature." *Pragmatics and Language Learning* 5 (1994): 247–65.

Hardy, Donald E., and Chris Newton. "Why Is She So Negative? Negation and Knowledge in Flannery O'Connor's *A Good Man Is Hard to Find.*" *Southwest Journal of Linguistics* 17, no. 2 (1998): 61–81.

Harris, Roy. "Communication and Language." In *The Foundations of Linguistic Theory: Selected Writings of Roy Harris,* edited by Nigel Love, 136–50. London: Routledge, 1990.

Hart, James Morgan. "The College Course in English Literature: How It May Be Improved." *Transactions of the Modern Language Association of America* 1 (1886): 84–95.

Havelock, Eric A. *The Muse Leans to Write: Reflections on Orality and Literacy from Antiquity to the Present.* New Haven: Yale University Press, 1986.

————. *Preface to Plato.* Cambridge: Harvard University Press, 1963.

Heidegger, Martin. *An Introduction to Metaphysics.* Translated by Ralph Manheim. New Haven: Yale University Press, 1959.

————. "What Is Metaphysics?," trans. R. F. C. Hull and Alan Crick, in *Existence and Being,* 325–61. Chicago: Henry Regnery Company, 1949.

Hockett, Charles F. "The Problem of Universals in Language." In *The View from Language: Selected Essays, 1948–1974,* 163–86. Athens: University of Georgia Press, 1977.

Hopper, Paul. "Aspect and Foregrounding in Discourse." In *Discourse and Syntax,* edited by T. Givón, 213–41. Syntax and Semantics, vol. 12. New York: Academic Press, 1979.

————. "Emergent Grammar." *Papers of the Annual Meeting of the Berkeley Linguistics Society* 13 (1987): 139–57.

————. "Emergent Grammar and the A Priori Grammar Postulate." In *Linguistics in Context: Connecting, Observation, and Understanding,* edited by Deborah Tannen, 117–34. Norwood, N.J.: Ablex, 1988.

Hopper, Paul, and Sandra A. Thompson. "Transitivity in Grammar and Discourse." *Language* 56 (1980): 251–99.

Horn, Laurence R. *A Natural History of Negation.* Chicago: University of Chicago Press, 1989.

Iser, Wolfgang. *The Act of Reading: A Theory of Aesthetic Response.* Baltimore: Johns Hopkins University Press, 1976.

Jakobson, Roman. "Closing Statement: Linguistics and Poetics." In *Style in Language,* edited by Thomas A. Sebeok, 350–77. Cambridge: MIT Press, 1960.

Johnstone, Barbara. *Stories, Community, and Place: Narratives from Middle America.* Bloomington: Indiana University Press, 1990.

Karttunen, Lauri. "Implicative Verbs." *Language* 47 (1971): 340–58.

Keenan, Edward. "Variation in Universal Grammar." In *Analyzing Variation in Language,* edited by Ralph Fasold and Roger Shuy, 136–48. Washington, D.C.: Georgetown University Press, 1975.

Keenan, Edward, and Bernard Comrie. "Noun Phrase Accessibility and Universal Grammar." *Linguistic Inquiry* 8, no. 1 (1977): 63–99.

Keller, Jane Carter. "The Figures of the Empiricist and the Rationalist in the Fiction of Flannery O'Connor." *Arizona Quarterly* 28 (1972): 263–73.

Kennelly, Laura B. "Exhortation in *Wise Blood:* Rhetorical Theory as an Approach to Flannery O'Connor." In *Flannery O'Connor: New Perspectives,* edited by Sura P. Rath and Mary Neff Shaw, 152–68. Athens: University of Georgia Press, 1996.

Kessler, Edward. *Flannery O'Connor and the Language of Apocalypse.* Princeton: Princeton University Press, 1986.

Kirsner, Robert S., and Sandra A. Thompson. "The Role of Pragmatic Inference in Semantics: A Study of Sensory Verb Complements in English." *Glossa* 10 (1976): 200–240.

Koffka, Kurt. *Principles of Gestalt Psychology.* New York: Harcourt, Brace and World, 1935.

Kurrik, Maire Jaanus. *Literature and Negation.* New York: Columbia University Press, 1979.

Labov, William. "The Transformation of Experience in Narrative Syntax." In *Language in the Inner City: Studies in the Black English Vernacular,* 354–96. Philadelphia: University of Pennsylvania Press, 1972.

Labov, William, and Joshua Waletzky. "Narrative Analysis: Oral Versions of Personal Experience." In *Essays on the Verbal and Visual Arts: Proceedings of the 1966 Annual Spring Meetings of the American Ethnological Society,* edited by June Helm, 12–44. Seattle: University of Washington Press, 1967.

Lakoff, George. *Women, Fire, and Dangerous Things: What Categories Reveal about the Mind.* Chicago: University of Chicago Press, 1987.

Lancashire, Ian et al. *Using TACT with Texts: A Guide to Text-Analysis Computing Tools.* New York: Modern Language Association of America, 1996.

Leech, Geoffrey N. *Principles of Pragmatics.* London: Longman, 1983.

Leech, Geoffrey N., and Michael H. Short. *Style in Fiction: A Linguistic Introduction to English Fictional Prose.* London: Longman, 1981.

Lehrer, Adrienne. "Polysemy, Conventionality, and the Structure of the Lexicon." *Cognitive Linguistics* 1–2 (1990): 207–46.

Levinson, Stephen C. *Pragmatics.* Cambridge: Cambridge University Press, 1983.

Longacre, Robert E. "A Spectrum and Profile Approach to Discourse Analysis." *Text* 1 (1981): 337–59.

Ludwig, Dale Leslie. "Controlled Distance: Internal Character Presentation in Flannery O'Connor's Short Stories." Ph.D. diss., University of Illinois at Urbana-Champaign, 1988.

Marston, Jane. "Epistemology and the Solipsistic Consciousness in Flannery O'Connor's 'Greenleaf.'" *Studies in Short Fiction* 21, no. 4 (1984): 375–82.

Mayer, David R. "'Like Ticks off a Dog': Flannery O'Connor's 'As If.'" *Christianity and Literature* 33, no. 4 (1984): 17–34.

McCarthy, John F. "Human Intelligence Versus Divine Truth: The Intellectual in Flannery O'Connor's Works." *English Journal* 55 (1966): 1143–48.

McEnery, Tony, and Andrew Wilson. *Corpus Linguistics.* Edinburgh: Edinburgh University Press, 1996.

McMullen, Joanne Halleran. *Writing against God: Language as Message in the Literature of Flannery O'Connor.* Macon, Ga.: Mercer University Press, 1996.

Mellard, James M. "Flannery O'Connor's Others: Freud, Lacan, and the Unconscious." *American Literature* 61 (1989): 625–43.

———. "Framed in the Gaze: Haze, *Wise Blood,* and Lacanian Reading." In *New Essays on Wise Blood,* edited by Michael Kreyling, 51–69. Cambridge: Cambridge University Press, 1995.

Meyer, William E. H., Jr. "Melville and O'Connor: The Hypervisual Crisis." *Stanford Literature Review* 4, no. 2 (1987): 211–29.

Miller, J. Hillis. "Narrative." In *Critical Terms for Literary Study,* edited by Frank Lentricchia and Thomas McLaughlin, 66–79. Chicago: University of Chicago Press, 1990.

Ming, Zhong. "Designed Shock and Grotesquerie: The Form of Flannery O'Connor's Fiction." *Flannery O'Connor Bulletin* 17 (1988): 51–61.

Mosher, Harold F., Jr. "The Narrated and Its Negatives: The Nonnarrated and the Disnarrated in Joyce's *Dubliners.*" *Style* 27 (1993): 407–27.

Mukarovsky, Jan. "Standard Language and Poetic Language." In *A Prague School Reader,* edited by Paul L. Garvin, 17–30. Washington, D.C.: Georgetown University Press, 1964.

Norris, Christopher. "Theory of Language and the Language of Literature." *Journal of Literary Semantics* 7, no. 2 (1978): 90–98.

Oates, Joyce Carol. "The Visionary Art of Flannery O'Connor." *Southern Humanities Review* 7 (1973): 235–46.

O'Connor, Flannery. *Collected Works.* New York: Library of America, 1988.

———. *The Complete Stories.* New York: Farrar, Straus and Giroux, 1971.

———. *The Correspondence of Flannery O'Connor and the Brainard Cheneys.* Edited by C. Ralph Stephens. Jackson: University Press of Mississippi, 1986.

———. *Everything That Rises Must Converge.* New York: Farrar, Straus and Giroux, 1965.

———. *A Good Man Is Hard to Find and Other Stories.* New York: Harcourt, Brace and World, 1955.

———. *The Habit of Being.* Edited by Sally Fitzgerald. New York: Vintage, 1979.

———. *Mystery and Manners: Occasional Prose.* Edited by Sally Fitzgerald and Robert Fitzgerald. New York: Farrar, Straus and Giroux, 1969.

———. *The Violent Bear It Away.* New York: Farrar, Straus and Cudahy, 1960.

———. *Wise Blood.* New York: Harcourt, Brace and World, 1952. Reprint, New York: Farrar, Straus and Cudahy, 1962.

Ong, Walter J. *Orality and Literacy: The Technologizing of the Word.* London: Methuen, 1982.

Orvell, Miles. *Invisible Parade: The Fiction of Flannery O'Connor.* Philadelphia: Temple University Press, 1972.

Parsons, Terence. *Events in the Semantics of English: A Study in Subatomic Semantics.* Cambridge: MIT Press, 1990.

Peer, Willie van. *Stylistics and Psychology: Investigations of Foregrounding.* London: Croom Helm, 1986.

Pratt, Mary Louise. *Toward a Speech Act Theory of Literary Discourse.* Bloomington: Indiana University Press, 1977.

Prince, Gerald. "The Disnarrated." *Style* 22 (1988): 1–8.

————. "On Presupposition and Narrative Strategy." *Centrum* 1 (1973): 23–31.

Quinn, M. Bernetta, O.S.F. "Flannery O'Connor, A Realist of Distances." In *The Added Dimension: The Art and Mind of Flannery O'Connor,* edited by Melvin J. Friedman and Lewis A. Lawson, 157–83. New York: Fordham University Press, 1966.

Quirk, Randolph, Sidney Greenbaum, Geoffrey Leech, and Jan Svartvik. *A Comprehensive Grammar of the English Language.* London: Longman, 1985.

Ragen, Brian Abel. *A Wreck on the Road to Damascus: Innocence, Guilt, and Conversion in Flannery O'Connor.* Chicago: Loyola University Press, 1989.

Ransom, John Crowe. *The World's Body.* Port Washington, N.Y.: Kennikat, 1938.

Reesman, Jeanne Campbell. "Women, Language, and the Grotesque in Flannery O'Connor and Eudora Welty." In *Flannery O'Connor: New Perspectives,* edited by Sura P. Rath and Mary Neff Shaw, 38–56. Athens: University of Georgia Press, 1996.

Reinhart, Tanya. "Principles of Gestalt Perception in the Temporal Organization of Narrative Texts." *Linguistics* 22 (1984): 779–809.

Rimmon-Kenan, Shlomith. *Narrative Fiction: Contemporary Poetics.* London: Routledge, 1983.

Rochester, Eric. "New Tools for Analyzing Texts." *Language and Literature* (London) 10 (2001): 187–91.

Rorty, Richard. *Philosophy and the Mirror of Nature.* Princeton: Princeton University Press, 1979.

Rupp, Richard H. "Fact and Mystery: Flannery O'Connor." *Commonweal* 79 (1963): 304–7.

Russell, Bertrand. "On Denoting." *Mind* 14 (1905): 479–93.

Sapir, Edward. *Language: An Introduction to the Study of Speech.* New York: Harcourt, Brace and World, 1921.

————. *Selected Writings of Edward Sapir in Language, Culture, and Personality.* Edited by David G. Mandelbaum. Berkeley: University of California Press, 1949.

de Saussure, Ferdinand. *Course in General Linguistics.* Edited by Charles Bally, Albert Sechehaye, and Albert Reidlinger. Translated by Wade Baskin. New York: Philosophical Library, 1959.

Schroeder, Michael L. "Ruby Turpin, Job, and Mystery: Flannery O'Connor on the Question of Knowing." *Flannery O'Connor Bulletin* 21 (1992): 75–83.

Shaw, Patrick W. "*The Violent Bear It Away* and the Irony of False Seeing." *Texas Review* 3, no. 2 (1982): 49–59.

Shloss, Carol. *Flannery O'Connor's Dark Comedies: The Limits of Inference.* Baton Rouge: Louisiana State University Press, 1980.

Sloan, Larue Love. "The Rhetoric of the Seer: Eye Imagery in Flannery O'Connor's 'Revelation.'" *Studies in Short Fiction* 25, no. 2 (1988): 135–45.

Smith, Barbara Herrnstein. *On the Margins of Discourse: The Relation of Literature to Language.* Chicago: University of Chicago Press, 1978.

Stalnaker, Robert C. "Pragmatic Presuppositions." In *Semantics and Philosophy,* edited by Milton K. Munitz and Peter K. Unger, 197–214. New York: New York University Press, 1974.

Strawson, P. F. *Introduction to Logical Theory.* London: Methuen, 1952.

———. "On Referring." *Mind* 59 (1950): 320–44.

Sullivan, M. *Chinese Art: Recent Discoveries.* London: Thames and Hudson, 1973.

Talmy, Leonard. "Figure and Ground in Complex Sentences." In *Syntax,* edited by Joseph H. Greenberg, Charles A. Ferguson, and Edith A. Moravcsik, 625–49. Universals of Human Language, vol. 4. Stanford: Stanford University Press, 1978.

Tannen, Deborah. *Talking Voices: Repetition, Dialogue, and Imagery in Conversational Discourse.* Cambridge: Cambridge University Press, 1989.

Tedford, Barbara Wilkie. "Flannery O'Connor and the Social Classes." *Southern Literary Journal* 13, no. 2 (1981): 27–40.

Thompson, Sandra A. "'Subordination' and Narrative Event Structure." In *Coherence and Grounding in Discourse,* edited by Russell S. Tomlin, 435–53. Amsterdam: John Benjamins, 1987.

Toolan, Michael. *Total Speech: An Integrational Linguistic Approach to Language.* Durham: Duke University Press, 1996.

Tottie, Gunnel. *Negation in English Speech and Writing: A Study in Variation.* New York: Academic Press, 1991.

Townsend, David J., and Thomas Gordon Bever. *Main and Subordinate Clauses: A Study in Figure and Ground.* Bloomington: Indiana University Linguistics Club, 1977.

Trowbridge, Clinton W. "The Symbolic Vision of Flannery O'Connor: Patterns of Imagery in *The Violent Bear It Away.*" *Sewanee Review* 76 (1968): 298–318.

Tyler, Stephen A. *The Unspeakable: Discourse, Dialogue, and Rhetoric in the Postmodern World.* Madison: University of Wisconsin Press, 1987.

Vosniadou, Stella. "Drawing Inferences from Semantically Positive and Negative Implicative Predicates." *Journal of Psycholinguistic Research* 11 (1982): 77–93.

Wallace, Steven. "Figure and Ground: The Interrelationships of Linguistic Categories." In *Tense-Aspect: Between Semantics and Pragmatics,* edited by Paul J. Hopper, 201–23. Amsterdam: John Benjamins, 1982.

Wason, Peter C. "The Contexts of Plausible Denial." *Journal of Verbal Learning and Verbal Behavior* 4 (1965): 7–11.

————. "The Processing of Positive and Negative Information." *Quarterly Journal of Experimental Psychology* 11 (1959): 92–107.

Watson, Greg. *Doin' Mudrooroo: Elements of Style and Involvement in the Early Prose Fiction of Mudrooroo.* Joensuu, Finland: University of Joensuu, 1997.

Weber, Jean Jacques. "The Foreground-Background Distinction: A Survey of Its Definitions and Applications." *Language and Literature* (San Antonio) 6 (1983): 1–15.

Werth, Paul. *Text Worlds: Representing Conceptual Space in Discourse.* London: Longman, 1999.

Zornado, Joseph Louis. "Flannery O'Connor: A Fiction of Unknowing." Ph.D. diss., University of Connecticut, 1992.

Index

negative uninformativeness, principle
of, 75–76
negatives: analytic, 86–87; typologies
of, 95. *See also* suppositions,
typologies of
New Criticism, 24, 81, 159, 162–63
Newton, Chris, 94
nonnarration, 40, 174n. 20(40)
Norris, Christopher, 161–62
Northern Illinois University,
173n. 7(19)

Oates, Joyce Carol, 7
O'Connor, Flannery: belief in sensory
knowledge, 142–43, 144; correspondence on faith, 94; on the
craft of fiction, 83, 122, 142; critique of reason, 45; dislike of literary interpretation studies, 1–2;
use of foregrounding/background-
ing, 39–42; letters and essays of,
2, 3; master's thesis, 3, 5, 43, 51;
relationship to southern audience,
68–69; style, 3, 43, 91–92,
148–57, 164; stylistic criticism of,
8; typical themes, 7, 8, 114–36,
167; use of negation, 88; use of the
words *negro, colored, nigger,*
175–76n. 12(64); on vision, 114,
118
Ong, Walter J., 17
onomastics, 170n. 4(8)
oral communication, 17, 18
ordinary language, 18, 161–63
Orvell, Miles, 117

paraphrasability, 162–63
"Parker's Back," 66–67

Parry, Milman, 17
Parsons, Terence, 131
participials, 30, 45, 126
Plato, 17
plot, 80
poetry, oral, 18
post-structuralism, 24, 160–62
Practical Extraction and Report
Language (PERL), 10–11
pragmatics, 129–30; distinct from
semantics, 131, 145–48
Pratt, Mary Louise, 19, 24
presupposition, 2, 11, 12, 35, 40, 45,
46–69, 96, 102, 133–34, 135,
164; backgrounding in, 131–32;
contrasted to background assumptions (supposition), 76–77; distinct from implication, 13–14,
130–36, 137; literary, 35–36,
69; manipulation of, 110–13,
178n. 16(110); marked, 54, 55,
56–58, 65, 69; in O'Connor style,
41, 56–58, 148–57; pragmatics
of, 125, 145–47; semantics of,
125; stylistic meanings of, 163;
triggers, 48, 49–51; typology of,
69, 163
Prince, Gerald, 164
the prophetic, 41

quasi simile. See *as if* construction
Quinn, M. Bernetta, 117–18
Quirk, Randolph, 119, 178n. 15(107)

rationality, limitations of, 7
reason, fallibility of, 45
Reinhart, Tanya, 38–39, 46–47
rejection/refusal, 95, 104